DEMCO

THE HISTORY OF NATIONS

Mexico

Adriane Ruggiero, *Book Editor*

Bruce Glassman, *Vice President*
Bonnie Szumski, *Publisher*
Helen Cothran, *Managing Editor*

GREENHAVEN
PRESS ®

THOMSON
GALE

San Diego • Detroit • New York • San Francisco • Cleveland
New Haven, Conn. • Waterville, Maine • London • Munich

For more information, contact
Greenhaven Press
27500 Drake Rd.
Farmington Hills, MI 48331-3535
Or you can visit our Internet site at http://www.gale.com

Cover credit: © Charles and Josette Lenars/CORBIS

LIBRARY OF CONGRESS CATALOGING-IN-PUBLICATION DATA
Mexico / Adriane Ruggiero, book editor.
p. cm. — (History of nations)
Includes bibliographical references and index.
ISBN 0-7377-1854-4 (lib. bdg. : alk. paper) —
ISBN 0-7377-1855-2 (pbk. : alk. paper)
1. Mexico—History. I. Ruggiero, Adriane. II. History of nations (Greenhaven Press)
F1226.M514 2004
972—dc21   2003054321

Printed in the United States of America

Contents

Chapter 3: From Independence to Empire to Republic, 1810–1848

cution. In 1822 Antonio López de Santa Anna proclaimed Mexico a republic.

4. Mexico at War with the United States

Chapter 4: Reform and Revolution, 1855–1920

1. Juárez's Plan for Reforming Mexico

2. The Porfirio Díaz Era

3. A Call for Revolt: The Plan of San Luis Potosi, 1910

4. Pancho Villa: Portrait of a Revolutionary

is allowing access to files that will likely reveal information about the protesters who disappeared without a trace after being arrested by the Mexican police in the 1970s.

FOREWORD

I n 1841, the journalist Charles MacKay remarked, "In reading the history of nations, we find that, like individuals, they
have their whims and peculiarities, their seasons of excite-
ment and recklessness." At the time of MacKay's observation,
many of the nations explored in the Greenhaven Press History
of Nations series did not yet exist in their current form. Nonetheless, whether it is old or young, every nation is similar to an
individual, with its own distinct characteristics and unique story.

The History of Nations series is dedicated to exploring these
stories. Each anthology traces the development of one of the
world's nations from its earliest days, when it was perhaps no
more than a promise on a piece of paper or an idea in the mind
of some revolutionary, through to its status in the world today.
Topics discussed include the pivotal political events and power
struggles that shaped the country as well as important social and
cultural movements. Often, certain dramatic themes and events
recur, such as the rise and fall of empires, the flowering and de-
cay of cultures, or the heroism and treachery of leaders. As well,
in the history of most countries war, oppression, revolution, and
deep social change feature prominently. Nonetheless, the details
of such events vary greatly, as does their impact on the nation
concerned. For example, England's "Glorious Revolution" of
1688 was a peaceful transfer of power that set the stage for the
emergence of democratic institutions in that nation. On the
other hand, in China, the overthrow of dynastic rule in 1912 led
to years of chaos, civil war, and the eventual emergence of a
Communist regime that used violence as a tool to root out opposition and quell popular protest. Readers of the Greenhaven
Press History of Nations series will learn about the common
challenges nations face and the different paths they take in response to such crises. However a nation's story may have developed, the series strives to present a clear and unbiased view of the
country at hand.

The structure of each volume in the series is designed to help
students deepen their understanding of the events, movements,

and persons that define nations. First, a thematic introduction provides critical background material and helps orient the reader. The chapters themselves are designed to provide an accessible and engaging approach to the study of the history of that nation involved and are arranged either thematically or chronologically, as appropriate. The selections include both primary documents, which convey something of the flavor of the time and place concerned, and secondary material, which includes the wisdom of hindsight and scholarship. Finally, each book closes with a detailed chronology, a comprehensive bibliography of suggestions for further research, and a thorough index.

The countries explored within the series are as old as China and as young as Canada, as distinct in character as Spain and India, as large as Russia, and as compact as Japan. Some are based on ethnic nationalism, the belief in an ethnic group as a distinct people sharing a common destiny, whereas others emphasize civic nationalism, in which what defines citizenship is not ethnicity but commitment to a shared constitution and its values. As human societies become increasingly globalized, knowledge of other nations and of the diversity of their cultures, characteristics, and histories becomes ever more important. This series responds to the challenge by furnishing students with a solid and engaging introduction to the history of the world's nations.

INTRODUCTION

"The history of Mexico is the history of a man seeking his parentage, his origins."
—Octavio Paz in *The Labyrinth of Solitude*

Mexico is a country with a vibrant blend of Indian and European cultures brought about by several hundred years of racial and cultural mixing. The blending was not the result of a peaceful encounter of peoples but of a violent collision between two different worlds, the Indian and the Spanish. In 1519 the Spanish conquistador Hernán Cortés landed on the Mexican Gulf Coast. By making alliances with local Indian chieftains and using superior Spanish weapons, Cortés and his army of five hundred men and many more Indian allies conquered the Aztec Empire in 1521. The violence of the conquest and the decimation of the Indian population by the smallpox, influenza, and measles that the conquistadores brought from Europe forever altered the development of Indian culture. Another important consequence of the conquest was the interracial mixing of the Indians and the Spanish, resulting in people called mestizos—men and women who were part Indian and part European.

Since the time of the Spanish conquest, Mexicans have tried to come to grips with what it means to be a people who are racially mixed yet divided socially and economically into castes created by the economic and political system imposed by the Spanish conquerors. Generally speaking, in Mexico today people who are fair-skinned and European-looking occupy the upper tiers of society. They are the well-to-do or the middle-class citizens who own houses and apartments, work in offices, send their children to universities, and travel abroad for pleasure. Those who are dark-skinned and Indian in appearance belong to another caste, occupying the lower strata of the social and economic structure. They tend to live in towns and villages; work in agriculture, ranching, or manufacturing for low pay; and have fewer economic opportunities. They are also the Mexicans who, often at great risk to themselves, illegally travel back and forth across the Mexico–U.S. border to work or reunite with family members. A third caste in Mexico consists of the indigenous people, the Indians. They are the descendants of the ancient tribes who never intermarried with other groups. They occupy the lowest rung of Mexican society and are also the poorest Mexicans, the ones with the fewest opportunities. As a result of their poverty and geographic remoteness, the indigenous people of Mexico depend heavily on the federal and state governments for help through social and economic programs. In sum, Mexican society still struggles with the restrictions of a centuries-old caste system even as it strives for political and economic equality for all. In the words of historians Mark Burkholder and Suzanne Hiles, "The Spanish Conquest irrevocably altered the social order of Mexico, by creating broad categories of victors and vanquished identified by race. It also facilitated the mixing of races."[1]

The Conquered and the Conqueror

The mixed-race Mexicans of the postconquest period were the result of the intermarriage of Spanish conquistadores (who, for the most part, did not bring Spanish women with them to America) and Indian women. The Spanish used the native women as concubines and acquired them as prisoners of war or as gifts from friendly Indian chieftains. Taking Indian women into their households was one of the ways the Spanish built alliances with surviving Indian groups. After the conquistadores had established themselves as colonists in New Spain, the Indian women married the Spanish men and gained the status of wives.

The Spanish had distinctive views of the culture with which they were comingling. In his book *Conquistadors*, Michael Wood explains the European attitude:

> To some, the Native Americans were untouched by the word of God and had been debased by the Devil; to others, they were a remnant from before the Fall [the fall of Adam and Eve as described in the Bible], living in innocence long lost by the corrupted West. Either way, it was almost impossible . . . for the indigenous peoples to be considered as humans in their own right.[2]

The Christian Spanish conquerors regarded the Aztecs as a brutal people and their religious ceremonies, with their emphasis on bloodletting and human sacrifice, as violent and inhuman. The Spanish belief that the Indians were less civilized allowed them to not only kill Indians but also to destroy the physical evidence of Indian culture with a single-minded vigor. Thus, countless codices, or books, from the Aztec Empire were burned by conquistadores and missionaries. Tenochtitlán, the Aztec capital city, was razed to make room for Mexico City, the capital of New Spain.

Once the conquest was accomplished, the Spanish realized that they needed the help of the Indians if they were to survive in their new circumstances and build a viable colony. As a result, many of the surviving Aztecs and other Indian peoples were put to work as laborers on *encomiendas*, the landholdings the individual Spaniards used to sustain themselves in the New World. Others were hauled off to mine the silver and gold that enriched the Spanish Empire. Still others were forced to work on the construction of Mexico City, begun by Cortés immediately after the conquest. Alonso de Zorita, a sixteenth-century Spanish judge in the colony of New Spain and author of *Life and Labor in Ancient Mexico*, describes how working for the Spanish under slave-like conditions weakened the Indian population:

> What has destroyed and continues to destroy the Indians is their forced labor in the construction of large stone masonry buildings in the Spaniards' towns. For this they are forced to leave their native climates . . . 20, 30, 40 more leagues away. Their whole tempo of life, the time and mode of work, of eating and sleeping are disrupted. They are forced to work many days and weeks, from dawn until after dusk, without any rest.[3]

Decimated by diseases such as smallpox and worn down by hard work, the Indian population eventually declined to a point where the indigenous peoples were no longer the majority.

Although many of the Spanish *encomenderos* (large landowners) saw the Indians as dull brutes fit only for labor in the fields or mines, they also believed they had an obligation to "save" the Indians by converting them to Christianity. As a result, Christian priests accompanied the conquistadores to the New World to win souls for the faith. Not all Indians capitulated to the Spaniards or went willingly into their service. Nor were all the Indians docile converts to Christianity. Mexico's early colonial history was marked by several uprisings, including that of the Maya of the Yucatán from 1546 to 1547. The uprising began when Mayan priests, fearing the destruction of their native religion, opposed the conversions carried out by the Franciscans, one of the first Catholic orders to arrive in Mexico. Indian uprisings were put down, often brutally, by the colonial government and its armies, and the missionaries were eventually able to win over Indian chiefs. Sons of chiefs were converted to the new faith, and their help was requested as the friars built monasteries in each region of the country. This development, accompanied by intermarriage, created a society that, according to historian Hugh Thomas, is composed of "men and women whose Spanish surnames and Christian culture have fused with their Indian blood and Indian features."[4]

The monasteries, or *conventos*, became the centers where the "spiritual conquest" of the Indians was carried out. Indian adults and children were Christianized through instruction in church doctrine and taught to read and write. They learned the Spanish culture within the walls of the monasteries, which were themselves built within pueblos, the towns established by the Spanish throughout Mexico. The Indians supplied the labor for the maintenance of the monasteries by working in monastery workshops and providing crops to the friars. The *conventos* also served as safe havens for the Indians against abuse by the *encomenderos*. In these settings, elements of Indian culture were passed on to the Europeans. These included the introduction of native American crops such as maize, beans, chiles, and squashes, the use of local herbs as medicines, and the native Aztec language Nahuatl, which introduced words such as *chocolate* and *tomato* into the vocabulary of the Spanish in Mexico.

The missionaries were aware that the destruction of ancient Indian texts carried out by the first churchmen in Mexico deprived them of any knowledge of Indian history. They therefore had the Indians write down the history of their people and illustrate it with drawings. These manuscripts, preserved over the centuries, became an important source of information for historians seeking to learn more about life in pre–Hispanic Mexico.

The Christian missionaries, mainly Franciscans, allowed the Indians to retain some of their ancient traditions (such as festivals linked to agriculture or the passage of the seasons) as long as the traditions did not interfere with Christian doctrinal teachings. As a result of the missionaries' methods of dealing with their Indian converts, Christianity in Mexico has a unique mixture of Spanish and Indian traditions. For example, the massive churches of Mexico were constructed by Indian artisans in the Spanish style but were embellished with the colors and details of their native regions.

In 1531 the missionary work of the Spanish friars received a huge push when an Indian peasant by the name of Juan Diego saw a vision of the Virgin Mary, mother of Jesus Christ, on a hill previously revered as sacred to the Aztec goddess Tonanzin. According to the legend that sprang up around Juan Diego, Mary asked him to go to the local bishop and demand that a church be built on the site. When Diego met the bishop and presented Mary's request, the churchman demanded a sign as proof of the veracity of Diego's story. The sign was given: Mary appeared again to Diego on a hill covered with flowers blooming out of season. Diego gathered the flowers, enfolded them in his cloak, and carried them to the bishop. When he opened his cloak before the bishop, the image of Mary appeared on it. As the story of Juan Diego and his vision spread, more Indians were convinced to convert. In time, they adopted the image of a dark-skinned Mary as their patron saint, calling her Our Lady of Guadalupe. Today, Our Lady of Guadalupe is the patroness of predominantly Roman Catholic Mexico.

The legend of Juan Diego and Our Lady of Guadalupe is one example of how the Indians adapted Christianity to suit their time and place. Once believed to be a real individual, Juan Diego is regarded today as a symbol of the pious Indian peasants who became the staunchest supporters of the church in Mexico. They became so devoted that when the revolutionary government of President Plutarco Elías Calles enforced governmental controls over the Catholic Church in the 1920s, the peasants rose in rebellion against the government and in support of the church.

Juárez, the Revolution, and Its Aftermath

By the late sixteenth century Mexico had developed into a highly stratified society with a strict hierarchy. At the top, the European-born Spanish and their children born in the New World (criollos) held power and wealth; at the bottom, Indians and African slaves (imported by the Spanish) provided the labor. In the middle was a small but growing group of people of mixed European-Indian-African background. Despite the division of Mexican society into these strata, it was possible for individuals of talent and ambition to rise from the lowest rungs to positions of power, if not wealth. Mexico's great nineteenth-century reformer and spokesperson for the plight of the Indians, Benito Juárez, came from the bottom group.

Juárez was a full-blooded Zapotec Indian from the Mexican state of Oaxaca. Through hard work and a singular focus, he transformed himself from a shepherd boy tending his uncle's flocks to a law student at the Institute of Arts and Sciences. From there, he entered politics and, in 1847, was elected governor of his state. He was the first Indian to hold that position. Fourteen years later Juárez became president of Mexico. One of his goals, simply stated in the following excerpt from a speech, reflected his pride in his Indian heritage and his desire to end the poverty and suffering of Mexico's Indian peoples:

> I am a son of the people and I will not forget it; on the contrary, I will stand up for their rights and take care that they learn, that they grow nobler and that they create a future for themselves and abandon the path of disorder, vice and misery to which they have been led by men who only in words call themselves friends and liberators but through their actions are the cruelest tyrants.[5]

As a national leader advocating Indian rights, Juárez was careful to include Indians and non-Indians in his description of "Mexicans."

Juárez's goal of lifting the Indians out of poverty remained a central concern of his liberal reform program. Although his death in 1872 cut short his plans, the ideals Juárez represented inspired a new generation of reformers. Those ideals survived during the long presidency of the dictatorial Porfirio Díaz (1876–1911) and helped ignite a revolution. The plight of the Indians, the peasantry, and urban workers were debated and fought over during the Mexican Revolution, which lasted from 1910 to 1920. Civil war devastated the country as politicians vied for control and regional warlords pursued their own plans for a new Mexico. In the chaos of the revolution, rebel leaders such as Emiliano Zapata seized the largest haciendas (self-contained estates), dismantled them, and distributed the land to the peasants. In the words of historian John Mason Hart, the Zapatistas (the followers of Zapata) "wanted modernity, better schools, roads, and health care. Zapata once complained that the horses in the stables of the elite where he worked were given better care than the people."[6] As an outgrowth of the revolution, Mexicans formulated a new constitution in 1917 that attempted to address the major social issues of the past decades. It established labor laws and gave the federal government sole control over education and natural resources. As a way to appease landless peasants, many of whom were Indians, the constitution allocated to villages formerly private or confiscated lands to be used as communal farms. Indian poverty was far from eliminated, however.

The political leaders of the 1920s and 1930s saw themselves as the heirs of the Mexican Revolution. As such, their goal was to rebuild the nation's economy as well as reform Mexican society without losing the ideals of the revolution. According to Hart, the reform of society was to take the form of "a revolution within a revolution . . . in which they [the reformers] embraced the new goal of Mexicanizing the nation. They [the new generation of reformers] scorned the Porfirian imitation of European high culture and sought to develop a new respect and pride in Mexican ways."[7] Mexico's indigenous peoples, who composed the majority of the population in some of the states (such as Chiapas), became the subject of educational and social reformers of the 1930s. Their movement, called *indigenismo*, or indigenism, aimed to advance Indian cultural values.

After years of feeling inferior to other nations (such as the United States), Mexicans, through a program of national education and revolutionary propaganda, gained a greater understanding of the singularity of their nation, its cultural diversity, and its accomplishments. At the forefront of the educational reform movement (and its main spokesperson and propagandist) was José Vasconcelos, minister of education during the presidency of Álvaro Obregón (1920–1924). Vasconcelos headed the National University of Mexico and worked to expand education throughout Mexico. He was also a writer who wanted to draw attention to the uniqueness of the Mexicans. In his 1925 essay *La raza cósmica* (*The Cosmic Race*), he wrote powerfully on behalf of the racial mixing that marked Mexican society, arguing that "even the most contradictory mixtures can always be beneficially resolved because the spiritual factor in each serves to elevate the whole."[8] The term *la raza* in the title means "the race" or "the people" and refers to the mixed culture of Spaniards and other Europeans, Indians, and Africans that was born out of the Spanish conquest of the indigenous people of Mesoamerica. Many scholars and indigenous people now reject Vasconcelos's ideas on race because they regard them as basically Eurocentric. They state that Vasconcelos had little tolerance for indigenous culture and that he believed indigenous people were Mexicans first and should be educated to become "Westernized."

Artists as well as writers and educators helped expand Mexicans' sense of themselves, their "*Mexicanidad*." During the 1920s and 1930s the murals painted on the sides of buildings and in grand public spaces by José Clemente Orozco, Diego Rivera, and Alfred Siqueiros recorded the peoples and circumstances of the Mexican Revolution in bold, bright images. The painter Frida Kahlo reveled in Mexican folklore and the culture of the indigenous people and used their themes in many of her works. Kahlo also used clothing to reflect her interest in all things Mexican, often dressing in the elaborate costumes worn by women in the different regions of Mexico. In music, Carlos Chavez followed a similar nationalist path by incorporating Indian materials into his modern compositions. His 1921 ballet *El fuego nuevo* (*The New Fire*) contains Aztec themes, and his *Sinfonía India* (1935–1936), based on Indian melodies, includes indigenous instruments such as drums, rasps, and rattles. Chavez was director of the Symphony Orchestra of Mexico and was also a dedicated teacher of many Mexican composers, including Silvestre Revueltas.

The Issue of Race and Indigenous Peoples Today

Today's Mexico—a nation of approximately 107 million—is a predominantly mixed-race nation in which the majority of the people have some Indian background. Despite this fact, old ideas about caste and status continue. Many Mexicans still pride themselves on their "Spanishness." In their eyes, Spanishness is equivalent to being white, European, and "modern" and is preferred over "Indianness," which is equated with dark skin and social and economic backwardness. Modern media in the form of television, movies, and glossy magazines promotes the allure of Western culture. Indigenous peoples, who number approximately 13 million, are not widely covered by the celebrity press. Although Mexico's ancient Indian cultures are esteemed (as visitors to the ruins of the great Mayan cities and Mexico City's National Museum of Anthropology can attest), the indigenous peoples of

Mexico remain poor. Their poverty is the result of several factors, including geographic isolation, the government's failure to find a realistic way of dealing with indigenous issues, and years of neglect by those in political power.

Most indigenous people today lack education and basic services, such as communication networks, that will enable them to support themselves in their traditional work (mainly farming) and compete in today's economy. One of the goals of the Mexican Revolution, to provide Indians with a better life, goes unfulfilled. Many rural people are unable to support themselves by farming their own plots of land and must take jobs as day laborers for large commercial farms in order to make any money at all. Their dependency on the large commercial farms (now often run by multinational corporations) makes it difficult if not impossible for them to advance or improve their lives. Each year more and more people leave the countryside in desperation and move to the cities in hope of finding work. They have to take the lowest-paying jobs and end up living in the numerous slums that surround Mexico City or other urban centers. Once in the cities, their lives change, becoming less Indian and more modern. According to Humberto Jurado, a teacher in one of the rare surviving Indian communities within Mexico City, "Modernization traps us [the Indians]; it destroys the communal life."[9] Other indigenous people end up migrating illegally across the border to the United States.

Can the indigenous people of Mexico maintain their traditional cultures while living in such dire circumstances? They and many of their supporters feel that Mexico's federal government merely talks about the rights of the indigenous and the importance of the native peoples to Mexican society but does little to help them. If such a situation continues to exist, the indigenous people will always be regarded as "the conquered," a remnant of a once-powerful and accomplished empire that disappeared long ago. The struggles of Mexico's indigenous people illustrate the continuing legacy of the Spanish conquest.

Notes

1. Mark Burkholder and Suzanne Hiles, "An Empire Beyond Compare," in *The Oxford History of Mexico*, ed. Michael C. Meyer and William H. Beezley. New York: Oxford University Press, 2000, p. 123.

2. Michael Wood, *Conquistadors.* Berkeley and Los Angeles: Univer-

sity of California Press, 2000, p. 20.

3. Alonso de Zorita, *Life and Labor in Ancient Mexico: The Brief and Summary Relation of the Lords of New Spain*. New Brunswick, NJ: Rutgers University Press, 1963, p. 205.

4. Hugh Thomas, *Aztecs*. London: Royal Academy of Arts, 2002, p. 79.

5. Quoted in Enrique Krauze, *Mexico: Biography of Power*. New York: HarperCollins, 1997, p. 167.

6. John Mason Hart, "The Mexican Revolution, 1910–1920," in *The Oxford History of Mexico*, ed. Michael C. Meyer and William H. Beezley. New York: Oxford University Press, 2000, p. 465.

7. Hart, "The Mexican Revolution, 1910–1920," p. 465.

8. José Vasconcelos, *The Cosmic Race: A Bilingual Edition*, trans. Didier T. Jaen. Baltimore: Johns Hopkins University Press, 1997, p. 40.

9. Quoted in Pablo Garibian, "Mexico City's Urban Indians Call for Autonomy," *Planet Ark*, October 7, 2003. www.planetark.org.

THE HISTORY OF NATIONS
Chapter 1

Great Indian Civilizations Flourish: Mexico Prior to 1517

The Earliest People of Mexico

By Robert Ryal Miller

In the following selection, Robert Ryal Miller traces the history of Mexico's earliest civilizations. The first people in ancient Mexico were nomadic hunters and gatherers who began to settle into farming communities around 7000 B.C. The Olmec, called the "mother culture" by Mexican archaeologist Alfonso Caso, established several customs and beliefs that influenced the cultures that came after them. Among these were calendars, the practice of human sacrifice, a ritual ball game, the building of pyramids and plazas, and the carving of stone into many ornamental and ceremonial objects.

The Amerindian civilization that stands out from those that rose and declined in the centuries before the arrival of the Europeans is the Maya. Like many scholars, Miller likens the Maya to the ancient Greeks in the level of their artistic and intellectual advances. Mayan accomplishments included a mathematical system, hieroglyphics, and the building of ceremonial cities. Other influential groups who played a role in shaping Mexico's Indian past were the Toltecs, the Zapotecs, and the Mixtecs. Around A.D. 800 the Toltecs began to build a large urban center in the Valley of Mexico, a high basin situated in the central part of the country. They ruled over the land south of the Valley of Mexico as well as the land east to the coast of the Gulf of Mexico. In the 1100s, the Toltec empire collapsed, clearing the way for another group to take control. This group was the Aztecs, who entered the Valley of Mexico in the mid-1200s.

Robert Ryal Miller is a former professor of Mexican history who has written extensively on Mexican and Latin American history and the history of the American West. He is the author of For Science and National Glory: The Spanish Scientific Expedition to America, 1862–1866 *and the translator of* Chronicle of Colonial Lima: The Diary of Josephe and Francisco Mugaburu, 1640–1697.

Robert Ryal Miller, *Mexico: A History*. Norman: University of Oklahoma Press, 1985. Copyright © 1985 by Robert Ryal Miller. Reproduced by permission.

M exico's human history began with the aboriginal people we call Indians—American Indians or Amerinds, to distinguish them from East Indians. Their archaeological records go back at least ten thousand years, and circumstantial evidence doubles that figure. Excavated sites reveal the presence of primitive men and women who used fire, had chipped-stone tools, and lived by hunting game and gathering wild plants. Over the centuries, hundreds of native tribes developed their own cultures, but only a few perfected an advanced civilization. Who were these "first Mexicans," and where did they come from? The records are meager; we must rely on scant archaeological evidence, oral traditions, comparison of artistic styles, and informed conjecture. . . .

Virtually all scholars believe that the primitive people of the Western Hemisphere originated in Asia. The most commonly held theory is that bands of hunters came to Alaska from northeastern Asia, using a land or ice bridge across the Bering Strait. This gradual movement from Siberia probably occurred thirty to forty thousand years ago during the Pleistocene Epoch (Ice Age), when the level of the oceans was much lower than today. Successive waves of Mongoloids, in pursuit of game or fleeing from danger, penetrated ever deeper into the New World, pushing earlier groups south and east. Assuming that the great majority of the first Americans came to this continent via the Bering Strait does not preclude the possibility of other arrivals by sea along the Aleutian Island chain, or transpacific crossings from Polynesia or Asia. And over the centuries there may have been a few people who crossed the Atlantic Ocean from Europe or Africa, sailing west on purpose or carried that direction by winds and currents. . . .

The scattered groups of nomadic hunters who first came to what is now called Mexico were in the Paleolithic (Stone Age) stage of development. Using traps, slings, throwing sticks (*atlatls*), and stone-tipped spears they slaughtered the now extinct species of mammoth, camel, and wild horse, as well as bison, bear, deer, and smaller mammals. . . .

As food gatherers and hunters, these earliest Mexicans wandered in bands or family groups, foraging for fruits, seeds, or roots of wild plants. They collected various berries, mesquite beans, onion bulbs, piñon nuts, sunflower seeds, and prickly pear cactus fruit (tunas). After the big game became extinct about 7000 B.C.—probably because of the dramatic shift to a desert-like cli-

mate that affected northern and central Mexico at that time—
they hunted deer, peccary, and smaller game, fished in lakes or
streams, and trapped armadillos, birds, gophers, iguanas, rabbits,
serpents, and turtles. Over the millennia, the bands were incorporated into tribes that grew in numbers, developed distinct languages, and elaborated more complex cultures. In domestic arts
the Indians fabricated nets for snaring fish and animals; made baskets; fashioned clothing from fur, feathers, or hides; and wove
fibers of cotton, yucca, sisal, and maguey.

The First Farmers

About 7000 B.C. some ancestral Mexicans discovered agriculture—that is, that seeds and roots could be planted to produce
more of the same kind. Very gradually they domesticated several
plants: beans, squash, and eventually maize or Indian corn. Maize
cultivation was a crucial step toward agriculture and an advanced
civilization. They planted the corn along with squash and bean
seeds in holes made with a fire-hardened digging stick. Their first
ears of maize were less than three centimeters (about an inch)
long and bore about fifty small kernels, but as time went on, the
cobs grew larger because of seed selection and careful cultivation. Eventually, the hybrid would not reproduce without man's
intervention. Indian women discovered several ways to prepare
maize for eating. They roasted or boiled the ears, or hulled the
corn and ground the dry kernels on a flat stone metate quern [a
kind of hand mill]. Parched, ground corn, sometimes mixed with
spices, was added to water for a nutritious drink, pinole; corn
flour dough was used for tamales or in a porridge called atole;
but most often the dough was patted out as tortillas, the thin un-
leavened cakes widely used as bread (even today), which they
cooked on stone slabs heated by charcoal fires.

Ultimately, the practice of agriculture liberated some of the
nomadic tribes from a constant search for food and permitted
them to settle down. They acquired additional land for cultivation by burning undergrowth or jungle, by terracing the slopes,
and by draining or filling suitable plots. This development was
accompanied by an increase in population. The combination of
an agricultural basis and village life gave the people more leisure
time, made possible vast public projects, and led to chiefdoms, or
hierarchical social systems wherein certain groups, such as the
chief and his relatives, were supported by the rest of the popula-

tion. It also became necessary to develop more elaborate rules or laws for land and water usage and to regulate societal behavior. . . .

As [Indian] society became more complex, so did their religion. To regulate planting and harvesting, shaman priests made astronomical observations and developed a calendar that involved mathematical calculations and some kind of record keeping. Priests organized celebrations related to fertility, rainmaking, and harvesting, and they presided over ceremonies connected with human birth, death, illness, and with civic affairs. Indian priests directed the construction of sacred mounds, usually built in the form of flat-topped pyramids, as centers for religious observances. At the pyramids and in their homes, Indians had idols made of wood, fired clay, bone, or stone to honor their deities or to serve as cult amulets. Evidence of human sacrifices shows an early concern with appeasing the forces of nature, and items associated with burials suggest that they had the concept of an afterlife.

Civilizations—generally defined as a relatively high level of human cultural and technological development—evolved in several parts of Mexico. Prominent features of these advanced cultures included: social stratification, labor specialization, monumental architecture, elaborate religious hierarchies closely integrated with the political structure, intensive agriculture, efficient methods for the distribution of food and other products, and a system of writing or record keeping. The evolution of civilized society was the culmination of millennia of cultural developments and ecological adaptation.

Phases of Development and Traits

Many archaeologists and historians divide pre-Columbian cultures into three distinct phases of development. The first, called the Formative or pre-Classic, dates from 2500 B.C. to A.D. 1; next is the Classic period, which embraced the first nine centuries of the Christian era; and finally the post-Classic from A.D. 900 to 1520. This scheme is useful for classifying artifacts and making cross-cultural comparisons, but since some of the civilizations span more than one period, it will be more convenient here to narrate the history of the principal advanced cultures, identifying them by their tribal names. Actually, we do not know what some of the people called themselves; for them we use names applied much later. . . .

Each Middle American [the region from central Mexico to

the Gulf of Nicoya in Costa Rica] Indian civilization had distinctive traits, but all had several things in common. They depended on maize as a staple food, as Mexicans still do; they cultivated maguey (agave) plants for fiber and for a beer-like beverage (*octli* or *pulque*); their polytheism was based on worshiping the forces of nature; they built truncated [flat-topped] pyramids which served as platforms for their temples and in at least one case also served as a burial place for a dignitary; they had dual calendars, ceremonial and solar; and their crafts had reached a high level of artistic style and technical competence. . . .

The Olmec

Ironically, one of the oldest pre-Columbian civilizations, the Olmec, is also the newest; that is, it was "discovered" and studied only since the late 1930s. This pre-Classic culture, which gradually emerged in the swampy lowlands of the Veracruz-Tabasco coast, flourished for hundreds of years in the first millennium B.C.; the most frequently cited dates are 1200 to 400 B.C. We do not know what these early people called themselves, but later dwellers in their homeland were called Olmecs (People of the Rubber Country). That area was long known for the latex extracted from native rubber trees (*guayule*) which was used for rubber balls and for waterproofing baskets and cloth. Olmecs ate seafood, aquatic birds, and toads, and they cultivated maize as well as harvested cacao trees. Their rise to civilization was related to an extensive trade network that may have been responsible for the emergence of a wealthy elite and the stratification of society.

The Olmecs did not build great cities, but they embellished their splendid, well-planned ceremonial centers with massive basalt monoliths. Three principal Olmec sites are called La Venta, San Lorenzo, and Tres Zapotes. . . .

Colossal stone heads, some measuring three meters (nine feet) high and weighing eighteen metric tons, are the most spectacular feature of Olmec art. Archaeologists have found more than a dozen of these enormous ovoid [egglike] monuments, which are believed to be portraits of actual Olmec leaders. The carved heads are topped by helmet-like caps that may have been worn in ritualistic ball games, and the faces have broad nostrils and thick lips like some Totonac Indians who still live in the general area. The question of how these monoliths were transported can only be answered with a guess that the ancients used rafts on artificial canals or waterways that have since disappeared. . . .

We know little about the daily life of the Olmecs, their political organization, or reasons for the collapse of their civilization. San Lorenzo was violently destroyed about 900 B.C., and five centuries later La Venta suffered a similar catastrophe. The deliberate mutilation of stone monuments at these sites suggests internal rebellion or external invasion. Olmec cultural achievements did not disappear with the loss of these centers; they remained viable in the homeland for several hundred years and were passed on to other Mesoamerican peoples. . . .

The Maya

The ancient Maya Indians created a spectacular civilization in southern Mesoamerica. In many ways their achievements surpass all other native American groups—certainly their superb monumental remains are more numerous. Some historians have compared the Maya to the ancient Greeks, noting that both made great intellectual advances, designed aesthetically pleasing works of art and passed their civilization on to other peoples. Millions of their descendants still inhabit parts of southeastern Mexico, Guatemala, Belize, Honduras, and El Salvador, where they cultivate indigenous plants, produce traditional folk art, and speak various dialects of the Maya language.

Their history in the early Formative era is obscure, but for more than a thousand years before A.D. 300 the Maya perfected their agriculture, religion, and arts. By the first century B.C. they lived in small agricultural villages and cultivated maize, beans, squash, and in some places harvested cacao, vanilla, sisal, and cotton. From the last two plants they made rope, mats, hammocks, and clothing. They also traded extensively by land and sea with people far to the north and south. Ecological adaptation, institutional order, and an understanding of higher mathematics were bases upon which the Maya civilization was built.

Within the vast Maya area archaeologists distinguish three geographical regions where different cultures evolved. The highlands of central Guatemala, adjacent El Salvador, and Honduras provided fertile land, a benign climate, and other resources to support a large population, then and now. Many early settlement sites, such as Kaminaljuyú, have been uncovered in the high intermountain valleys. The low-lying Yucatán peninsula was a second ecological zone settled by the Maya. It is a tropical plain, virtually treeless, with shallow soil deposits and very little rainfall; nevertheless, an adequate supply of sub-surface water and natural wells (*cenotes*) along with man-made cisterns makes cultivation possible. Settled by humans long ago, this northern lowland region still has a high population. Between Yucatán and the highlands is a third Maya region that is scarcely inhabited today, the central lowlands with its Petén jungle core and adjacent uplands in Chiapas, Belize, and Honduras. Mostly covered by dense tropical forests interspersed by rivers and swamps, and with heavy rainfall and humidity that make even slash and burn agriculture difficult, this region seems least suitable for human settlement; yet it was here that the Maya civilization flowered early and reached its highest peak.

The golden age of the Maya occurred from A.D. 300 to 900, when their culture flourished in the central lowlands. During this Classic period they built the great ceremonial centers known today as Bonampak, Copán, Palenque, Piedras Negras, Tikal, Uaxactún, and a dozen others. A remarkable system of causeways (*sacbeob*) connected some of these places, facilitating collection of tribute and exchange of trade items. These "cities" were not typical urban communities; instead they were civic-religious centers that had some elite dwellings, and dispersed in the surrounding area were scattered hamlets where the bulk of the peasants lived.

The genius of the Maya is revealed in their extant monuments at the Classic era sites. Here are handsome limestone temples with mansard-type roofs topped with decorative combs; stone-faced pyramids that usually served as a base for temples; cut-stone buildings that seem to have been used as government headquarters and official residences; ball courts, gateways, plazas, carved stone pillars (stelae); and water-reservoirs—all constructed without metal tools. . . .

A Number System and Writing

The Maya numerical system was a brilliant achievement that paved the way for their advancements in astronomy, engineering, and calendrical calculations. With only three symbols—a dot for one, a bar for five, and a shell-like figure for zero—they made complicated computations by using a positional mode that increased by twenties from bottom to top (unlike our decimal system, which increases by tens from right to left of the decimal point). The bottom, or units, position recorded numbers from 0 through 19; the second position sub-total was multiplied by twenty; the third position multiplied by 400 (20×20); and so on. . . .

Maya numerals also had an alternative form, a glyph that was the head of an animal, a bird, or a mythological creature. Numerical symbols were only part of the written communication pattern.

Maya hieroglyphic writing was the most sophisticated of all the American Indian inscription systems. More than four hundred glyphs, representing numbers, dates, colors, and more complicated matters, were chiseled in stone, painted in wet plaster and on pottery, and drawn in primitive books made from paper derived from the inner bark of the wild fig tree. These paper records, or codices, were folded accordian-fashion. Only three of them survive today. . . . The glyphs, only partly deciphered today, recorded data and abstract knowledge related to chronology, astronomy, religion, and highlights of the rule of certain leaders.

Maya Society

Classic Maya society was stratified. At the top was an elite hereditary nobility composed of priests and ranking officials and their families; the middle sectors were the majority, the families of craftsmen and specialists, commoners, and peasant farmers; and at the bottom was a large component of slaves who were convicted criminals, or prisoners of war, or those who sold themselves or were sold by their families into servitude. Children of slaves were born free. Many scholars believe that the Classic Maya political organization was theocratic; others maintain there was a secular ruler and a high priest. Certainly there was a hierarchy of priests who were carried on litters and whose functions included prophesy, medicine, education of candidates for the priesthood, and religious rituals. . . .

After six hundred years of splendor in the central lowlands, development suddenly ceased and the Maya centers were abandoned. No inscriptions dated later than A.D. 950 have been found there. Although there is some evidence of foreign intruders at the end of the Classic period, it is not believed that military conquest caused the collapse. Scholars have suggested several possible reasons: a maize virus, soil exhaustion, prolonged drought, epidemic disease, hurricanes, or supernatural visions perceived by leaders who were told to move elsewhere. But the best evidence

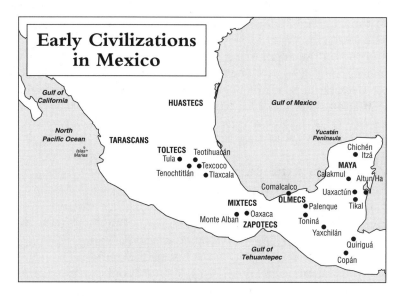

points to peasant insurrections. Apparently the workers, oppressed by an increasing tax and work load to support the nobles and priests, retreated into the jungle, whereupon the whole society collapsed. The demographic and vital center of lowland civilization then shifted to northern Yucatán. The Maya highland petty states and chiefdoms, which had lagged far behind Classic era lowland developments, continued to exist.

A Maya renaissance occurred in northern Yucatán beginning in the tenth century. During this post-Classic period old centers in Yucatán were rebuilt and new ones were established near natural wells, the only reliable source of fresh water. Culture, techniques, and traditions from the south were transplanted in the north, perhaps carried there by priests or refugees. But the striking feature of this period was the influence from central Mexico that came with an actual invasion by Nahuatl-speaking Toltecs who settled down and fused their culture with the Maya. The architecture of this renascent Maya-Toltec period is not as refined as the Classic period, but it has a grandeur based on magnitude coupled with a simplicity of decoration. . . .

Maya-Toltec Culture

Maya-Toltec culture flourished for a few hundred years in Yucatán before it disintegrated. Oral traditions suggest that political stability was first maintained through a confederation or league of three cities: Chichén Itzá, Mayapán (a walled city), and Ux-mal. Then about A.D. 1200 Mayapán destroyed Chichén Itzá and dominated the area until it was annihilated in a revolt in the mid–fifteenth century. Thereafter, small independent chiefdoms were established, but their intermittent civil wars hastened the cultural decline. The final blow to Maya civilization came from the Spanish, who first overran the highland Maya chiefdoms and then invaded the northern lowlands. . . .

Zapotecs and Mixtecs

Between Maya territory and the highland Valley of Mexico is the cultural crossroads of Oaxaca, home of the distinctive Za-potec and Mixtec Indians. Both of these groups developed ad-vanced cultures that were as complex as any Mesoamerican civ-ilization. The origins of each society are clouded—a felicitous word since both called themselves "Cloud People."

The Zapotec heydey occurred during the Classic era (A.D. 200–900), when their principal center was at the hilltop of Monte Albán. This crest, which overlooks the city of Oaxaca, is located at the junction of three valleys; it had been a ceremonial center for hundreds of years before the Zapotecs shaped it into an urban complex. The top of the hill was leveled to form a gi-gantic plaza more than three hundred meters (330 yards) long, surrounded by pyramids, palaces, a ball court, elaborately deco-rated tombs, and an observatory. The slopes and adjacent hills were residential zones. Artifacts found here show influences from the Gulf Coast, Yucatán, and the central highlands. Like other ad-vanced cultures, the Zapotecs had a vigesimal [based on twenty] counting system using bar and dot number glyphs, and they had dual calendars, a ceremonial one of 260 days and another one based on the solar year.

About A.D. 900 the empire radiating from Monte Albán col-lapsed, and the hilltop complex was abandoned. Perhaps the cause of this disintegration was related to the rise of militaristic soci-eties and the contemporary turmoil throughout Mesoamerica. In the succeeding post-Classic era rival Zapotec groups remained in the Oaxaca valleys—their political chiefs sometimes at Zaachila and their priests at Mitla (Place of the Dead), an old sacred site and necropolis forty-five kilometers (twenty-seven miles) south-east of Monte Albán. Mitla's temple architecture is unique, with handsome fitted stone mosaic friezes in forty geometric designs, including step frets, scrolls, and squared spirals. At the end of the thirteenth century a few Mixtecs moved south into the Valley of Oaxaca, where some of their elite intermarried with Zapotecs. Then, in the following century, the Mixtecs conquered Zaachila and forced the principal Zapotec ruler to seek refuge in Tehuantepec. Subsequently, the Mixtecs expanded their control over the region from their political center of Cuilapan (also called Sayacu).

The Mixtecs, whose cultural crucible seems to have been in the mountains between the Valley of Oaxaca and southern Puebla (or perhaps farther north), reached their zenith in the post-Classic era. Eight extant codices, painted in bright colors on deerskin, trace their dynastic history from the late seventh century to the coming of the Spaniards. These pictographs contain data on genealogies of various officials, plants and animals utilized, gods and temples, human sacrifice, and the conquest of towns. It is clear that the Mixtecs created several militaristic states or princedoms based on subjugation of peoples in order to exact tribute. . . .

Sometime in the second half of the fifteenth century Aztec (Mexica) armies marched into Oaxaca, where, after much resistance, they subdued Cuilapan, Zaachila, and other cities. During this period there were various battles between combinations of Aztecs, Mixtecs, and Zapotecs. Finally, the region was politically unified by the Spaniards, who conquered it in the 1520s.

Teotihuacán

Northwest of the Mixtec-Zapotec country is the beautiful Valley of Mexico, a vast oval basin where several pre-Columbian civilizations developed and where Mexico City was eventually built. On the valley floor were five interconnected lakes (now reduced to one), and ringing it were snow-covered volcanos, notably Popocatépetl and Iztaccíhuatl. Although it is in the tropics, this large valley has a temperate climate because of its elevation of about 2,200 meters (7,200 feet). There were Formative era settlements at several valley sites such as Tlatilco and Cuicuilco, the latter abandoned after a volcanic eruption, but the earliest advanced civilization flowered in the Classic period in the northeast part of the valley. We do not know what the inhabitants called the place, but the Aztecs later named the abandoned urban site Teotihuacán (Place of the Gods), and the Spaniards renamed it San Juan de Teotihuacán.

The ruins of the vast complex of Teotihuacán, called simply

"the Pyramids" by modern tourists, lie about forty kilometers (twenty-five miles) northeast of the present capital of Mexico. This site was occupied by a sedentary agricultural society for a thousand years before its rise as a Classic era city. From the beginning of the Christian era it grew rapidly until its peak about six centuries later, when it covered an area of twenty square kilometers (7.7 square miles) and had a population of at least 100,000—perhaps double that figure. Besides being the most highly urbanized place of its time in the New World it was also a preeminent temple center, seat of a powerful state, and focus of a far-reaching trade network. . . .

Mystery surrounds the downfall of Teotihuacán, which seems to have occurred in the eighth century. Many of the buildings show traces of burning and destruction—was the city plundered and put to the torch by invaders? Or was there an internal struggle between religious and military or secular forces? Clearly, the city was abandoned, but what happened to the former inhabitants after the catastrophe? So far, archaeologists have found insufficient evidence to answer these questions. After the fall of Teotihuacán another Indian civilization, the Toltec, began to use the deserted city for ceremonies and as a burial place for its leaders.

The Toltecs

In many ways the Toltec empire, which flourished in the post-Classic period, spans the gap between the fall of Teotihuacán and the rise of Aztec predominance in central highland Mexico. . . . The Toltecs were composed of two distinct ethnic groups: the Nonoalcas, who came to central highland Mexico from the Gulf Coast, and the Tolteca-Chichimecas, who moved southeast into settled areas in and around the Valley of Mexico. Their primary base was at Tula (Tollan in Nahuatl), about eighty kilometers (forty-eight miles) north of the present capital of Mexico and not far from the abandoned city of Teotihuacán. Here, where the junction of two rivers made irrigated agriculture possible, beginning about A.D. 800 the Toltecs developed a prosperous urban center with a peak size three centuries later of perhaps 65,000 inhabitants plus a sizeable rural population. Tula had a large ball court, various temples with friezes depicting jaguars and eagles eating human hearts, and those intriguing Chacmool statues of reclining figures with their elbows on the ground and knees raised. Most impressive of all is an extant truncated pyramid topped by giant stone Atlantean columns that once supported a temple roof. These pillars, carved to resemble warriors, are appropriate symbols for the militaristic state.

From their base at Tula the Toltecs created a tributary empire that extended south through the Valley of Mexico to Cuernavaca and Xochicalco, east to Tulancingo and Huachinango (halfway to the Gulf Coast), and west perhaps as far as Toluca. They seemed to have had an alliance with two city-states, Otumba and Culhuacán, the latter located near the southern shore of Lake Texcoco. There were also some Toltec colonies, probably on the Gulf Coast, but certainly at Chichén Itzá, Yucatán.

In the twelfth century, Tula suffered a series of crises and disasters that led to the dispersal of many inhabitants and the collapse of Toltec imperial power. Bands of semi-nomadic Chichimecs invaded from the northwest; the ceremonial center of the city was damaged and burned; and later, Huastecas from the Gulf Coast attacked the city. An internal schism culminated about A.D. 1125 with the departure of a certain faction that ultimately took possession of Cholula.

At this time other Chichimecs under the leadership of Mixcoatl moved into the Valley of Mexico, where they intermarried with Toltecs and established a new Toltec dynasty based at Culhuacán. About A.D. 1150, Mixcoatl was assassinated and his position usurped. . . . In the resulting chaos a major portion of the population left Tula, and Toltec power collapsed. There followed an extended period of conflict between various groups in the central highlands. No single state dominated the area until the Aztecs created a confederation in the fifteenth century.

Possible Explanations for the Rise of the Maya

By Robert J. Sharer

The most brilliant society to emerge in the ancient Americas was the Maya. During the peak of their civilization—around the A.D. 700s— the Maya built numerous cities in what is today southern Mexico, Guatemala, Belize, and Honduras. The history of the Maya and the depth of their accomplishments—which include richly decorated temples, palaces, and pyramids, systems of writing and mathematics, a way of keeping track of time, and a complex system of beliefs—has been revealed first through the work of explorers and archaeologists who uncovered the physical artifacts of the Maya and, second, through the efforts of anthropologists and ethnohistorians who reconstruct past civilizations. The Mayan story is incomplete, however, and is being filled in gradually and systematically by the current generation of scholars and scientists.

One scientist familiar with the ancient Maya is Robert J. Sharer, the author of the following selection. Sharer is a professor of anthropology and curator of the American section of the University Museum of Archaeology and Anthropology at the University of Pennsylvania. He provides an anthropological perspective on the history of the Maya and offers possible reasons for the great rise of the Mayan civilization.

There were many reasons for the meteoric rise of the Maya, and archaeologists have by no means uncovered all of them. But recent research has tended to emphasize the search for "causes," and we can now identify many of the more important forces in the development of Maya civilization. The

Robert J. Sharer, *The Ancient Maya*. Stanford, CA: Stanford University Press, 1994.

34

most significant of these factors—ecological adaptation, temporal and spatial diversity, unity of elite subculture, networks of interaction, competition, and ideology—merit some examination. They did not operate in isolation, of course, but rather in concert, to shape this remarkable civilization.

Making Use of the Land

Ecological adaptation comprises the interrelated factors of environment, subsistence, and population growth. These are obviously important to an understanding of any human society, for environmental conditions and the means used to produce food largely determine the characteristics of a human population, including its health and nutritional status and whether or not it can sustain growth in size, density, or organizational complexity. The Maya experience is in many ways an excellent illustration of these relationships, for the Maya area presented its inhabitants with an extremely diverse environment, one that is rich in resources and blessed with a variety of opportunities for developing means to obtain food, and the Maya, for much of their history at least, made the most of their environmental opportunities. The earliest means of human subsistence, hunting and gathering, was greatly facilitated in this environment. Rich in food resources, the area in time came to support permanent villages in the most productive coastal environments and connecting river valleys. Throughout Maya prehistory, in fact, hunting and gathering continued to provide essential protein. Later refinements may have included the development of artificial ponds for the raising of fish, such as those that have been identified along the west coast of the Yucatan Peninsula.

One of the earliest forms of cultivation in the Maya area was undoubtedly swidden agriculture, whereby fields were cleared, burned off, and planted with a variety of food crops, including maize, beans, squash, chilis, and such root crops as manioc and sweet potatoes. But whatever the crop, tropical soils become exhausted after several years of cultivation, and new fields must be cleared and planted while the old lie fallow. Swidden agriculture is nonetheless adaptable to a wide range of environments, from highland valleys and mountain slopes to lowland jungle and scrub forest. For the modern Maya farmer, in fact, it remains the most common method of cultivation, and it is still practiced from the highlands of Guatemala to the lowlands of Yucatan.

Swidden cultivation is an example of *extensive* agriculture: large areas are needed to produce rather low yields per unit area, since a large proportion of land must remain fallow at any given time. More *intensive* agricultural methods usually require some means of replenishing the soils. Under certain favorable circumstances, such as the periodic flooding that revives alluvial river valleys, the replenishment is the gift of nature. But in their household gardens, the Maya did their own replenishing, using what is probably the oldest intensive method of cultivation: a plot of land adjacent to the family dwelling is fertilized by household refuse. Household gardens are still in use in many Maya communities today. Important garden cultigens include tree crops such as avocado, cacao, guava, papaya, hog plum, palm, and ramon (breadnut), and some small plots are given over to the many crops grown in the swidden fields. Such crops, however, were not confined to the household gardens of the ancient Maya; those with commercial value, such as cotton, cacao, and probably oil palm may well have been grown in large stands located in favorable areas like (in the case of cacao) the Pacific coast, the lower Motagua Valley, and the Caribbean coast.

Other intensive methods, techniques found rarely or not at all in this area today, included agricultural terracing and raised fields. Evidence for ancient terracing has been found in parts of the Maya highlands and in hilly portions of the lowlands. Raised fields, similar to the *chinampas* ("floating gardens") of Central Mexico, allowed productive use of swampy or poorly drained land. Crops were grown on parallel or intersecting ridges of well-drained, fertile soil built up from the swamp floor. The canals between the raised fields provided drainage and served as a source for rich soil that was periodically scooped up to renew the growing areas. The canals may also have been used for raising fish and other aquatic life. These raised fields could support a variety of crops, including nonfood items such as cotton and tobacco for local consumption or, more importantly, commercial production for export to other areas. It has been suggested that many of the raised fields whose remains have been found in northern Belize were used for growing cacao as well as maize. Relic raised-field systems have also been identified in the western lowlands, along the lower Río Usumacinta and Río Candelaria, in the eastern lowlands, and possibly in the *bajos* (seasonal swamps) of the central Peten.

How do these subsistence adaptations help us to understand the development of Maya civilization? To begin with, given the diversity of the environment within the Maya area, it follows that there would have been a corresponding variety in the subsistence modes and resources available from one locale to the next and, consequently, a diversity of potentials for growth and for exchanges with neighboring areas. Although each of the subsistence methods had its own, distinct origins—some at an early date, others much later—all undoubtedly followed a similar pattern of development. As a given area was colonized, its environmental potentials led to a sequence of cultural responses: initial experimentation with known resource-acquisition methods, followed either by acceptance (with or without modification), if they proved successful, or by rejection and renewed experimentation with new methods. Ultimately, areas suitable for increased food production and rich in other resources supported population growth and expanded settlements, which in turn produced powerful incentives for still more intensified agriculture. . . .

The Diverse Maya

The spatial and cultural diversity of Classic Maya civilization originated in and was maintained by boundaries that were set by both natural and cultural factors. Many of the qualities of diversity within Maya civilization no doubt derive primarily from environmental limits, reinforced and perpetuated by social boundaries. Ascribing cultural diversity to environmental diversity and limits is particularly justified in the much more broken topography of the Maya highlands, but, although the impact of the environment is less dramatic in the lowlands (and was, until recently, often ignored), it was important there as well. Still, social boundaries in the lowlands stemmed chiefly from a pattern that saw multiple groups expanding and settling the landscape and, in the process, creating social and political groups that discourage both fissioning [splitting] from within and incursions from without.

One important consequence of environmental and cultural boundaries may be found in the Maya political structure. *It seems clear that the Maya were never politically unified;* from beginning to end, their society was fragmented into scores of independent polities [organized states]. The basis of this organizational and political diversity has been sought from several perspectives, often by drawing upon analogies from non-Maya ethnographic or historical sources. These include models of Classic Maya sociopolitical organization as a "chiefdom-like" ranked society integrated by vertical patron-client obligations (these based on ethnographic analogies with East African or similar preindustrial kingdoms) or as a feudal system with a more stratified organization integrated by both vertical obligations and horizontal marriage alliances (these derived from analogies with a variety of societies, including medieval Western Europe, feudal Japan, and

BALL GAMES

The presence of ball courts is one of the most interesting aspects of ancient Mayan cities. Archaeologists working in the 1800s and 1900s identified these spaces among the ruins of Chichén Itzá, Uxmal, Copán, Palenque, and Tikal. A typical ball court consisted of long, parallel walls several feet apart that rose to deep embankments on both sides. The walls formed an open alley at each end. Rings were fitted along the walls of the alley. Archaeologists found images of the ball game in Mayan sculpture and painted ceramics. Their findings led them to imagine that the Maya used the court to play a game involving a rubber ball being thrown through the rings. The ball game was also popular among the Aztecs and through them became known to the Spanish, who wrote about it in their histories of the Spanish Conquest.

Games have been part of human culture for thousands of years. From ancient Egypt to China, Greece, Rome and early Europe, people have competed with each other on the field of sports. However in these early civilizations most sports were based on individual tests of skill and strength. Even the early Olympic tradition placed its emphasis on an individual's competence in sports. It was in the Americas, particularly in prehispanic Mexico, that the focus of games became team sports, not personal prowess.

In Mesoamerica, long before the arrival of the Spanish, there was an amazing enthusiasm for team sports, an enthusiasm unequaled in any other place until recent times.

contemporary East Africa). And more recently, [noted historian] Jeremy Sabloff has viewed the Classic Maya as a system of peer polities, or a cluster of independent petty states where proximity and competition checked the growth of any single polity and discouraged political unification. In contrast to these models, which tend to see political power as deriving from control over production, [historian] David Freidel has proposed a more dispersed and subtle system of political authority maintained by

This vying of one group against another in team competition is still a phenomenon of American life and modern games still carry on many traditions established over 3000 years ago in the New World. The heritage of these ancient games still exists in the traditions and rituals of modern sports. The actual concept of playing on a team, formal court/stadium settings, special rituals, standardized equipment, formal gear or uniforms, gambling, professional players, the creation of heroes and the use of a rubber ball were all part of the sporting world of [3000 years ago] just as they are today. . . .

Scholars have learned much about this game through chronicles of the colonial era, archaeological remains of ball courts and game paraphernalia, and contemporary ethnographic practices among Maya peoples. The Mesoamerican ballgame challenges our understanding of the secular nature of sports because of its intimate connection with cosmology and ritual sacrifice to the gods.

Precolumbian ball courts were usually built at the heart of sacred ceremonial centers in cities. The ballgame was often played for ritual purposes and the outcome of these games resulted in the sacrifice of defeated players. . . . The sacrifice of slaves or prisoners of war, who were forced to participate in ritual ballgames, was seen as something necessary for sustaining a sense of balance with the gods and with the Maya cosmos.

Jane Stevenson Day, "The Precolumbian Ballgame," exhibit at the Birmingham Museum of Art, May 5–October 20, 1996.

control over distribution (he draws his model from analogies of pilgrimages and market fairs). . . .

One difficulty of all such models derived from analogies with other societies is that they often portray Classic Maya sociopolitical organization as uniform in character, right across the lowlands. The available archaeological and ethnohistorical data from the Maya themselves, however, clearly indicate that the independent Maya polities varied in their organizational structure and changed through time. . . .

Maya polities appear to have been mostly small-scale localized states, and we are just beginning to address questions concerning the organizational diversity, among these polities, and the delineation of their individual developmental trajectories. Important integrative factors—forces tending to link polities rather than divide them—also operated throughout the course of Maya civilization. Some of these were economic or ideological. Others involved political aggrandizement—brought about either by marriage alliances or by conquest and military alliances—although expansions of this sort appear to have been relatively fragile and short-lived. . . .

Thus, far from being a monolithic entity, Maya civilization was a vast and diverse manifestation, flowering over a varied geographical area and across an extensive temporal span. Though the Classic period is traditionally defined as ca. A.D. 250–900, many characteristics of Maya civilization originated during the previous 800 or so years of the Middle and Late Preclassic, and persisted for more than 600 years beyond the Classic, through the Postclassic. During this long span of time the character of Maya civilization constantly changed. But at no point in time can we recognize a unified system, for what we term Maya civilization always comprised many linguistic, social, and political groupings. . . .

Upper-Class Innovators

Our definition of Maya civilization rests heavily on the material manifestations of the elite subculture, the class within each Maya polity that managed and directed the course of that polity. And to the degree that these polities formed an interdependent system of states (or peer polities), the economic, social, and ideological ties that created this network were maintained by the elite. Seen in a dynamic perspective, it was these elite-directed activities, both within and between the independent Maya polities, that fueled the evolutionary course of Maya civilization. Elites sponsored the innovations—recognizable in the archaeological record—that stimulated the cycles of growth and decline we can see throughout the course of Maya civilization. These range from the intensification of agriculture to more efficient political institutions. During the Classic period, authority centered on the position of the Maya king, or *ahau*, who ruled in each of the major lowland polities. The *ahau's* power was legitimized [made legal] by a synthesis of preexisting and innovative forms, including the erection of monuments for the display of genealogies and momentous events, the hereditary transmission of power within the ruling lineage, and the construction of a monumental funerary temple dedicated to veneration of the ruler's divinity. Smaller or less-successful centers may never have adopted all these Classic-period mechanisms of political authority, and their perpetuation of older (Preclassic) elite institutions, and the evolution of new institutions of political power after the Classic period, would then have contributed to the contrasting organizational diversity of Maya civilization.

Trade Among the Maya

As we have seen, the Maya were not isolated, but were active participants in a network of interconnections with the rest of Mesoamerica to the west, and Central America to the east. These networks moved principally people and goods, but they were also the conduits for the interchange of ideas. Of course trade, the exchange of goods, is the activity most apparent in the archaeological record. Trade among the ancient Maya embraced a complex of economic activity involving the acquisition and transport of goods and the exchange of goods and services (often in centralized markets). Although no conclusive physical evidence of ancient markets exists, trade centers were noted by the Spaniards at the time of the Conquest, and their antiquity is assumed. But direct archaeological evidence for trade itself, in a variety of commodities, does exist.

A distinction is often made between *localized* trade, that *within* a single environmental zone, such as a highland valley, and *long-distance* trade, that *between* environmental zones. The ancient Maya were a crucial part of a system of long-distance trade routes that ran the length and breadth of Mesoamerica and beyond. The primary long-distance trade routes in the Maya area were those that connected Central Mexico (to the northwest of the Maya) with Central America (to the southeast of the Maya). There were three primary route systems: the southern route, running along the Pacific coastal plain; the central route, running across the Peten; and the northern route, following the Yucatan coast. . . . North–south trade routes tied together the Maya area, connecting northern Yucatan and its plentiful salt resources, for instance, with the highland and coastal regions to the south. As intermediaries between Mexico and Central America, and as producers of highly desirable resources (jadeite, obsidian, salt, quetzal feathers, and much more), the Maya were inescapably the middlemen and the masters of much of the Mesoamerican economic system.

Centralized Markets

The development of centralized markets was undoubtedly a crucial factor in the growth of Maya society. Because goods could be exchanged in a single, central location, a village could engage in specialized production (of textiles or pottery, for example, according to its environmental potential), take its products to the market center, and exchange them for other necessities from other villages. The result was an economic unity and interdependence focused on the market center, and each such market was linked to others by means of long-distance trade, as well. The long-distance trade networks also furnished exotic goods that were often reserved for limited segments of society, the most important being the items that furnished wealth and symbols of status for the elite class.

Together, these economic factors were a powerful stimulus for social organization and development. The market centers, to which the villages were tied, were controlled by the emerging elite class, and the resulting economic power accorded the elites became a crucial foundation for their local status and authority. . . .

Maya Warfare

Even in the initial, expansive colonization of the Maya area, competition for land and other resources could have been expected to ensue as soon as areas suitable for agriculture and settlement began to be scarce. . . . By the Middle Preclassic [ca. 1000 B.C.], the Maya had begun raiding neighboring groups to take captives, which they used for labor and for ritualized sacrifices. These sporadic conflicts expressed and maintained the dominance of one polity over another and increased the prestige of the victorious leaders—while often eliminating the vanquished leaders as sacrifices. Eventually, the ultimate competitive option was taken up: open military conflict between polities, with the goal of expanding the victor's control over people, land, and resources.

But military activity necessarily involves certain developmental consequences. In the first place, it creates the need for a new specialty, ultimately a new occupational class, the warrior. In time, the Maya warrior class seems to have become part of the "middle class," between farmer and elite, that had initially consisted of craftsmen, merchants, and bureaucrats. In the second place, conflict between centers creates new demands on social organization; and centralized authority is usually the most efficient means of directing a society and its military forces, in either an aggressive or a defensive situation. Thus, for the Maya, as with all societies, competition and conflict were a major factor in the development of a more complex society and an increase in centralized authority. . . .

Belief System of the Maya

The ancient Maya made no distinction between the natural and supernatural worlds, as we do, and there can be no doubt that their ideology—their belief system, which explained the character and order of the world—was a significant factor in the development of their civilization. . . .

The supernatural guided all aspects of life, even the daily activities of individual people and the ways by which food and other resources were acquired. Economic transactions, political events, and social relationships, including family and village life, were seen to be subject to supernatural control. Thus ideology was embedded in ecological adaptation and in the organization of society, trade, and competition, the very factors considered crucial underpinnings of social evolution.

The structure of Maya society was defined and sanctioned by an elaborate cosmological system. The Maya cosmos was an animate, living system in which invisible powers governed all aspects of the visible world—all that was to be seen in the earth and the sky—and even the underworld hidden beneath. Each individual and social group had its role to play in this system, and the whole elaborate hierarchy of social classes, surmounted [headed by] by the elite and ruling lords, existed simply to maintain this cosmological order. . . . Any individual, from farmer to king, who deviated from an appointed task or failed in an obligation to the supernatural powers, would be punished by misfortune, illness, or even death. There were, of course, supernatural specialists, intermediaries between humans and the supernatural world, who could intervene to gain favor, or to discover the meaning of events and what the future would hold (this pursuit is called *divination*).

The Role of Shamans

The earliest supernatural intermediaries were village shamans, part-time specialists who cured illness and divined the future. But as Maya society grew and elaborated, an elite class with priestly powers emerged: full-time specialists with both supernatural and political authority, conferring on themselves the prerogatives of mediating between the supernatural and the rest of society. In essence, the Maya ruler was the supreme shaman for the society he governed, and as such was responsible for the prosperity, health, and security of all his subjects. In ancient Maya society, therefore, kings were both political leaders and priests, and the ruling elite thereby came to direct *all* community activities—the giving of tribute, the building of temples and palaces, the maintenance of long-distance trade, the launching of military expeditions, and the performance of the complex of rituals that nourish and placate the gods—all as ordained by the cosmological order.

Within such a system, success bred success, for with each bumper crop of maize, or with each victory over a rival power, the allegiance to the ruler by the ruled was strengthened, and the morale of the entire society was bolstered. But although successes increased the power and prestige of the ruler, failures did not necessarily diminish them; for minor failures could be explained away, laid against other factors, rather than be taken as signs of supernatural disfavor toward the ruler. Thus, as long as the belief in the ruler's supernatural connections remained intact, the system would not be threatened. Sudden catastrophes, of course, such as the capture of the ruler by a rival power, or long-term disasters, such as repeated crop failures, could—and often did—shake belief in the ruler's powers and place the entire system in jeopardy.

The Arrival of the Aztecs

BY MICHAEL D. COE AND REX KOONTZ

The history of the period A.D. 900 to 1521 is dominated by the Aztecs, the Amerindian people who rose to prominence in central Mexico. They were one of a group of tribes who vied for influence and control of trade after the decline of the great Mayan centers. It took the Aztecs only two hundred years from the time of their arrival in the Valley of Mexico in the late 1100s to evolve into a highly complex, differentiated society.

In the following selection, authors Michael D. Coe and Rex Koontz present a broad view of the rise of Aztec power. They describe the situation in the Valley of Mexico before the arrival of the Aztecs and explore how the Aztecs gathered power through a series of conquests of surrounding peoples. The authors also examine the Aztec rulers who created the empire that astounded the Spanish invaders who eventually conquered their society.

Michael D. Coe is a professor of anthropology at Yale University. He is the author of The Maya, Breaking the Maya Code, *and* Reading the Maya Glyphs. *Rex Koontz lectures on art history at the University of Houston and has written about ancient Mexican art, architecture, and aesthetics. He is the author of* Landscape and Power in Ancient Mesoamerica.

The beginnings of the Aztec nation, as we know them from their own accounts, were so humble and obscure that their rise to supremacy over most of Mexico in the space of a few hundred years seems almost miraculous. It is somehow inconceivable that the magnificent civilization witnessed and destroyed by the Spaniards could have been created by a people who were not many generations removed from the most abject barbarism, yet this is what their histories tell us.

But these histories, all of which were written down in Nahuatl (the Aztec language) or in Spanish early in the Colonial period [1524–1767], must be considered in their context, and rigorously evaluated. First, given the nature of central Mexican chronology during the Post-Classic [1000–1492], which was based on the 52-year Calendar Round, it is clear that at least some of the supposedly historical data we are given in the chronicles [a history of the Aztecs] is cyclical rather than linear: that is, an event which occurs at one point in a given cycle could also have taken place, and will take place, at similar points in other such cycles. Secondly, there were ample opportunities for the Aztec royal dynasty to rewrite its own history and the history of the nation as changing times demanded; we are told that this was done in the reign of the ruler Itzcoatl, but it apparently was done on a far larger scale during the course of the sixteenth century to cope with the cataclysm of the Spanish invasion and Conquest. The fully developed Aztec state had a cosmic vision of itself and its place in the universe which demanded a certain kind of history, and we now realize that even royal genealogies could be tailored to fit this vision.

The Valley of Mexico Before the Aztecs

It is thus no easy task to reconcile the often-conflicting native chronicles into a coherent story of Aztec origins and rise to power; yet there is considerable agreement on the broad outlines. The story begins with events which followed Tula's destruction in the twelfth century. Refugees from this center of Toltec civilization managed to establish themselves in the southern half of the Valley [of Mexico], particularly at the towns of Colhuacan and Xico, both of which became important citadels transmitting the higher culture of their predecessors to the savage groups who were then streaming into the northern half. Among the latter were the band of Chichimeca under their chief Xolotl, arriving in the Valley by 1244 and settling at Tenayuca; the Acolhua, who founded Coatlinchan around the year 1160; the Otomi at Xaltocan by about 1250; and the powerful Tepanecs, who in 1230 took over the town of Atzcapotzalco, which much earlier had been a significant Teotihuacan settlement. There is no question that all of these with the exception of the Otomi were speakers of Nahuatl, now the dominant tongue of central Mexico. Thus, by the thirteenth century, all over the Valley there had sprung up a group of modestly sized city-states, those in the north founded by Chichimec upstarts eager to learn from the Toltecs in the south.

According to [historian] Edward Calnek, this was a time of relative peace in the Valley. The Toltec refugees, occupying the rich lands in the south and west, introduced the organization and ideology of rule by the elite (called *pipiltin* in Nahuatl); its guiding principle was that only someone descended from the ancient royal Toltec dynasty could be a ruler or *tlatoani* ("speaker"). Those who lacked such descent could demand—if they were powerful enough—women of royal rank as wives. As time passed, the *pipiltin* came to hold a nearly complete monopoly of the highest offices in each city-state. As for the non-Toltec groups, some adopted the system sooner than others; the Aztecs were to prove the last hold-outs.

Into this political milieu stepped the Aztecs themselves, the last barbaric tribe to arrive in the Valley of Mexico, the "people whose face nobody knows." The official Aztec histories claimed that they had come from a place called "Aztlan" (meaning "Land of White Herons"), supposedly an island in a lake in the west or northwest of Mexico, and thus called themselves the "Azteca." One tradition says that they began their migration toward central Mexico in A.D. 1111, led by their tribal deity Huitzilopochtli ("Hummingbird on the Left"), whose idol was borne on the shoulders of four priests called *teomamaque*. Apparently they knew the art of cultivation and wore agave fiber clothing, but had no political leaders higher than clan and tribal chieftains. It is fitting that Huitzilopochtli was a war god and representative of the sun, for the Aztecs were extremely adept at military matters, and among the best and fiercest warriors ever seen in Mexico.

Along the route of march, Huitzilopochtli gave them a new name, the Mexica, which they were to bear until the Conquest. Many versions of the migration legend have them stop at Chicomoztoc, "Seven Caves," from which emerge all of the various ethnic groups which were to make up the nascent Aztec nation. There is a further halt at the mythical Coatepec ("Snake Mountain") where, somewhat confusingly, Huitzilopochtli is miraculously born as the sun god—a supernatural tale of supreme importance.

It needs no saying that none of the above is to be taken literally: like many other Mesoamerican peoples, such as the highland Maya, the Aztecs had myths and legends describing a migration from an often vague land of origin to a historically known place where they settled, inspired by the prophecy of a god. Similar legends can be found in the Book of Genesis [in the Bible] and among a number of tribal states in Africa and Polynesia. Their function seems clear: to tell the world that the rule by a particular elite was given by history and supported by divine sanction.

From Serfs to Mercenaries

Exactly when these Aztecs arrived in the Valley of Mexico is far from clear, but it must have already taken place by the beginning of the fourteenth century. Now, all the land in the Valley was already occupied by civilized peoples; they looked with suspicion upon these Aztecs, who were little more than squatters, continually occupying territory that did not belong to them and continually being kicked out. It is a wonder that they were ever tolerated since, women being scarce as among all immigrant groups, they took to raiding other peoples for their wives. The cultivated citizens of Colhuacan finally allowed them to live a degraded existence, working the lands of their masters as serfs, and supplementing their diet with snakes and other vermin. In 1323, however, the Aztecs repaid the kindness of their overlords, who had given their chief a Colhuacan princess as bride, by sacrificing the young lady with the hope that she would become a war goddess. Colhuacan retaliated by expelling these repulsive savages from their territory.

We next see the Aztecs following a hand-to-mouth existence in the marshes of the great lake, or "Lake of the Moon." On they wandered, loved by none, until they reached some swampy, unoccupied islands, covered by rushes, near the western shore; it was claimed that there the tribal prophecy, to build a city where an eagle was seen sitting on a cactus, holding a snake in its mouth, was fulfilled. By 1344 or 1345, the tribe was split in two, one group under their chief, Tenoch, founding the southern capital, Tenochtitlan, and the other settling Tlatelolco in the north. Eventually, as the swamps were drained and brought under cultivation, the islands became one, with two cities and two governments, a state of affairs not to last very long.

The year 1367 marks the turning point of the fortunes of the Aztecs: it was then that they began to serve as mercenaries for the mightiest power on the mainland, the expanding Tepanec kingdom of Atzcapotzalco, ruled by the unusually able Tezozomoc. One after another the city-states of the Valley of Mexico fell to the joint forces of Tezozomoc and his allies; sharing in the resulting loot, the Aztecs were also taken under Tepanec protection.

Up until this time, the Aztec system of government had essentially been egalitarian, and there were no social classes: the *teo-mamaque* and the other traditional leaders had remained in control. But in 1375, Tezozomoc gave them their first ruler or *tla-toani*, Acamapichtli ("Bundle of Reeds"), although during his reign there was still a degree of tribal democracy, in that he was not allowed to make or execute important decisions without the consent of the tribal leaders and the assembly. During these years, and in fact probably beginning as far back as their serfdom under Colhuacan, the Aztecs were taking on much of the culture that was the heritage of all the nations of the Valley from their Toltec predecessors. Much of this was learned from the mighty Tepanecs themselves, particularly the techniques of statecraft and empire-building so successfully indulged in by Tezozomoc. Already the small island kingdom of the Aztecs was prepared to exercise its strength on the mainland.

The Aztecs Triumph

The chance came in 1426, when the aged Tezozomoc was succeeded as Tepanec king by his son Maxtlatzin, known to the Aztecs as "Tyrant Maxtla" and an implacable enemy of the growing power of Tenochtitlan. By crude threats and other pressures, Maxtlatzin attempted to rid himself of the "Aztec problem"; and in the middle of the crisis, the third Aztec king died. Itzcoatl,

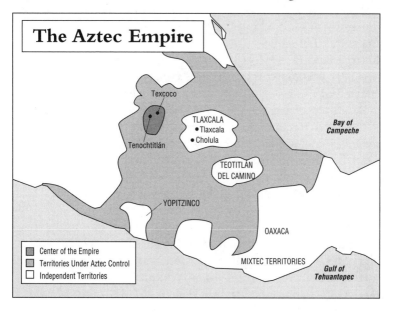

"Obsidian Snake," who assumed the Aztec rulership in 1427, was a man of strong mettle. More important, his chief adviser, Tlacaelel, was one of the most remarkable men ever produced by the Mexicans. The two of them decided to fight, with the result that by the next year the Tepanecs had been totally crushed and Atzcapotzalco was in ruins. This great battle, forever glorious to the Aztecs, left them the greatest state in Mexico.

In their triumph, and with the demotion of the traditional leaders, the Aztec administration turned to questions of internal polity, especially under Tlacaelel, who remained a kind of grand vizier to the Aztec throne through three reigns, dying in 1475 or 1480. Tlacaelel introduced a series of reforms that completely altered Mexican life. The basic reform related to the Aztec conception of themselves and their destiny; for this, it was necessary to rewrite history, and so Tlacaelel did, by having all the books of conquered peoples burned since these would have failed to mention Aztec glories. Under his aegis, the Aztecs acquired a mystic-visionary view of themselves as the chosen people, the true heirs of the Toltec tradition, who would fight wars and gain captives so as to keep the fiery sun moving across the sky.

This sun, represented by the fierce god Huitzilopochtli, needed the hearts of enemy warriors; during the reign of Motecuhzoma Ilhuicamina, "the Heaven Shooter" (reigned 1440–1469), Tlacaelel had the so-called "Flowery War" instituted. Under this, Tenochtitlan entered into a Triple Alliance with the old Acolhua state of Texcoco (on the other side of the lake) and the dummy state of Tlacopan in a permanent struggle against the Nahuatl-speaking states of Tlaxcala and Huexotzingo. The object on both sides was purely to gain captives for sacrifice.

Besides inventing the idea of Aztec grandeur, the glorification of the Aztec past, other reforms relating to the political-juridical and economic administrations were also carried out under Tlacaelel. The new system was successfully tested during a disastrous two-year famine which occurred under Motecuhzoma Ilhuicamina, and from which this extraordinary people emerged more confident than ever in their divine mission.

Given these conditions, it is little surprise that the Aztecs soon embarked with their allies on an ambitious program of conquest. The elder Motecuhzoma began the expansion, taking over the Huaxteca, much of the land around Mount Orizaba, and rampaging down even into the Mixteca. Axayacatl (1469–1481) subdued neighboring Tlatelolco on trumped-up charges and substituted a military government for what had once been an independent administration; he was less successful with the Tarascan kingdom of Michoacan, for these powerful people turned the invaders back. Greatest of all the empire-builders was Ahuitzotl (1486–1502), who succeeded the weak and vacillating Tizoc as sixth king. This mighty warrior conquered lands all the way to the Guatemalan border and brought under Aztec rule most of central Mexico. Probably for the first time since the downfall of Tula, there was in Mexico a single empire as great as, or greater than, that of the Toltecs. Ahuitzotl was a man of great energy; among the projects completed in his reign was a major rebuilding of the Great Temple of Tenochtitlan, completed in 1487, and the construction of an aqueduct to bring water from Coyoacan to the island capital.

The Last Aztec

Ahuitzotl's successor, Motecuhzoma Xocoyotzin ("The Younger") (1502–1520), is surely one of history's most tragic figures, for it was his misfortune to be the Aztec ruler when Mexican civilization was destroyed. He is described in many accounts, some of them eye-witness, as a very complex person; he was surely not the single-minded militarist that is so well typified by Ahuitzotl. Instead of delighting in war, he was given to meditation in his place of retreat, the "Black House"—in fact, one might be led to believe that he was more of a philosopher-king, along the lines of Hadrian. Like that Roman emperor, he also maintained a shrine in the capital where all the gods of captured nations were kept, for he was interested in foreign religions. In post-Conquest times, this was considered by Spaniards and Indians alike to have been the cause of his downfall: according to these *ex post facto* sources, when [Spanish explorer Hernan] Cortés arrived in 1510, the Aztec emperor was paralyzed by the realization that this strange, bearded foreigner was Quetzalcoatl himself, returned from the east as the ancient books had allegedly said he would, to destroy the Mexican peoples. All of his disastrous inaction in the face of the Spanish threat, his willingness to put himself in the hands of Cortés, was claimed to be the result of his dedication to the old Toltec philosophy. The triumphant Spaniards were only too glad to spread the word among their new subjects that this was Motecuhzoma's destiny, and that it had been foretold by a series of magical portents that had led to an inevitable outcome.

THE HISTORY OF NATIONS
Chapter 2

Spanish Conquest and Rule, 1517–1810

Hernán Cortés: Conquistador

By Hugh Thomas

After arriving in Cuba in 1511, Spanish explorers rapidly began to colonize the island in the name of the Spanish king. Naturally, these conquistadores looked to the west for new lands to explore, subdue, and settle. Expeditions under Francisco Hernández de Córdoba (1517) and Juan de Grijalva (1518) revealed a land not far from Cuba that was rich in gold and inhabited by native peoples: Mexico's Yucatán Peninsula. Plans for additional explorations were made. The governor of Cuba, Diego Velázquez de Cuéllar, granted the leadership of a third expedition to Hernán Cortés (1485–1547), who, like many of his fellow conquistadores, had migrated from Spain to the New World to seek fame and fortune. Although Cortés and Velázquez shared the financing of the expedition and apparently agreed on its goals, Cortés's planning revealed his intentions to do more than merely explore and trade. Velázquez became suspicious of Cortés's actions and tried to stop him, but Cortés set sail too soon for the governor to take any action.

Hugh Thomas, the author of the following selection, describes the events surrounding the launch of the Cortés expedition. Thomas believes that Cortés planned to conquer and colonize Mexico all along and depicts him as a masterful planner who applied considerable energy to buy, equip, and assemble eleven ships from around Cuba and persuaded a group of approximately five hundred adventurers to accompany him. Above all, Cortés was a man of bold action who chose to set sail rather than wait for the governor to replace him.

Hugh Thomas is an English historian and scholar who specializes in Hispanic culture. His book Conquest: Montezuma, Cortés, and the Fall of Old Mexico *is a classic in the field. Thomas's other works include books on the Spanish civil war and Cuban revolution.*

Hugh Thomas, *Conquest: Montezuma, Cortés, and the Fall of Old Mexico.* New York: Simon and Schuster, 1993. Copyright © 1993 by Hugh Thomas. All rights reserved. Reproduced by permission of the publisher.

Cortés left Santiago [a city on the southeast coast of Cuba] with six ships. He left a seventh one behind being careened [repaired]. He did not have much food—being especially short of bread. He therefore stopped at the small port of Macaca (probably the modern Pilón) on Cape Cruz. He there picked up a thousand rations of cassava bread from his friend, Francisco Dávila, who had a property there. Cortés seems to have obtained some supplies from a royal farm there, too. He sent a ship to Jamaica for wine, eight hundred flitches [sides] of bacon, and two thousand more rations of cassava bread.

Cortés next stopped at Trinidad, the little settlement founded in the centre of Cuba, not far from where, a few years before, [Bartolomé de] Las Casas [a chronicler of the Spanish Conquest] had had his farm. Here the magistrate was Francisco Verdugo, who had married Inés, a sister of [Diego] Velázquez [the governor of Cuba]. He was a hidalgo [nobleman] of Cojes de Iscar, a village a short distance from Cuéllar. Just as Cortés arrived, Verdugo received a letter from the Governor requiring him to delay the armada [fleet]. Velázquez had decided to replace Cortés with Vasco Porcallo de Figueroa. Similar letters were received by the captains of two of Cortés' ships, Francisco de Morla and Diego de Ordaz. The first, who came from Jerez, had been steward, *camarero*, to Velázquez. The second, Ordaz, came from Castroverde de Campos in León. His first adventure in America had been in Colombia in 1510, with the disastrous expedition of Alonso de Ojeda when the cartographer, Juan de la Cosa, had been killed by a poisoned arrow at the battle at Turbaco, prior to a disgraceful massacre of Indians. Ordaz had taken part in the conquest of Cuba. He was famous for having been left behind by his brother Pedro in a swamp. In 1518 he had probably been asked by the Governor to join Cortés in order to prevent mutiny on Cortés' expedition—by its commander most of all. His mother was a Girón, a grand family, and he was connected by blood to Velázquez, as were most of that Governor's officials. In 1518, he was nearly forty, he had a slight stammer, a thin black beard, rode badly, but had a strong face. On this expedition he financed his own ship of sixty men, with meat, cassava bread, wine, chickens and pigs. Though he was a poor horseman (and would often remain in command of foot soldiers), he was literate, being an excellent, often caustic, letter-writer. Like several other leaders of Cortés' expedition, Ordaz seems to have been involved in various disputes over debts (perhaps in respect of the pearl trade) which made it desirable for him to leave Cuba.

Attempts to Stop Cortés

Cortés heard of these letters of Velázquez and, using powers which nobody previously knew him to possess, not only persuaded Ordaz and Morla to continue to collaborate with him but prevailed upon the first to arrange with Francisco Verdugo to provide the fleet with some horses, several loads of fodder, and more bread. One of Velázquez's messengers, Pedro Laso, was even persuaded to enlist in Cortés' fleet. This was an early example of Cortés' skill with words which would be one of his most formidable weapons. Years later, Verdugo explained that he had given Cortés these goods since Velázquez had asked him to. No doubt that meant that he was obeying an earlier request of the Governor's, and turning a blind eye to his latest one.

Cortés then sent Ordaz with a brigantine, the *Alguecebo*, to seize a ship which he had heard was on its way carrying provisions to Darien [a place southeast of the Yucatan]. Ordaz was successful. He secured the load of four thousand *arrobas* [Spanish measurement of weight—about 10 kilos] of bread and fifteen hundred flitches of bacon or salted chicken. The owner, a merchant of Madrid, Juan Núñez Sedeño, who was on board, with a mare and a colt, decided to throw in his lot with Cortés. Talking of these incidents to Las Casas years later (in Spain in 1542), Cortés admitted, "By my faith, I carried on over there as if I had been a gentlemanly pirate."

Cortés was involved in at least one non-piratical activity: his page, Diego de Coria, saw him writing for the first eight nights after leaving Santiago. What was he working on? Letters to Spain? To his father and to the judge, Licenciado Céspedes, telling them what he was planning? Or to merchants in Hispaniola or Seville, forewarning them of their new opportunities? The page never knew.

Some of those who had been on [Juan, nephew of Velázquez] Grijalva's expedition joined Cortés at Trinidad. From there, Cortés sent down some messages forty miles away to Sancti Spiritus, from where he was joined by others who had farms in the neighbourhood. These included one of the most important members of the expedition: a fellow citizen of Medellín, Alonso Hernández Portocarrero, a cousin of the Count of that city.

Though this conquistador could scarcely speak without swearing, and though his military qualities were unproven, Cortés was evidently pleased to have with him a grandee from his own *pueblo* [town]. Portocarrero was also a nephew of Judge Céspedes. He had a small farm and a hundred and fifty Indians in Cuba. But he could not have been rich, for Cortés bought him a horse by selling the gold tassels from his own velvet cloak. He also recruited at Trinidad two other men from Medellín, Rodrigo Rangel and Gonzalo de Sandoval. The latter was only about twenty-one years old. When about fourteen, he had been a page to Velázquez. His capacity for endurance would make him in the end the most successful of Cortés' captains. All of them (and there were others) contributed whatever they could from their properties, particularly cassava bread and smoked ham. Much of the latter was now available since, by that time, the wild pigs of Cuba were prospering as much as they did in Extremadura [a region of Spain].

By now at last Cortés had learned of Grijalva's return: he heard of it when at Macaca. Grijalva had with him many interesting and beautiful gold objects beyond what Alvarado [a conquistador in the company of Cortés] had brought. He also had his girl slave, with her splendid ornaments, several men and, surprisingly for someone so apparently rational, some tantalising information about Amazons. All this made Velázquez even more concerned to bring Cortés' imminent expedition to a swift end.

But from Trinidad Cortés sailed on to the little port of San Cristóbal de la Habana on the south coast of Cuba....

Cortés in Havana

Havana, then a new city, was loyal to Velázquez. Most of its few settlers refused to help Cortés. But all the same, Cortés stayed in the house of Pedro Barba, who had also journeyed with Grijalva (he had given his name to the Mayan interpreter) and was in command of the town. Cortés displayed his banner in the street. He also had his expedition announced by the town crier. In consequence, he gained the backing not only of one or two more adventurers, but also of Cristóbal de Quesada, collector of tithes [donations] for the bishop, who declared himself willing to assist. So did Francisco de Medina, the collector, on the Crown's behalf, of the tax known as "*la cruzada*" ("the bull of crusade", in theory a voluntary contribution to the expenses of the war against Islam, but now an ordinary tax extended to the New

World). These two sold Cortés another five thousand rations of bread, two thousand flitches of bacon, and many beans and chickpeas, as well as wine, vinegar and six thousand loaves of bread made from cassava—one of the few Caribbean products which the Castilians deigned to eat: wisely, for it lasted much longer without deterioration than bread made from wheat.

Yet one more intimate of Velázquez, Gaspar de Garnica, appeared by ship in Havana. He brought another letter for Cortés from the Governor. It required him to wait. Garnica carried other letters from Velázquez for his cousin Juan Velázquez de León, who had joined Cortés at Trinidad, and for Diego de Ordaz. Fr. Bartolomé de Olmedo, a Mercedarian [friar] who had agreed to accompany Cortés, received a letter from a fellow friar in Velázquez's circle. All these communications asked their recipients to delay Cortés. The letter to Ordaz even requested him to seize Cortés and bring him back a prisoner to Santiago. Ordaz asked his commander to dine on the caravel in which Garnica had come. But Cortés suspected a trap. He feigned a stomach ache. Garnica wrote to Velázquez that he had not dared to seize Cortés, since he was too popular with his soldiers. . . .

Velázquez was in as weak a position as ever, since it would have been impossible for him to have gathered a new fleet quickly to sail either against or in collaboration with Cortés. Cortés was evidently not to be dissuaded. He had invested his fortune in the enterprise, as had some others. . . .

The Expedition

This expedition, like most in those times, was an adventure of private enterprise. The model, like most things in the history of the establishment of the Spanish empire, derived from medieval practice. The Crown had (indirectly) given permission; and the Crown's governor had nominated the commander. The commander was responsible for fitting things out. Those who volunteered for the journey were on it because they hoped to make their fortunes. Only the forty or fifty sailors and the five pilots were paid—by Cortés. The soldiers, whether captains or humble infantrymen, lived, as usual, on expectations. Yet once they had agreed to join the "army" of the *Caudillo* [highest-ranking general], they assumed the obligation under pain of death not to abandon it.

Cortés held a muster of his expedition just short of the extreme west point of Cuba, at Cape Corrientes. In this at least he was following his instructions.

He now had eleven ships. But only four were of substance—the flagship, *Santa María de la Concepcion,* a *nao* [a ship with a broad beam and deep keel] of a capacity of a hundred tons, and three others with a capacity of sixty to eighty tons. The rest were small open ships or brigantines. All the bigger ships, and perhaps some of the brigantines, would have been built in Spain. One of the *naos,* that captained and apparently paid for by Pedro de Alvarado, failed to be present at the muster. Cortés decided to sail without him. Another ship which Cortés had bought was, it may be remembered, still being careened in Santiago.

Counting the men who later sailed with Alvarado, Cortés had with him about five hundred and thirty Europeans, of whom thirty were crossbowmen. Twelve had arquebuses. These last were men who belonged to a different order of society from the captains or the infantrymen. Yet they were as important as the captains. There had been *condottieri* [mercenaries] in Italy who had opposed their introduction: Paolo Vitelli had put out the eyes and cut off the hands of captured German *schiopettieri,* because he thought it unworthy that a knight should be laid low by common men with guns. Cortés had no such reluctance to use modern technology. He also had fourteen pieces of artillery of the same type that Grijalva had taken: probably ten culverins of bronze, with four falconets. But Cortés probably also had with him some breech-loading cannon, lombards, such as were often found then on ships. These could sustain a higher rate of fire than the other muzzle-loaders. These weapons, most of which had names (San Francisco, Juan Ponce, Santiago and so on), were in the hands of specialists: Francisco de Mesa; a Levantine named Arbenga; Juan Catalan, one of the few Catalans to be found in the Indies; and Bartolomé de Usagre, from his name an Extremeño. The captain of this little unit of artillery was Francisco de Orozco, "who had been a good soldier in Italy": the magical experience which was supposed to guarantee everything. Similar responsibilities in respect of the crossbowmen went to Juan Benítez and Pedro de Guzmán, masters in the art of repairing those weapons.

There may have been as many as fifty sailors, many of them, as was common in those days on Spanish ships, foreigners—Portuguese, Genoese, Neapolitans, and even a Frenchman.

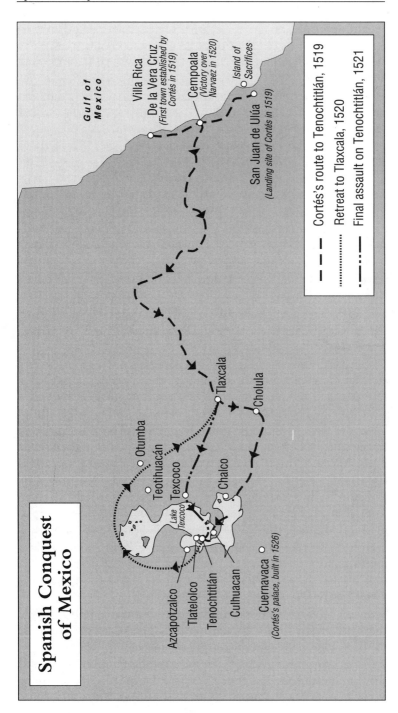

Spanish Conquest
of Mexico

Gulf of
Mexico

Villa Rica
De la Vera Cruz
(First town established by
Cortés in 1519)

Cempoala
(Victory over
Narvaez in 1520)

Island of
Sacrifices

San Juan de Ulúa
(Landing site of Cortés in 1519)

Tlaxcala

Cholula

Otumba

Teotihuacán

Texcoco

Chalco

Lake
Texcoco

Azcapotzalco

Tlatelolco

Tenochtitlán

Culhuacan

Cuernavaca
(Cortés's palace, built in 1526)

— — — Cortés's route to Tenochtitlán, 1519

· · · · · · · Retreat to Tlaxcala, 1520

— · — · — Final assault on Tenochtitlán, 1521

About a third of Cortés' expedition probably originated in Andalusia, almost a quarter from Old Castile, and only sixteen per cent from Extremadura. Seville and Huelva were far the most frequent birthplaces of the men concerned. But as so often, many commanders were Extremeños [residents of the Extremadura region of Spain]. A few Spanish women also travelled: these were two sisters of Diego de Ordaz, three or four maids, and one or two women who went as housekeepers. The exact role of these particular *"conquistadoras"*—the word was used by Andrea del Castillo, Francisco de Montejo's daughter-in-law, in a subsequent enquiry—is unclear. But no doubt that lady was correct when she said that, when women of her quality did take part in these engagements, their work was considerable. One or two of these women certainly later fought effectively. . . .

There were a dozen men with some kind of professional training, though only one doctor, Pedro López. There were several notaries, whose services Cortés later would use indiscriminately. Perhaps there were half a dozen carpenters. Apart from the sailors, there were a few Greeks, Italians, some Portuguese, and several other foreigners.

Despite Velázquez's prohibition, there were with Cortés several hundred Cuban Indians, including some women, as well as a few African freemen and black slaves. (It is possible that Juan Garrido, a free black African who had become a Christian in Lisbon, later famous as the first man to grow wheat in Mexico, was among these.) One citizen of Cuba said later that he thought that every one of Cortés' expedition had two Cuban servants. The fisherman "Melchor", one of the cross-eyed Mayas captured in Yucatan by Hernández de Córdoba, accompanied the fleet (though his comrade, the melancholy Julián, who had accompanied Grijalva, had died). "Francisco", the Nahuatl-speaking Indian who had been captured by Grijalva, was also on board Cortés' ship.

Horses and Dogs

Sixteen horses were loaded: the important innovation of this voyage. These were, as [Lucas Fernandez de] Piedrahita, the historian of the conquest of Nueva Granada, would put it, "the nerves of the wars against the natives." Those taken by Cortés were probably the same breed as those which a later Diego Velázquez painted in his equestrian portraits: sturdy, short-backed, legs not too long, strong enough to carry a man in armour and a heavy, comfortable Moorish saddle. For the riders would have ridden *á la gineta*, that is with stirrups long, a powerful bit and a single rein. The legs of the riders would have pressed back, the heads of the horses turned by pressure at the neck, not at the mouth. On the crossing from Cuba to Yucatan these horses would have been hoisted on to the decks by pulley and remained there for the voyage. The horses were expensive: each one cost at least three thousand pesos: even an African slave cost less. No doubt some of the horses were descendants of those carried to Hispaniola by Columbus on his second voyage. The names of some of them were recalled by Bernal Díaz: El Rey ("the King"); Roldanillo ("little Roland"); Cabeza de Moro ("Moor's head").

There were also numerous dogs—presumably either Irish wolfhounds or mastiffs, the difference in breeds being then obscure. Dogs had fought effectively, and had been used brutally, in establishing other parts of the Spanish empire, as they had in the wars against the Moors. Cortés would not have dreamed of depriving himself of their use. His father might have told him that a dog, Mohama, had fought so valiantly at Granada that he received a horseman's share of the spoil. Indeed, the use of dogs in war in Europe was common. Henry VIII would soon send four hundred mastiffs to Charles V for use against the French, some of them wearing light armour. In the conquest of Puerto Rico, Ponce de León's dog Becerrillo ("little calf") had played an important part, with his "reddish fur and black eyes". Becerrillo's son, Leoncillo ("little lion"), had been with [Vasco Núñez de] Balboa when he first saw the Pacific.

Friends and Enemies

The captains on the expedition presented some political difficulties to Cortés. Several were more experienced than he in wars in the Indies. Others were close friends of Diego Velázquez. Most prominent among these last was, of course, Diego de Ordaz, whose equivocal role at Havana had already distinguished him. Other "Velázquistas", as they came to be known, were Francisco de Montejo, the Salamantino commander of one of the four *naos;* Francisco de Morla; and Juan Velázquez de León. The latter, a strong fighter with a well-kept curly beard, and a harsh voice which stuttered, was a spirited man, very grand in his ways, whose attachment to his kinsman, the Governor, had slackened when he did not receive a good grant of Indians.

There were also men who would rarely say a good word for Cortés. The most prominent of these was Juan Escudero, that constable, *alguacil,* of Asunción de Baracoa who had seized Cortés in 1515 and imprisoned him during one of his rows with the Governor.

At the same time, the *Caudillo,* to use Velázquez's word for him, had some dedicated friends. Most were Extremeños. These included Alonso Hernández Portocarrero and Gonzalo de Sandoval, who came from Medellín; Juan Gutiérrez de Escalante, who had been with Grijalva; Alonso de Grado, "a man of many graces but not much of a soldier" [Torquemada], an *encomendero* [a holder of land and Indians] on a small scale in Hispaniola, who had been born in Alcántara; and, above all, Pedro de Alvarado and his four brothers, who, from the beginning of the journey, were the strongest backers of the new *Caudillo.* Two Castilian supporters of Cortés were Francisco de Lugo, a bastard son of Álvaro de Lugo, the lord of Fuencastín, near Medina del Campo, and Bernardino Vázquez de Tapia, Grijalva's standard-bearer, who could also be counted at this time in this category. But these men compensated neither in seniority nor in numbers for the friends of the Governor. Thus Cortés had to make a practice of attempting to win over the first group, by promoting and seeking to inspire them without losing his own friends. It was a delicate task.

Cortés' task was made easier by the fact that he had established by this time a household of his own, modelled on the kind of staff that the Count of Medellín or some other Extremeño baron would have had, though Ovando and Velázquez would have had the same: Cristóbal de Guzmán was master of his household; Rodrigo Rangel was chamberlain (*camarero*); and Joan de Cáceres, a man of experience who was nevertheless illiterate, was his majordomo [steward]. The first of these was from Seville, the other two Extremeños. Rangel was from Medellín. People noticed that Cortés, having "established a household, lived as a lord". All the same, for some time more he remained, in the memory of Juan Núñez Sedeño, "almost as a companion" to the rest of the expedition. . . .

The backbone of Cortés' army was undoubtedly composed of . . . men who wanted more money and were prepared to go to a lot of trouble to find it. Most would have come out to the

Indies, either to Cuba, Hispaniola, or Tierra Firme, since 1513. But some would have been elderly survivors of the early expeditions to Hispaniola, and perhaps there were some with clipped ears or noses—indicating that they had once been convicted robbers in Castile. Several expeditionaries (Cristóbal Martín de Gamboa, Joan de Cáceres) had first gone to the Indies with Ovando in 1502, and had taken part in the conquest of Cuba.

Supplies for the Voyage

On board there was enough bread, smoked or salted meat, bacon, salt, oil, vinegar and wine to last the five hundred or so men for a few weeks. The maize, chillis and yucca were no doubt looked on as a reserve. Fresh water was carried in barrels, though they often leaked, because the European wood from which they were usually made did not survive the tropics well (very soon, water, like wine, began to travel in earthenware jars). No more water was taken than was estimated would last the crossing to Yucatan.

The weapons, apart from the cannon, arquebuses and crossbows, and the ammunition needed, were mostly swords and lances. Cortés had intelligently ordered cotton armour for use against arrows, such as he had learned was favoured for its lightness by the Indians in Yucatan. This had been made for him near Havana, where cotton was available and where Cuban Indian women were adept at weaving. But those who considered themselves, or were, of knightly class had brought the traditional steel helmets, breastplates and bucklers which, heavy as they were, made, as Cortés had discovered from stories from men on the earlier expeditions, a strong impression on their opponents. He must have had many spare parts: not just for the soldiers, but for the horses who required spare bridles, saddles, stirrups and of course horse-shoes, a surprisingly expensive item.

A final cargo consisted of the presents which the conquistadors took to give to the Indians: the same things which Hernández de Córdoba and Grijalva had taken, including glass beads, bells, mirrors, needles, pins, leather goods, knives, scissors, tongs, hammers, iron axes, as well as some Castilian clothes: handkerchiefs, breeches, shirts, capes, and stockings. Some of these objects such as scissors were of real interest to people who had not reached the age of iron, much less that of steel, yet whose capacity to adapt and learn about new technology was soon shown to be remarkable. Most of these things probably came originally from Germany, Italy or Flanders, though perhaps there were oyster shells from the Canaries, and there were, as will be seen, one or two pearls from what is now Venezuela.

According to Cortés chaplain, [Francisco] López de Gómara, [in his work *La Conquista de Mexico*], Cortés started the expedition to Mexico with a speech. Perhaps he did, though it is hard to believe that he made the full-blooded appeal to the desire for fame and fortune which that author, well versed in the oratory of the later Italian Renaissance, published. The speech, according to López de Gómara, purported to say that the expedition would win for the conquistadors "vast and wealthy lands", kingdoms "greater than those of our monarchs", and "great rewards wrapped around with hardships". Had Cortés spoken so directly, the friends of Velázquez under his command might have overthrown him there and then. Still, Cortés would probably have known that modern generals often made speeches to their assembled troops. But it is uncertain to whom Cortés could have spoken. Merely his own ship's company? Or to his captains, especially carried over from their ships to hear him?

Cortés all the same permitted his men to have an inkling of what he was privately thinking, by displaying, on a banner which he flew from the masthead of his flagship, and which he had had prepared in Santiago, a blue cross and a slogan in Latin: "*Amici, sequamur crucem, et si nos fidem habemus, vere in hoc signo vincemus*", which, being translated, might be said to read, "Friends, let us follow the cross and, if we have faith, let us conquer under this banner". To those who had been educated, or who wished to be thought educated, this motto of course recalled the sign of the cross which, in legend, appeared to the [Roman] Emperor Constantine's army before the battle of the Milvian bridge. . . .

Cortés' Intentions

The subject of Cortés' religious beliefs baffles all but the fortunately simple who, like the first historian of the Mexican church, Fr. Mendieta, believe that Cortés was chosen by God to carry out His purposes. The evidence is as conflicting as that relating to the colour of his hair. "Even though he was a sinner, he had faith and did the work of a good Christian", wrote the Franciscan priest [Toribio de Benavente] Motolinía, who knew him well (being his confessor) in later life, adding [in his work *Historia de las Indies de Nueva España*] that "he confessed with many tears and placed his soul and treasure in the hands of his confessor". His favourite oath was "by my conscience". Yet Diego de Ordaz, who saw him most days for the next eighteen months, would write in 1529 that Cortés had "no more conscience than a dog". [*Diego de Ordaz, compañero de Cortés*]. He was "addicted to women in excess", greedy, and loved the "worldly pomp" of which he would speak disdainfully in his will; yet he preached well, prayed often, and usually wore a gold chain with a picture of the Virgin on one side and John the Baptist on the other.

The truth seems to be that, though a sincere Christian, Cortés was quite able to combine Christian beliefs, and actions, with a realisation that these things were useful. The motives of Cortés, like those of Columbus, were inextricably mixed: above all, no doubt, he wanted glory, he also wanted wealth and, where appropriate, or convenient, he also wanted to serve God. "For God and Profit" was the slogan of the merchant of Prato, Francesco Datini. The Roman Church before the Counter-Reformation, and before the establishment of the Jesuits [an order of priests], was a more relaxed enterprise than it subsequently became. Cortés forgave [voyage members] Sandoval and Portocarrero for blasphemy since they were intimates; but he ostensibly punished others for the same crime (Cristóbal Flores, Francisco de Orduña). He gambled. He loved, as a show above all, the material things of life, of which he had seen too few in his childhood. He liked having a court of assistants. He would contemplate any tactic, even one which might (given his time) have been with justification called Machiavellian. These things show his priorities. But he naturally developed as his expedition gathered strength. He probably became more God-fearing as he faced more and more challenges. The Church often afforded a convenient pretext for action—more so (though this is to anticipate) than was the case in respect of other conquests in the Caribbean, for the obvious reason that the religions of old Mexico and its subordinate territories were more formidable than those of the West Indies. Christianity, after all, was the philosophy of Cortés' expedition, even if it was decorated with Castilian honour. It was the morality which offered morale, the sense of community which sustained the individual in battle, and the faith which might even comfort prisoners who would meet their death on the sacrificial stone.

The departure of five hundred men left Cuba exposed. It seems doubtful whether the whole Castilian population of the island could in 1518 have been more than a thousand males. In Baracoa there were only one or two Castilian households remaining. Had the indigenous population had a leader, or had the French been as willing then to attack the Spanish empire as they already were beginning to be to attack ships on the high seas, Velázquez would have been hard pressed to protect his little kingdom.

Cortés sent a respectful letter of goodbye to that proconsul before he left. But neither respect nor obedience were in his heart. Cortés kept his own counsel. He never allowed himself to talk about his intentions before he left Cuba. The evidence is, though, that he intended to colonise and conquer, as well as to discover (*poblar* as well as *descubrir*). Bernal Díaz [a member of the expedition] recalled him saying so before he left Santiago. No one, after all, takes horses and cannon if they are going merely to trade.

So it was that the third Castilian expedition finally set off for Yucatan on 18 February 1519.

An Eyewitness Account of the Spaniards' Dealings with the Indians

By Bernal Díaz del Castillo

The Spanish conquistador Hernán Cortés led the expedition to Mexico that resulted in the conquest of the Aztecs. Cortés first landed at Cozumel in the Yucatán Peninsula in 1519. From there, he and his party of five hundred sailed around the peninsula north to the Maya town of Potonchan. After vanquishing the Maya inhabitants in battle, Cortés and his company rested before setting sail for the empire of the Aztecs. According to the Maya, this was a place of unparalleled riches. As Cortés journeyed toward the Aztec empire, he encountered envoys sent by the Aztec emperor Montezuma (also called Moctezuma or Moteuc-zoma). The envoys offered the foreigners food and gifts and took special note of the Spaniards' horses, cannon, rifles, swords, lances, and armor. They also asked Cortés not to advance to the Aztec capital of Tenochti-tlán. Cortés refused and continued his march. At each stopping point along their way, the Spanish met Indian groups who, Cortés soon learned, were unhappy with paying the Aztecs the tribute they demanded. Cortés enlisted these Indians as allies against the Aztecs.

The following selection is taken from the eyewitness account of Bernal Díaz del Castillo (1495–1584), a member of Cortés's expedition. He describes a battle between the Spanish and the Tlaxcalans, an Indian tribe Cortés and his men met on their march inland. The Tlaxcalans were hostile to the Aztecs and were also the first military force to seriously challenge the Spanish. Díaz del Castillo wrote his account of the Spanish conquest of Mexico in his old age. His work was first published in 1632 and was soon accepted as an authoritative work on the conquest.

Bernal Díaz del Castillo, *The Discovery and Conquest of Mexico, 1517–1521*, translated by A.P. Maudslay. New York: Da Capo Press, 1956.

From the little town belonging to Xalacingo [an Indian chief], where they gave us a golden necklace and some cloth and two Indian women, we sent two Cempoalan [an Indian group] chieftains as messengers to Tlaxcala, with a letter, and a fluffy red Flemish hat, such as was then worn. We well knew that the Tlaxcalans could not read the letter, but we thought that when they saw paper different from their own, they would understand that it contained a message; and what we sent to them was that we were coming to their town, and hoped they would receive us well, as we came, not to do them harm, but to make them our friends. We did this because in this little town they assured us that the whole of Tlaxcala was up in arms against us, for it appears that they had already received news of our approach and that we were accompanied by many friends, both from Cempoala and Xocotlan, and other towns through which we had passed. As all these towns usually paid tribute to Montezuma [the Aztec king], the Tlaxcalans took it for granted that we were coming to attack Tlaxcala, as their country had often been entered by craft and cunning and then laid waste, and they thought that this was another attempt to do so. So as soon as our two messengers arrived with the letter and the hat and began to deliver their message, they were seized as prisoners before their story was finished, and we waited all that day and the next for an answer and none arrived.

Then Cortés addressed the chiefs of the town where we had halted, and repeated all he was accustomed to tell the Indians about our holy religion, and many other things which we usually repeated in most of the towns we passed through, and after making them many promises of assistance, he asked for twenty Indian warriors of quality to accompany us on our march, and they were given us most willingly.

After commending ourselves to God, with a happy confidence we set out on the following day for Tlaxcala, and as we were marching along, we met our two messengers who had been taken prisoner. It seems that the Indians who guarded them were perplexed by the warlike preparations and had been careless of their charge, and in fact, had let them out of prison. They arrived in such a state of terror at what they had seen and heard that they could hardly succeed in expressing themselves.

According to their account, when they were prisoners the Tlaxcalans had threatened them, saying: "Now we are going to kill those whom you call Teules [an Indian group the Spanish encountered during their march inland], and eat their flesh, and we will see whether they are as valiant as you announce; and we shall eat your flesh too, you who come here with treasons and lies from that traitor Montezuma!"—and for all that the messengers could say, that we were against the Mexicans, and wished to be brothers to the Tlaxcalans, they could not persuade them of its truth.

When Cortés and all of us heard those haughty words, and learned how they were prepared for war, although it gave us matter for serious thought, we all cried: "If this is so, forward—and good luck to us!" We commended ourselves to God and marched on the Alferez Corral, unfurling our banner and carrying it before us, for the people of the little town where we had slept, as well as the Cempoalans assured us that the Tlaxcalans would come out to meet us and resist our entry into their country. . . .

A Battle with the Indians

The next day, as we marched on, two armies of warriors approached to give us battle. They numbered six thousand men and they came on us with loud shouts and the din of drums and trumpets, as they shot their arrows and hurled their darts and acted like brave warriors. Cortés ordered us to halt, and sent forward the three prisoners whom we had captured the day before, to tell them not to make war on us as we wished to treat them as brothers. He also told one of our soldiers, named Diego de Godoy, who was a royal notary, to watch what took place so that he could bear witness if it should be necessary, so that at some future time we should not have to answer for the deaths and damages which were likely to take place, for we begged them to keep the peace.

When the three prisoners whom we had sent forward began to speak to the Indians, it only increased their fury and they made such an attack on us that we could not endure it. Then Cortés shouted:—"Santiago—and at them!" and we attacked them with such impetuosity that we killed and wounded many of them with our fire and among them three captains. They then began to retire towards some ravines, where over forty thousand warriors and their captain general, named Xicotenga, were lying in ambush, all wearing a red and white device for that was the badge and livery of Xicotenga.

As there was broken ground there we could make no use of

the horses, but by careful manœuvring we got past it, but the passage was very perilous for they made play with their good archery, and with their lances and broadswords did us much hurt, and the hail of stones from their slings was even more damaging. When we reached the level ground with our horsemen and artillery, we paid them back and slew many of them, but we did not dare to break our formation, for any soldier who left the ranks to follow some of the Indian captains and swordsmen was at once wounded and ran great danger. As the battle went on they surrounded us on all sides and we could do little or nothing. We dared not charge them, unless we charged all together, lest they should break up our formation; and if we did charge them, as I have said, there were twenty squadrons ready to resist us, and our lives were in great danger for they were so numerous they could have blinded us with handfuls of earth, if God in his great mercy had not succoured [aided] us.

While we found ourselves in this conflict among these great warriors and their fearful broadswords, we noticed that many of the strongest among them crowded together to lay hands on a horse. They set to work with a furious attack, laying hands on a good mare known to be very handy either for sport or for charging. The rider, Pedro de Moron, was a very good horseman, and as he charged with three other horsemen into the ranks of the enemy the Indians seized hold of his lance and he was not able to drag it away, and others gave him cuts with their broadswords, and wounded him badly, and then they slashed at the mare, and cut her head off at the neck so that it hung by the skin, and she fell dead. If his mounted companions had not come at once to his rescue they would also have finished killing Pedro de Moron. We might possibly have helped him with our whole battalion, but I repeat again that we hardly dared to move from one place to another for fear that they would finally rout us, and we could not move one way or another; it was all we could do to hold our own and prevent ourselves from being defeated. However, we rushed to the conflict around the mare and managed to save Moron from the hands of the enemy who were already dragging him off half dead, and we cut the mare's girths, so as not to leave the saddle behind. In that act of rescue, ten of our men were wounded and I remember that at the same time we killed four of the (Indian) captains, for we were advancing in close order and we did great execution with our swords. When this had happened, the enemy began to retire, carrying the mare with them, and they cut her in pieces to exhibit in all the towns of Tlaxcala, and we learnt afterwards that they made an offering to their idols of the horseshoes, of the Flemish felt hat, and the two letters which we had sent them offering peace. . . .

The place where this battle took place is called Tehuacingo, and it was fought on the 2nd day of the month of September in the year 1519. When we saw that victory was ours, we gave thanks to God who had delivered us from such great danger. . . .

A Night Attack

After the battle which I have described was over, in which we had captured three Indian chieftains, our Captain Cortés sent them at once in company with the two others who were in our camp and who had already been sent as messengers and ordered them to go to the Caciques [chiefs] of Tlaxcala and tell them that we begged them to make peace and to grant us a passage through their country on our way to Mexico, and to say that if they did not now come to terms, we would slay all their people, but that as we were well disposed towards them we had no desire to annoy them, unless they gave us reason to do so; and he said many flattering things to them so as to make friends of them, and the messengers then set out eagerly for the capital of Tlaxcala and gave their message to all the Caciques already mentioned by me whom they found gathered in council with many other elders and priests. They were very sorrowful both over the want of success in the war and at the death of those captains, their sons and relations, who had fallen in battle. As they were not very willing to listen to the message, they decided to summon all the soothsayers, priests, and those others called *Tacal naguas*, and they told them to find out from their witchcraft, charms, and lots what people we were, and if by giving us battle day and night without ceasing we could be conquered, and to say if we were Teules, as the people of Cempoala asserted, and to tell them what things we ate, and ordered them to look into all these matters with the greatest care.

When the soothsayers and wizards and many priests had got together and made their prophecies and forecasts, and performed all the other rites according to their use, it seems that they said that by their divinations they had found out we were men of flesh and blood and ate poultry and dogs and bread and fruit, when we had them, and that we did not eat the flesh nor the hearts of the Indians whom we killed. It seems that our Indian friends whom we had brought from Cempoala had made them believe that we were Teules, and that we ate the hearts of Indians, and that the cannon shot forth lightning, such as falls from heaven and that the Lurcher, which was a sort of lion or tiger, and the horses, were used to catch Indians when we wanted to kill them, and much more nonsense of the same sort.

The worst of all that the priests and wizards told the Caciques was, that it was not during the day, but only at night that we could be defeated, for as night fell, all our strength left us. When the Caciques heard this, and they were quite convinced of it, they sent to tell their captain general Xicotenga that as soon as it was possible he should come and attack us in great force by night. On receiving this order Xicotenga assembled ten thousand of the bravest of his Indians and came to our camp, and from three sides they began alternately to shoot arrows and throw single pointed javelins from their spear throwers, and from the fourth side the swordsmen and those armed with macanas and broadswords approached so suddenly that they felt sure that they would carry some of us off to be sacrificed. Our Lord God provided otherwise, for secretly as they approached, they found us well on the alert. . . .

That night, one of our Indian friends from Cempoala was killed and two of our soldiers were wounded and one horse, and we captured four of the enemy. When we found that we had escaped from that impetuous attack we gave thanks to God, and we buried our Cempoala friend and tended the wounded and the horse, and slept the rest of the night after taking every precaution to protect the camp as was our custom.

When we awoke and saw how all of us were wounded, even with two or three wounds, and how weary we were and how others were sick and clothed in rags, and knew that Xicotenga was always after us, and already over forty-five of our soldiers had been killed in battle, or succumbed to disease and chills, and another dozen of them were ill, and our Captain Cortés himself was suffering from fever as well as the Padre de la Merced, and what with our labours and the weight of our arms which we always carried on our backs, and other hardships from chills and the want of salt, for we could never find any to eat, we began to wonder what would be the outcome of all this fighting, and what we should do and where we should go when it was finished. To march into Mexico we thought too arduous an undertaking because of its great armies, and we said to one another that if those Tlaxcalans, which our Cempoalan friends had led us to believe were peacefully disposed, could reduce us to these straits, what would happen when we found ourselves at war with the great forces of Montezuma? . . .

One and all we put heart into Cortés, and told him that he must get well again and reckon upon us, and that as with the help of God we had escaped from such perilous battles, our Lord Jesus Christ must have preserved us for some good end; that he [Cortés] should at once set our prisoners free and send them to the head Caciques, so as to bring them to peace, when all that had taken place would be pardoned, including the death of the mare. . . .

A Peace Offering

While we were in camp and were busy polishing our arms and making arrows, each one of us doing what was necessary to prepare for battle, at that moment one of our scouts came hurrying in to say that many Indian men and women with loads were coming along the high road from Tlaxcala, and were making for our camp. Cortés and all of us were delighted at this news, for we believed that it meant peace, as in fact it did, and Cortés ordered us to make no display of alarm and not to show any concern, but to stay hidden in our huts. Then, from out of all those people who came bearing loads, the four chieftains advanced who were charged to treat for peace, according to the instructions given by the old Caciques. Making signs of peace by bowing the head, they came straight to the hut where Cortés was lodging and placed one hand on the ground and kissed the earth and three times made obeisance [a sign of respect] and burnt copal [tree resin], and said that all the Caciques of Tlaxcala and their allies and vassals, friends and confederates, were come to place themselves under the friendship and peace of Cortés and of his brethren the Teules who accompanied him. They asked his pardon for not having met us peacefully, and for the war which they had waged on us, for they had believed and held for certain that we were friends of Montezuma and his Mexicans, who have been their mortal enemies from times long past, for they saw that many of his vassals who paid him tribute had come in our company, and they believed that they were endeavouring to gain an entry into their country by guile and treachery, as was their custom to do, so as to rob them of their women and children; and this was the reason why they did not believe the messengers whom we had sent to them; that now they came to beg pardon for their audacity, and had brought us food, and that every day they would bring more and trusted that we would receive it with the friendly feeling with which it was sent; that within two days the captain Xicotenga would come with other Caciques and give a further account of the sincere wish of all Tlaxcala to enjoy our friendship.

As soon as they had finished their discourse they bowed their heads and placed their hands on the ground and kissed the earth. Then Cortés spoke to them through our interpreters very seriously, pretending he was angry, and said that there were reasons why we should not listen to them and should reject their friendship, for as soon as we had entered their country we sent to them offering peace and had told them that we wished to assist them against their enemies, the Mexicans, and they would not believe it and wished to kill our ambassadors; and not content with that, they had attacked us three times both by day and by night, and had spied on us and held us under observation; and in the attacks which they made on us we might have killed many of their vassals, but he would not, and he grieved for those who were killed; but it was their own fault and he had made up his mind to go to the place where the old chiefs were living and to attack them; but as they had now sought peace in the name of that province, he would receive them in the name of our lord the King and thank them for the food they had brought. He told them to go at once to their chieftains and tell them to come or send to treat for peace with fuller powers, and that if they did not come we would go to their town and attack them.

He ordered them to be given some blue beads to be handed to their Caciques as a sign of peace, and he warned them that when they came to our camp it should be by day and not by night, lest we should kill them.

Then those four messengers departed, and left in some Indian houses a little apart from our camp, the Indian women whom they had brought to make bread, some poultry, and all the necessaries for service, and twenty Indians to bring wood and water. From now on they brought us plenty to eat, and when we saw this and believed that peace was a reality, we gave great thanks to

God for it. It had come in the nick of time, for we were already lean and worn out and discontented with the war, not knowing or being able to forecast what would be the end of it.

As our Lord God, through his great loving kindness, was pleased to give us victory in those battles in Tlaxcala, our fame spread throughout the surrounding country, and reached the ears of the great Montezuma in the great City of Mexico; and if hitherto they took us for Teules, from now on they held us in even greater respect as valiant warriors, and terror fell on the whole country at learning how, being so few in number and the Tlaxcalans in such great force, we had conquered them and that they had sued us for peace. So that now Montezuma, the great Prince of Mexico, powerful as he was, was in fear of our going to his city, and sent five chieftains, men of much importance, to our camp at Tlaxcala to bid us welcome, and say that he was rejoiced at our great victory against so many squadrons of warriors, and he sent a present, a matter of a thousand dollars' worth of gold, in very rich jewelled ornaments, worked in various shapes, and twenty loads of fine cotton cloth, and he sent word that he wished to become the vassal of our great Emperor, and that he was pleased that we were already near his city, on account of the good will that he bore Cortés and all his brothers, the Teules, who were with him and that he [Cortés] should decide how much tribute he wished for every year for our great Emperor, and that he [Montezuma] would give it in gold and silver, cloth and chalchihuites [green stones], provided we would not come to Mexico. This was not because he would not receive us with the greatest willingness, but because the land was rough and sterile, and he would regret to see us undergo such hardships which perchance he might not be able to alleviate as well as he could wish. Cortés answered by saying that he highly appreciated the good will shown us, and the present which had been sent, and the offer to pay tribute to His Majesty, and he begged the messengers not to depart until he went to the capital of Tlaxcala, as he would despatch them from that place, for they could then see how that war ended.

An Aztec Account of the Fall of Tenochtitlán

By Miguel Leon-Portilla

The Spanish conquistador Hernán Cortés, accompanied by about three hundred of his company and a few thousand Indian allies, first entered the Aztec capital of Tenochtitlán on November 8, 1519. After he failed to keep the Spaniards away from the city with offerings of gifts and requests to halt their advance, the Aztec emperor Montezuma (also spelled "Motecuhzoma") met Cortés in person on the outskirts of the city. Montezuma had been emperor since 1502 and ruled over approximately 20 million people at the time of his meeting with Cortés. Not all his subjects were loyal to Montezuma, however, and the emperor feared that the Spaniards' arrival in the capital might increase dissension among these groups. It was also the harvest season, and the Aztec emperor was not prepared to wage war.

If Montezuma's position was precarious, so was Cortés's, despite the fact that the Aztec emperor may have believed Cortés to be a god returning to Mexico from across the sea. Tenochtitlán's location—on an island in the middle of a vast lake situated in an immense valley—posed special problems for the invading force. The only routes in and out of the capital were across three causeways guarded by bridges. Cortés's Indian allies remained outside the city. Cortés believed that if he left the city the Aztecs might assume that he was weak and attack. Inside the city, he was completely dependent on the inhabitants for food and shelter. Cortés decided to preempt any Aztec assault by seizing Montezuma and controlling the Aztecs through him. This action diminished the emperor's power and ultimately sealed his fate. During a battle between the Aztecs and the Spaniards, Montezuma was killed either at the hands of his own people or by the Spanish. Cortés and his men barely escaped from Tenochtitlán but returned in the spring of 1521 with more supplies and their Indian allies. Following a three-month siege, Cortés and his army reentered the city and killed the remaining Aztec defenders.

The following selection is taken from Miguel Leon-Portilla's retelling of the conquest of Mexico. His account is derived from a translation of the Florentine Codex, *the name scholars gave to the manuscript written by Friar Bernardino de Sahagun and translated under the title* General History of the Things of New Spain. *Leon-Portilla also includes material from other sources and Indian songs. Leon-Portilla is the director of the Inter-American Indian Institute in Mexico. He is an expert on the origins, culture, and histories of the pre-Hispanic Indian peoples of Mesoamerica. His other works include* Fifteen Poets of the Aztec World, Aztec Thought and Culture: A Study of the Ancient Nahuatl Mind, *and* The Language of Kings: An Anthology of Mesoamerican Literature, Pre-Columbian to the Present.

The Spaniards arrived in Xoloco, near the entrance to Tenochtitlan. That was the end of the march, for they had reached their goal.

Motecuhzoma now arrayed himself in his finery, preparing to go out to meet them. The other great princes also adorned their persons, as did the nobles and their chieftains and knights. They all went out together to meet the strangers.

They brought trays heaped with the finest flowers—the flower that resembles a shield; the flower shaped like a heart; in the center, the flower with the sweetest aroma; and the fragrant yellow flower, the most precious of all. They also brought garlands of flowers, and ornaments for the breast, and necklaces of gold, necklaces hung with rich stones, necklaces fashioned in the petatillo style.

Thus Motecuhzoma went out to meet them, there in Huitzillan. He presented many gifts to the Captain [Cortes] and his commanders, those who had come to make war. He showered gifts upon them and hung flowers around their necks; he gave them necklaces of flowers and bands of flowers to adorn their breasts; he set garlands of flowers upon their heads. Then he hung the gold necklaces around their necks and gave them presents of every sort as gifts of welcome.

The Emperor's Greeting

When Motecuhzoma had given necklaces to each one, Cortes asked him: "Are you Motecuhzoma? Are you the king? Is it true that you are the king Motecuhzoma?"

And the king said: "Yes, I am Motecuhzoma." Then he stood up to welcome Cortes; he came forward, bowed his head low and addressed him in these words: "Our lord, you are weary. The journey has tired you, but now you have arrived on the earth. You have come to your city, Mexico. You have come here to sit on your throne, to sit under its canopy.

"The kings who have gone before, your representatives, guarded it and preserved it for your coming. The kings Itzcoatl, Motecuhzoma the Elder, Axayacatl, Tizoc and Ahuitzol ruled for you in the City of Mexico. The people were protected by their swords and sheltered by their shields.

"Do the kings know the destiny of those they left behind, their posterity? If only they are watching! If only they can see what I see!

"No, it is not a dream. I am not walking in my sleep. I am not seeing you in my dreams. . . . I have seen you at last! I have met you face to face! I was in agony for five days, for ten days, with my eyes fixed on the Region of the Mystery [place of Cortes's origin]. And now you have come out of the clouds and mists to sit on your throne again.

"This was foretold by the kings who governed your city, and now it has taken place. You have come back to us; you have come down from the sky. Rest now, and take possession of your royal houses. Welcome to your land, my lords!"

When Motecuhzoma had finished, La Malinche [called Doña Marina by the Spaniards] translated his address into Spanish so that the Captain could understand it. Cortes replied in his strange and savage tongue, speaking first to La Malinche: "Tell Motecuhzoma that we are his friends. There is nothing to fear. We have wanted to see him for a long time, and now we have seen his face and heard his words. Tell him that we love him well and that our hearts are contented."

Then he said to Motecuhzoma: "We have come to your house in Mexico as friends. There is nothing to fear."

La Malinche translated this speech and the Spaniards grasped Motecuhzoma's hands and patted his back to show their affection for him.

The Spaniards' Curiosity

The Spaniards examined everything they saw. They dismounted from their horses, and mounted them again, and dismounted again, so as not to miss anything of interest.

The chiefs who accompanied Motecuhzoma were: Cacama, king of Tezcoco; Tetlepanquetzaltzin, king of Tlacopan; Itzcuauhtzin the Tlacochcalcatl, lord of Tlatelolco; and Topantemoc, Motecuhzoma's treasurer in Tlatelolco. These four chiefs were standing in a file.

The other princes were: Atlixcatzin [chief who has taken captives]; Tepeoatzin, The Tlacochcalcatl; Quetzalaztatzin, the keeper of the chalk; Totomotzin; Hecateupatiltzin; and Cuappiatzin.

When Motecuhzoma was imprisoned, they all went into hiding. They ran away to hide and treacherously abandoned him!

When the Spaniards entered the Royal House, they placed Motecuhzoma under guard and kept him under their vigilance. They also placed a guard over Itzcuauhtzin, but the other lords were permitted to depart.

Then the Spaniards fired one of their cannons, and this caused great confusion in the city. The people scattered in every direction; they fled without rhyme or reason; they ran off as if they were being pursued. It was as if they had eaten the mushrooms that confuse the mind, or had seen some dreadful apparition. They were all overcome by terror, as if their hearts had fainted. And when night fell, the panic spread through the city and their fears would not let them sleep.

In the morning the Spaniards told Motecuhzoma what they needed in the way of supplies: tortillas, fried chickens, hens' eggs, pure water, firewood and charcoal. Also: large, clean cooking pots, water jars, pitchers, dishes and other pottery. Motecuhzoma ordered that it be sent to them. The chiefs who received this order were angry with the king and no longer revered or respected him. But they furnished the Spaniards with all the provisions they needed—food, beverages and water, and fodder for the horses.

The Treasure House

When the Spaniards were installed in the palace, they asked Motecuhzoma about the city's resources and reserves and about the warriors' ensigns and shields. They questioned him closely and then demanded gold.

Motecuhzoma guided them to it. They surrounded him and crowded close with their weapons. He walked in the center, while they formed a circle around him.

When they arrived at the treasure house called Teucalco, the

MALINCHE

*An Amerindian woman named Malinche (called Doña Marina by
the Spanish) served Hernán Cortés as his translator with the Aztecs.
According to Cortés's companion-in-arms, Bernal Díaz del Castillo,
Malinche was the daughter of a lord and chief. When her father died,
she was given to Indians from another region, who in turn gave her
to the people of Tabasco. The Tabasco people gave her to Cortés, with
whom she remained before and during the conquest. She and Cortés
had a son together. Following the fall of Tenochtitlán in 1521 Malinche married one of Cortés's men, with whom she had a daughter.
Malinche died in either 1551 or 1552.*

*The following excerpt, from Bernardino de Sahagún's compila-
tion of the Indians' history of the Spanish Conquest, describes Malinche's role as an interpreter during the first meeting between Montezuma (also called Moctezuma) and Cortés.*

Here it is recalled how Moctezuma went in peace and calm
to meet the Spaniards at Xoloco, where the house of Alvarado now stands, or at the place they call Huitzillan.

And when the Spaniards had arrived at Xoloco, Moctezuma dressed and prepared himself to meet them with other
great rulers and princes, his major men and nobles. They
then went to meet him [Cortés]. They arranged beautiful
flowers in gourds used for vases, in the midst of sunflowers
and magnolias, they placed popcorn flowers, yellow magnolias, and cacao blooms. . . .

And when Moctezuma went to meet them at Huitzillan,
he bestowed gifts on Cortés; he gave him flowers, he put
necklaces on him; he hung garlands around him and put
wreaths on his head. . . .

Then Cortés asked him: "Is it not you? Are you not he?
Are you Moctezuma?"

And Moctezuma responded: "Yes, I am Moctezuma."
Then he stood up to welcome Cortés, to meet him face to
face. He bowed his head low, stretched as far as he could, and
stood firm.

Then he addressed him in these words: "Our lord, you are very welcome in your arrival in this land. You have come to satisfy your curiosity about your noble city of Mexico. You have come here to sit on your throne, to sit under its canopy, which I have kept for awhile for you. For the rulers and governors [of past times] have gone: Itzcoatl, Moctezuma I, Axayacatl, Tiçocic, and Ahuitzotl. [Since they are gone], your poor vassal has been in charge for you, to govern the city of Mexico. Will they come back to the place of their absence? If even one came, he might witness the marvel that has taken place in my time, see what I am seeing, as the only descendant of our lords. For I am not just dreaming, not just sleepwalking, not seeing you in my dreams. I am not just dreaming that I have seen you and have looked at you face to face. I have been worried for a long time, looking toward the unknown from which you have come, the mysterious place. For our rulers departed, saying that you would come to your city and sit upon your throne. And now it has been fulfilled, you have returned. Go enjoy your palace, rest your body. Welcome our lords to this land."

When Moctezuma finished his speech, which he directed toward the Marquis, Marina explained and interpreted it for him. And when the Marquis heard what Moctezuma had said, he spoke to Marina in a babbling tongue: "Tell Moctezuma to not be afraid, for we greatly esteem him. Now we are satisfied because we have seen him in person and heard his voice. For until now, we have wanted to see him face to face. And now we have seen him, we have come to his home in Mexico, slowly he will hear our words."

Thereupon, Cortés took Moctezuma by the hand and led him by it. They walked with him, stroking his hair, showing their esteem. And the Spaniards looked at him, each examining him closely. They walked on foot, then mounted and dismounted in order to look at him.

Bernardino de Sahagún, "Malinche Interprets Moctezuma's Speech for the Spaniards," *General History of the Things of New Spain*, 2nd ed. Santa Fe, NM: School of American Research, 1900.

riches of gold and feathers were brought out to them: ornaments made of quetzal feathers, richly worked shields, disks of gold, the necklaces of the idols, gold nose plugs, gold greaves [leg guards] and bracelets and crowns.

The Spaniards immediately stripped the feathers from the gold shields and ensigns. They gathered all the gold into a great mound and set fire to everything else, regardless of its value. Then they melted down the gold into ingots. As for the precious green stones, they took only the best of them; the rest were snatched up by the Tlaxcaltecas. The Spaniards searched through the whole treasure house, questioning and quarreling, and seized every object they thought was beautiful.

Next they went to Motecuhzoma's storehouse, in the place called Totocalco [Place of the Palace of the Birds], where his personal treasures were kept. The Spaniards grinned like little beasts and patted each other with delight.

When they entered the hall of treasures, it was as if they had arrived in Paradise. They searched everywhere and coveted everything; they were slaves to their own greed. All of Motecuhzoma's possessions were brought out: fine bracelets, necklaces with large stones, ankle rings with little gold bells, the royal crowns and all the royal finery—everything that belonged to the king and was reserved to him only. They seized these treasures as if they were their own, as if this plunder were merely a stroke of good luck. And when they had taken all the gold, they heaped up everything else in the middle of the patio.

La Malinche called the nobles together. She climbed up to the palace roof and cried: "Mexicanos, come forward! The Spaniards need your help! Bring them food and pure water. They are tired and hungry; they are almost fainting from exhaustion! Why do you not come forward? Are you angry with them?"

The Mexicans were too frightened to approach. They were crushed by terror and would not risk coming forward. They shied away as if the Spaniards were wild beasts, as if the hour were midnight on the blackest night of the year. Yet they did not abandon the Spaniards to hunger and thirst. They brought them whatever they needed, but shook with fear as they did so. They delivered the supplies to the Spaniards with trembling hands, then turned and hurried away.

Spanish Rule Is Established

BY MARK A. BURKHOLDER, WITH SUZANNE HILES

After conquering the Aztecs, Hernán Cortés renamed their former empire New Spain. Cortés appointed himself governor of the Spanish colony until he was replaced by an official appointed by the king of Spain. The colony was an area about twice the size of present-day Mexico and rose from the ashes of the Aztec empire. The capital, Mexico City, established in 1535 and built on the site of the Aztec capital of Tenochtitlán, became a thriving urban center with a cathedral, a university, a newspaper, shops brimming with imported goods, and large houses of the former conquistadores. Here, the Spaniards enjoyed a way of life similar to that of their home country.

In the following viewpoint, Mark A. Burkholder, professor of history at the University of Missouri at St. Louis, and coauthor Suzanne Hiles describe the branches of Spanish government in Mexico during the three hundred years after the Spanish Conquest. The Council of the Indies, located in Madrid, formulated laws for the Spanish colonies in the Americas. The members of the council were appointed by the king to hear civil cases emanating from the colonies and also to put forth names for government and religious offices. Across the Atlantic in Mexico City, viceroys ruled the colony of New Spain in the name of the king, carried out his laws, maintained order, administered justice, and were generally responsible for all facets of colonial life. The vast distance between the colony and the mother country gave the viceroys great discretion in the administration of laws dictated by the Council of the Indies. The viceroys were assisted in their work by judicial bodies known as audiencias *located in each region of New Spain. Members of the* audiencias *also ruled in the king's name. Ruling at the local level and subordinate to the viceroy and the* audiencias *of their area were officials called* alcaldes.

Appointment to high offices in New Spain was based on birth and the favor of the king, and not necessarily on merit. Viceroys came from the Spanish aristocracy, and officeholders at the lower rungs of the imperial ad-

ministration were usually criollos, *those of Spanish parentage born in the colonies. While there was great opportunity for viceroys to enrich themselves, many, as Burkholder points out, were conscientious bureaucrats.*

As early as the 1570s, the political and administrative stability that would characterize post-Conquest New Spain until the 19th century was firmly established. Evident as well was social stability, based primarily on a racially determined hierarchy. Spaniards from the Iberian Peninsula and their New World descendants (criollos) were at the apex, Indian commoners and black slaves at the base, and a small but growing number of persons of mixed racial background occupied the middle range. The arrival of clergy, the creation of a university in Mexico City to prepare the Spanish youth of the colony for ecclesiastical and civil positions, and the establishment of the tribunal of the Inquisition [a Catholic organization to combat and punish heresy] rounded out a kingdom that half a century after the conquistadores' arrival was in many ways truly a "New Spain."

The consolidation of Spanish rule, the increasing flow of Mexican silver into Spain's royal coffers, and the perfection of a transatlantic trading system based upon the regular sailing of fleets from Seville to Veracruz coincided with the reign of Philip II (1556–98) and the pinnacle of Spanish power in Europe. However, economic and financial problems in Spain, military defeats with their corresponding loss of Spanish influence, and the progressive collapse of the fleet system from the early 1620s onward soon altered the colonial relationship.

As Spain floundered toward second-power status in Europe, New Spain relinquished its primitive dependence on the mother country. Isolated from military conflict, the colony experienced social tranquility, administrative stability, long-term economic growth, and, after about 1630, an overall increase in population. Although the Crown in Madrid retained administrative oversight, colonial merchants, miners, large landowners, and officeholders forged social, economic, and political relationships and focused their primary attention on personal rather than royal interests. Able to produce everything needed for subsistence and to import luxury items in exchange for [silver] bullion, Mexico achieved a measurable degree of economic independence. At the same time, however, the unquestioned legitimacy of Spanish rule provided a solid basis for political stability. . . .

The Governing of New Spain

Colonial Mexico was the core of the viceroyalty of New Spain established in 1535. The *gobierno* [government] of New Spain, administered directly by the viceroy as governor, was the colony's heartland. East of the Isthmus of Tehuantepec on the Pacific Coast and extending into the Gulf of Mexico was the gobierno of Yucatán. North and west of the gobierno of New Spain lay New Galicia. Further expansion led to the creation of gobiernos of New Vizcaya (1562), New León (1580), and New Mexico (1598). Additional subdivision of frontier regions occurred from the late 17th century until the early 19th century.

The physical size and population of the gobiernos resulted, particularly in New Spain and New Galicia, in their division into the provincial units known most commonly as *alcaldías mayores*. The number of subdivisions peaked in the 1570s, then fell substantially as a result of a declining native population and administrative consolidation, especially in the late 17th century. Within each of these jurisdictions a municipality housed the provincial administrator, or *alcalde mayor*.

The most numerous territorial units were the municipalities. The Crown confirmed the existence of the native municipalities and their dependent villages and emphasized their central role. In addition, it required that new municipalities be founded when native villages were consolidated or "congregated." Within the native municipalities, Indian officials handled administrative matters and served as essential links with the Spanish overlords (*encomenderos*) and royal officials. . . .

Time and distance profoundly affected administration of the colony, by forcing the Crown to delegate more authority to colonial officials than was customary in Spain. Thus, despite institutional checks on their behavior, officeholders in New Spain enjoyed a latitude and flexibility that their Spanish counterparts lacked. An order sent from Madrid in early July typically did not reach Mexico City until late September. The response normally did not leave New Spain until late spring, to arrive in Madrid in the fall. And this lengthy cycle might mark only the first round of communication in resolving an issue. Thus, the distance covered by mounted couriers and sailing ships ensured leisurely communications between Spain and Mexico. . . .

The highest-ranking official resident in Mexico was the viceroy of New Spain. To inaugurate the office, Charles I selected

Antonio de Mendoza, a younger son of one of Castile's most illustrious noble families and thus someone with the political connections and social rank that would overawe the conquistadores
and early settlers. During his unusually long 15-year tenure (1535–
50), Mendoza firmly established royal authority in Mexico.

As personal representatives of the monarch, Mendoza and subsequent viceroys lived in a palace located on the central plaza
(plaza mayor) of Mexico City, had numerous servants, extended

THE ENCOMIENDA SYSTEM

*One of the main reasons why young Spanish adventurers—the fu-
ture conquistadores—joined Hernán Cortés in the conquest of the
Aztec empire was to gain wealth and status. When the conquest was
completed and the spoils divided, Cortés bestowed upon his cohorts
parcels of land as payment for their efforts. These parcels were called*
encomiendas *and the holder of the land, the* encomendero. *The*
encomienda *system enabled the Spanish to control and subjugate
the Indians, a conquered people of a formerly great empire.*

Through a formal grant of encomienda, designated Indian
families, usually the inhabitants of a town or of a cluster of
towns, were entrusted to the charge of a Spanish colonist,
who thus became the *encomendero.* In the characteristic
phrase, he "held" these Indians "in encomienda." The first
encomenderos were permitted to exact both commodity tribute and labor service from the Indians whom they "held."
In this way they derived an income and were able to control
labor groups without risk or effort. In return they were expected to render military service (a traditional obligation for
the privileged as well as a consequence of the fear of Indian
uprisings) and to provide for the Christianization of the Indians committed to their charge. Technically the term encomienda referred to the conditions of trust under which
Indian peoples were granted; they were *entrusted* to an *encomendero's* care as a responsibility and favor, in return for military and religious obligations on his part. . . .

lavish hospitality, and projected an image of royalty. While it encouraged the keeping up of such regal appearance, the Crown simultaneously imposed important restraints on its territorial governors. Among the devices used to curtail viceregal power were limited terms of service, instructions issued by the Council of the Indies, occasional special inspections, prohibitions against establishing local social and economic ties, and a formal judicial review following the viceroys' terms of service. Most important,

From the time of the conquest of Mexico through the "age of conquest" and after, encomienda flourished openly in the Spanish colonies of America. Everywhere the soldiers of the conquest armies repeated the demands of the soldiers of [Hernán] Cortés [leader of the conquistadors who defeated the Aztecs]. It was everywhere accepted that the largest and most remunerative grants were to be assigned to those whose military services had been most substantial. Cortés became the foremost *encomendero* of all, with his holdings in the Valley of Oaxaca and scattered additional grants elsewhere. His tremendous riches—it is likely that he was at one time the wealthiest person in the entire Spanish world—depended chiefly on encomienda, which furnished him a large annual tribute income and labor for his various enterprises. . . .

Encomienda Indians were made to perform many new tasks. Spanish agriculture required plows, draft animals, and new crops. Sugar milling, a standard *encomendero* operation in the tropical zones, involved methods of work previously unknown to American natives. The prodigious construction labors likewise followed Spanish rather than native techniques. But it would be idealistic to suppose that Indians in encomienda developed private skills or otherwise derived personal benefit from their training. Most labor remained routine, unskilled, mass labor. Abundant records of the early post-conquest period testify to the abuses—the punishments, tortures, exorbitant tribute demands, labor cruelties, enslavement, and other excesses—committed by *encomenderos* and their overseers.

Charles Gibson, *Spain in America*. New York: Harper & Row, 1966.

other colonial institutions and representatives—for example, the *Audiencia* [highest court of appeals] of Mexico, the archbishop of Mexico, treasury officials, and the city council of Mexico City— served as checks on viceregal behavior by virtue of their over- lapping responsibilities and their privilege of communicating in- dependently with the king and the Council of the Indies.

As New Spain's chief executive the viceroy had extensive re- sponsibilities, which included preventing "unjust" exploitation of the natives and overseeing defense, exploration, and settlement; the administration of justice, civil administration; and tax collec- tion and disbursement, as well as encouraging economic expan- sion and remitting surplus revenue to Spain. Above all, the monarch measured his representative's success by that official's ability to remit a sizable amount of surplus revenue to Spain....

The broad responsibilities and regal lifestyle of the viceroys gave them a presence that exceeded their actual power. Ranked lower, but at times collectively more important, were the mem- bers of the *audiencias* of Mexico and Guadalajara, the high courts and advisory bodies to the viceroy of New Spain and the presi- dent of the *Audiencia* of New Galicia. The Crown named viceroys to term appointments, whereas audiencia ministers were appointed for life unless they advanced within a tribunal or to another court.... Their local ties and appreciation of local agen- das gave the audiencias substantial power. Wise chief executives heeded their recommendations.

The Crown established audiencias in Mexico in 1527 and Guadalajara in 1547. Royal legislation specified that all audiencia ministers be men of legitimate birth (all claimed noble status), at least 25 years of age, and recipients of a university degree in law. While the first ministers named were born in Spain, beginning in 1585, a sprinkling of criollos received appointments....

Provincial Officials

Provincial officials formed the most numerous category of royal appointees. Originally named to oversee Native Americans pre- viously living in *encomiendas* (grants of Indian labor and tribute) that had reverted to the Crown, these officials also had judicial and military responsibilities. Their number fluctuated consider- ably, but the pinnacle was more than 270 in the 1570s. Subse- quent consolidation reduced this number until on the eve of their replacement by the intendant system in the late 1780s there

were 129 alcaldías mayores in the gobierno of New Spain, 62 alcaldías mayores and 7 gobiernos on the northern frontier of the
colony, and a few others in the southeastern region.

From Antonio de Mendoza's tenure until the 1670s, the
viceroys named most of the provincial officials. The immediate
descendants of conquistadores and the early settlers sought these
appointments based on their fathers' services; royal legislation issued in 1538 supported their claims. By the end of the 16th century more than 40 percent of such officials were born in New
Spain. Viceregal patronage, however, also benefited retainers who
accompanied the chief executives to Mexico. . . .

Municipalities

Beneath these various colonial administrative layers, each municipality, whether of native or Spanish origin, had a local government and local officials. Municipal councils typically had four
or more aldermen (*regidores*) and two local judges and council-
men (*alcaldes*). In addition, municipalities had a variety of officials
who policed the area; supervised local revenues, expenditures, and
retailing; and performed a host of general administrative tasks. Indian municipalities also had responsibility for collecting tribute,
maintaining treasuries and communal properties, supporting the
local church, adjudicating petty crimes, handling local land and
water cases, and litigating to protect local rights and property. Independent Indian villages (head towns) also had local governors.
Not surprisingly, the locally born participated extensively at the
municipal government level. The largest municipality, Mexico
City, had a majority of such aldermen from 1590 on. . . .

In maintaining Spanish rule through recourse to law with only
minimal reliance on military force, balancing the conflicting interests of Crown and colonists, conquerors and conquered, and
remitting surplus revenues to Spain, the bureaucrats of New
Spain were generally quite successful. Although many enriched
themselves through illegal means, their involvement in local economic affairs and social ties through marriage, kinship, and as
godparents made them sensitive to local interests and thus tem-
pered their implementation of royal dictates. The political stability they helped create and maintain through this balance between
royal and colonial interests contrasted sharply with the instability
that followed independence.

From Independence to Empire to Republic, 1810–1848

A Revolt Against Spanish Rule Is Launched

By Enrique Krauze

Mexico in the early 1800s was a nation of vast natural resources and great social inequalities. The descendants of the Spanish conquistadores held most of the wealth in the form of haciendas (large estates) and silver mines. The Indians and the mestizos (those of both Indian and Spanish or European parents) labored for them in poverty and ignorance. Divisions also existed between criollos (those born in Mexico of European back-ground) and peninsulares *(Spanish-born settlers). Politically, Mexico was splintered into many different factions. Liberal reformers wanted greater autonomy from Spain. Conservatives wanted to preserve ties with Spain and Mexico's Spanish heritage. Moderates stood between the two poles.*

In the following selection, journalist and historian Enrique Krauze describes one of the leading figures in Mexican history: the priest Miguel Hidalgo y Costilla. His call for a revolt against Spanish rule on September 16, 1810, began Mexico's war for independence. Inspired by the revolutions in the United States (1776), France (1789), and Haiti (1804), many reform-minded Mexicans, mainly criollos but also mestizos and Indians, looked forward to greater political independence from Spain. When French emperor Napoléon Bonaparte invaded Spain in 1808 and placed his brother on the throne, criollos saw this as an opportunity to overthrow Spanish rule and the control the peninsulares *exerted over Mexican life. Miguel Hidalgo, a criollo and a political radical, led the first widespread uprising against colonial rule. The uprising faded and Hidalgo was arrested and later executed.*

Enrique Krauze was born in Mexico City in 1947 and edited the intellectual journal Vuelta. *He has written numerous essays and articles on present-day Mexico and is a supporter of democratic reform.*

Enrique Krauze, "The Insurgent Priests," *Mexico: Biography of Power, a History of Modern Mexico, 1810–1996,* translated by Hank Heifetz. New York: Harper-Collins, 1997.

F ather Miguel Hidalgo was part of an old tradition of cre- ole [those born in the New World of Spanish background] patriotism common to all of Spanish America but dating back, in New Spain, to the sixteenth century and strongly rein- forced by the work of the creole Jesuits of the Enlightenment in the mid–eighteenth century. He himself was part of the regular clergy, not a member of any order, but when the Bourbon kings [of Spain] (wary of their prestige and influence and interested in their wealth) had expelled the Jesuits in 1767, Hidalgo was a stu- dent at Valladolid, a major center of Jesuit influence, and he would always remember those priests who had placed so much value on the history and natural riches of Mexico. Almost half a century later, Hidalgo declared: "We will freely exploit the in- credibly rich products of our country and within a few years its inhabitants will enjoy all the delights of this vast continent."

Hidalgo had other, less idealistic reasons for demanding that the creoles be granted their rights. Through the *Consolidación de Vales Reales* of 1804, the Spanish Crown had put a lien on Hi- dalgo's haciendas [estates] and those of his family, threatening to auction them off unless the sudden, exorbitant demands for pay- ment were met. Hidalgo had been pushed to the edge of bank- ruptcy, and his younger brother Manuel had been so disturbed that he went mad and would die within a few years, in 1809.

Professor and Priest

When he launched his revolution in 1810, Miguel Hidalgo had long been recognized as "one of the best theologians in his dio- cese," "a man deeply versed in literature and with a very broad range of knowledge in all areas." The son of the manager of a hacienda, he was born in 1753 on the Hacienda de Corralejo, in the state of Guanajuato. He studied theology in the city of Val- lodolid (now called Morelia), where he witnessed the expulsion of the Jesuits. His fellow students called him "the Fox," a nick- name that, according to the Conservative [Lucas] Alamán, cor- responded "perfectly to his crafty personality." Graduating in 1782, he became a professor (for ten years) and ultimately Rec- tor at the famous seminary of San Nicolás in the same city. . . .

Later, in his own parishes, though he was still a man much ad- mired, somewhat different views were also expressed about him. At the beginning of the century, the Inquisition [church court convened to fight heresy] began to receive accusations against

Hidalgo, who was then priest of the rich parish of San Felipe Torres Mochas. The complaints were of two kinds: moral and theological. His accusers did not doubt that he had a "fine brain," a "cheerful" disposition, and was "shrewd in the area of letters," but he also had some extravagant habits. He was a "professional gambler and as such was dissolute," "free in his treatment of women," and given to "continual amusement" to such a degree that "in the house of this Hidalgo there has been enough riotous celebration to turn it into a little France," a place where you find "male and female musicians, games of chance and dancing"; "he keeps an entire orchestra on salary, whose directors dine with him and are treated like family." The problem, nevertheless, was not so much what Hidalgo did as what he thought. To judge by the denunciations, the curate was almost a heretic. Among the many charges raised against him, Hidalgo was said to have denied the existence of hell. ("Don't believe that, Manuelita," a close friend—perhaps too close—confessed to have heard him say. "These things are deceptions.") He mocked Saint Teresa [a Spanish nun and mystic] ("a deluded woman, who, because she whipped herself, fasted a lot and did not sleep, saw visions"). He preached intellectual licentiousness (the Bible ought to be "studied with the freedom of mind to discuss what we want without fearing the Inquisition")....

The cycle of denunciations ended shortly afterward, and though they began again in 1807, none of them did any practical harm to the priest. Aside from the fact that many of the accusations—particularly the theological ones—were probably exaggerated and distorted, Hidalgo could count on important support: He was highly esteemed by the civil and ecclesiastical authorities of his district and diocese, who for the most part looked kindly on the new air of liberty at the beginning of the new century. Hidalgo's biographers from every age have discounted these indictments, putting them down to envy or associating them with subsequent events in his life (the Inquisition file was in fact reopened during the final trial to which he was subjected). But at least with the moral charges, these accusations show an internal agreement that suggests they were true. Hidalgo was not only a restless priest but an eccentric one, a free and brilliant man, who attracted—and seduced—the most enlightened of his contemporaries but unsettled the more rigid and conservative. They vaguely sensed in him the seed of something new and disconcerting.

The Many Hidalgos

Within Hidalgo there were many Hidalgos, and all of them were equally eccentric. As a priest, while ministering to his flock (in the parishes of Colima, San Felipe, and, finally, Dolores), he showed very little interest in administrative work or in celebrating many masses. Instead he enjoyed preaching, where he could apply his knowledge of theology, and he showed great care and concern in taking confessions from the sick and the dying. This paternal attitude of the priest Hidalgo showed above all in his treatment of the Indians. He learned their language and he taught them various crafts and trades. It was as if he were trying to transform theology into charity.

If in his youth he had been primarily a contemplative person, over time he grew more active and became an innovative and hardworking businessman. Besides managing the small family haciendas, he developed an interest in beekeeping, curing skins, manufacturing pottery, cultivating vineyards, and in his last parish, the village of Dolores, he planted an extensive acreage of mulberry trees in order to raise silkworms. . . .

The reverse side of this display of activity was his spendthrift and disorganized character. Evidence abounds of his procrastination in paying off debts and, later, of his appetite for gambling and extravagance. On the point of departure from Colima for San Felipe, he forgot to pay off money he owed. Once in San Felipe, he incurred another debt with a certain Sr. Ignacio Soto, who pressured the bishop until he finally confiscated a third of Hidalgo's official earnings to settle the grievance. The Colegio de San Nicolás demanded payment of a sum of money, and the tedious inquiries went on for years. In another case of an upaid debt, the vicar-general himself had to reprimand Hidalgo. Overall, this priest's activities were as incessant as they were unreflective. . . .

Hidalgo's Intellectual Roots

Bishop Manuel Abad y Queipo [of Michoacan] was one of the most fascinating intellectual personalities of the Enlightenment in New Spain. He kept abreast of the latest developments and political theories in Europe while at the same time composing his famous series of "Representations" in which he outlined the socioeconomic problems of New Spain and warned of the dangers of a social uprising. Hidalgo was one of his friends and a member of his intellectual circle.

Despite their closeness, the secular classics valued by Hidalgo were not those (Adam Smith, Jovellanos, the Physiocrats) esteemed by Abad. Still less was Hidalgo concerned with [eighteenth-century philosophers] Voltaire, Rousseau, or the French Encyclopedists, whose writings he probably did not know at all. Hidalgo's century was the seventeenth rather than the eighteenth. He translated Racine and Molière (*Tartuffe* was his favorite work), read La Fontaine, and played Rameau on the violin. The "little France" of his house in Dolores was more an art center than an intellectual salon. He liked to read history—and not only ecclesiastical history—but his favorite historian continued to be [Jacques Benigne] Bossuet with his belief in Divine Providence. It was not Montesquieu—frequently quoted by Abad—but the Spanish neoscholastic thinkers of the sixteenth and seventeenth centuries who guided Hidalgo in political matters. Despite recent censorship by the Crown, students of the seminary where Hidalgo had studied were by no means unfamiliar with the assertion of the Jesuit Francisco Suárez (1548–1617) that "sovereignty lies essentially with peoples and not with kings; the kings exercise it by consent of the people and with the understanding and indispensable condition that it should be exercised for the benefit and utility of the people, and in the event of its abuse, kings can be deposed and war may even be declared upon them, because peoples are superior to kings."

These surprising, pre-Rousseauian theories on the tyrannical nature of domination . . . were the theoretical and moral reservoir that the creoles of Mexico City's *ayuntamiento* (municipal council) used to support their claim that the people were now sovereign, after Napoleon's invasion of Spain in September of 1808 and the imprisonment of King Ferdinand VII. Even the viceroy, José de Iturrigaray, agreed to the devolution [the passing on] of legal authority to the *ayuntamiento* (a quasi-democratic body that had represented the *vox populi* in Spain ever since the Middle Ages), but a coup d'état against him led by wealthy Spanish merchants thwarted this first bid for creole autonomy.

Two years after these events, which had become well known throughout New Spain (the viceroy had been deposed, the members of the *ayuntamiento* imprisoned and some of them killed), Hidalgo was doing some highly specialized reading: *A Dictionary of Arts and Sciences* that included an article on artillery tactics and the manufacture of cannons and also the book of Bossuet's *Uni-*

versal History that dealt with the conspiracy of Catiline against the Senate of Rome. His purpose was not innocently intellectual. He was himself conspiring with several creole officials against the Spanish government. In September, moved to sudden action

MEXICO IN THE EARLY NINETEENTH CENTURY

Alexander von Humboldt (1769–1859) was a German natural-ist, botanist, explorer, and geographer. In 1799 Humboldt journeyed to South America on a scientific expedition during which he explored Venezuela's Orinoco River and climbed Mount Chimborazo, a vol-cano in Ecuador. He also measured the ocean current flowing along the continent's west coast. This current bears his name—the Hum-boldt Current. In 1803, Humboldt visited Mexico, where he ad-vised the government on mining reform and lectured at the mining academy. He also observed the structure of Mexican society and com-mented on its inequalities. The following selection is taken from Alexander von Humboldt's essay on New Spain.

Mexico is the country of inequality. Nowhere does there ex-ist such a fearful difference in the distribution of fortune, civ-ilization, cultivation of the soil, and population.... The Mex-ican Indians, when we consider them *en masse*, offer a picture of extreme misery. Banished into the most barren districts, and indolent from nature, and more still from their political situation, the natives live only from hand to mouth. We should seek almost in vain among them for individuals who enjoy anything like a certain mediocrity of fortune. Instead, however, of a comfortable independency, we find a few fam-ilies whose fortune appears so much the more colossal....

The Indians are exempted from every sort of indirect impost [customs duty]. They pay no *alcavala* [tax]; and the law allows them full liberty for the sale of their productions. ... If the legislation of Queen Isabella and the Emperor Charles V [rulers of Spain] appears to favour the Indians through a betrayal of the rebellion he was planning (and the rumor of an invasion by the forces of Napoleonic France), he launched an attempt to claim power for the people. But this time—though Hidalgo used the same theories to justify his ac-

---

with regard to imposts, it has deprived them, on the other hand, of the most important rights enjoyed by the other citizens. In an age when it was formally discussed if the Indians were rational beings, it was conceived granting them a benefit to treat them like minors, to put them under the perpetual tutory of the whites, and to declare null every act signed by a native of the copper-coloured race, and every obligation which he contracted beyond the value of 15 francs. These laws are maintained in full vigour; and they place insurmountable barriers between the Indians and the other castes, with whom all intercourse is almost prohibited. Thousands of inhabitants can enter into no contract which is binding; and condemned to a perpetual minority, they become a charge to themselves and the state in which they live. . . .

Amongst the inhabitants of pure origin the whites would occupy the second place, considering them only in the relation of number. They are divided into whites born in Europe, and descendants of Europeans born in the Spanish colonies of America or in the Asiatic islands. The former bear the name of *Chapetones* or *Gachupines*, and the second that of *Criollos*. The natives of the Canary islands, who go under the general denomination of *Islenos* (islanders), and who are the *gerans* [supervisors] of the plantations, are considered as Europeans. The Spanish laws allow the same rights to all whites; but those who have the execution of the laws endeavour to destroy an equality which shocks the European pride. The government, suspicious of the Creoles [descendants of Europeans born in the Spanish colonies], bestows the great places exclusively on the natives of Old Spain.

Alexander von Humboldt, *Political Essay on the Kingdom of New Spain*, trans. John Black. London: Longman, Hurst, Rees, Orme, and Brown, 1811.

tions—power was to be seized not by their creole representatives on the Mexico City council, but by the people themselves, by the masses. He was acting [according to historian Hernandez y Davalos] "on the authority of my nation"; he had been chosen "by the Mexican nation to defend its rights"; and he would seek the restitution of "the holy rights granted by God to the Mexicans, usurped by cruel, bastard and unjust conquerors."

"Death to the Spaniards!"

On the morning of September 16 [1810], he rang the cathedral bell to summon his Indian parishioners into the church square of Dolores and delivered his famous cry (the *grito*): "Death to the Spaniards! Long live the Virgin of Guadalupe!" (though disagreements exist on exactly what he did say). We know he called on the Indians to open the jails of Dolores, free the prisoners, and lock up the Spaniards, and that he authorized the sacking of houses and haciendas belonging to the Spanish-born (*gachupines*) and allowed his followers to kill and satisfy their instincts for revenge. That same day, Hidalgo, possessed by what he would later call his "frenzy," had taken a canvas of the Virgin of Guadalupe from the nearby sanctuary of Atotonilco and attached it to a stick, creating a standard for his struggle. In San Miguel El Grande, it is certain that he did cry out, "Take! My children! Because everything is yours!" Within days, the whole central region of the country, the Bajío, went up in flames. Following close at the heels of the undermanned and disorganized official regiments commanded by creole officers (Hidalgo never even had a hundred creole followers) came nearly twenty thousand men of the humblest origins, his flock, Hidalgo's army. . . .

With Hidalgo approaching, most of the Spanish population in the city of Guanajuato shut themselves up behind the stone walls of the Alhóndiga de Granaditas, a building used for storing grain. As if history were taking an atrocious revenge for the massacres of Indians by the conquistadors at Cholula and the great temple of Tenochtitlan, Indians and Castes [mestizos] from the city itself joined Hidalgo's Indian brigades in slaughtering all the Spanish men. Captives were beaten to death. . . . A mob ran wild, looting and wrecking houses and businesses. It was a frenzy fueled by racial and social hatred.

When a fellow priest asked him to explain the nature of his struggle, Hidalgo, already acclaimed as the "Captain-General of

America," answered that "he would have found it much easier to explain what he would have liked the revolution to be, but even he did not really understand what it was." His personal motive was something nearly every creole wanted: to gain independence from Spain. What he presumably "would have liked" was to incorporate the creoles into his army, but they would not follow him, because for them the events from the very beginning were an upheaval aimed at eliminating the entire white population of the country, creoles and native Spaniards alike (about a million out of a total population of six million). Hidalgo would later confess that he knew of no way to ignite the war other than the one he put into effect: using the prestige of his priesthood to appeal to the elemental passions of his Indian parishioners, among them plunder and revenge.

Hidalgo had no broader military strategy. . . . The intensity of Hidalgo's actions steadily mounted—based on a single, fevered purpose. He wanted to destroy the old order, to cure its social and ethnic injustices, to avenge the old grievances of the creoles and to avenge Manuel, the brother who had died. He wanted a universal conflagration [a large fire that destroys everything]. When Hidalgo occupied Valladolid, and his old friend Abad y Queipo excommunicated him, he responded by issuing a decree to abolish slavery. This must have been one of the earliest of such formal declarations, if not the very first, in the Americas. His conscience was clear: He was the leader of a just war. . . .

At the end of October, that caravan of an army [Hidalgo's followers] halted at Monte de Las Cruces, near Mexico City. Following Hidalgo was his horde of at least eighty thousand Indians (and Castes) armed with lances, stones, and sticks, so thoroughly ready to plunder Mexico City that they had brought sacks with them for carrying off what they would seize. Suddenly, the fire of the royalist artillery spread real fear, for the first time, among Hidalgo's soldiers, who in their desperation tried to charge the big guns and stop up the smoking mouths of the cannon with their huge, straw sombreros. Hidalgo . . . refused to make a direct assault on the capital. Was it his Spanish roots that made him make this decision, to prevent another massacre of Spaniards? Or his discretion, an unwillingness to see the deaths mount up among his Indians? The reasons remain a mystery. But his failure to act was the beginning of his downfall.

Hidalgo withdrew toward the west and set up his headquarters in Guadalajara. While in that city, he issued two important decrees meant to remedy social and agrarian injustices. One abolished taxes . . . the other ordered the restitution of lands to Indian communities. . . . And [according to writer Hernandez y Davalos] he envisioned summoning a congress, "to be made up of representatives from all cities, towns and places in this kingdom, who—while keeping as their principal goal the maintenance of our religion—would pass mild and benevolent laws suited to the particular circumstances of each *pueblo:* then they will govern with the gentleness of priests, will treat us like their brothers, will banish poverty. . . ."

Hidalgo, the "Sun King"

By then an imperial use of the first person had become habit. Hidalgo was letting himself be treated like a sovereign. He lavishly made official appointments; he lived surrounded by guards; he would walk arm in arm with a lovely young woman and allow himself to be addressed with the title "Most Serene Highness." He attended banquets, dances, ceremonies, plays, parades, gala functions where he accepted the homage of politicians, military men, and priests in the midst of banners, flags, exquisite refreshments, bursts of music, and peals of bells. Guadalajara was now his "little France," and Hidalgo was the Sun King [name given to King Louis XIV of France].

That priest-king could be munificent to some and terrible to others. "In Guadalajara," [José Maria Luis] Mora writes, "according to decisions that Hidalgo made in secret . . . a bullfighter named Marroquín would take out groups of Spaniards at night, while the city was quiet, and bring them to the Salto ravine . . . and there he would cut their throats." Through an offering of immunity and protection, Hidalgo had attracted *gachupines* [Spaniards living in Mexico] from the surrounding area and concentrated them in the Colegio de San Juan and in the local seminary. Some had brought their families with them. When the real reason behind this assembly was revealed—Marroquín appeared with his knife—[Ignacio] Allende [Hidalgo's second-in-command], who for some time had disagreed with "that rogue of a priest" as he called him, entertained the idea of poisoning Hidalgo. He did not do it, nor could he prevent the month of massacres that ran from the Feast of the Virgin of Guadalupe on December 12, 1810, to January 13, 1811. . . .

The Uprising Fades

During the colonial period, on the whole, truly indigenous uprisings were fires that quickly went out. In Guadalajara, through exhaustion, satiation, or for motives as mysterious as the sudden disappearance—which Hidalgo could not explain—of the image of the Virgin from their hats (the truth seems to be that some of his soldiers were removing it, as a sign of their displeasure at his failure to attack Mexico City), the Indians began to leave him. For this and other reasons—disorder among the remaining recruits, the vagueness and therefore limited appeal and power of his program, disagreements among his commanders, the emergence of a burdensome and extortionate bureaucracy, and the firm resistance of the royalist troops who defeated his disorganized armies at Puente de Calderon—Hidalgo was forced north toward the interior eastern provinces.

In Saltillo he was welcomed by two groups of Insurgents—under Captains Menchaca and Colorado—whose ranks included contingents of Comanche Indians. On seeing them, Hidalgo was enraptured. "They had their bodies painted with differently colored stripes," a witness noted, "and they were wearing buffalo hides." It would be the last time that the creole priest would be able to preach to an indigenous flock, as different as they were from his parishioners in Dolores. His words touched on the key theme of creole self-identity, the connection of the creoles with the Indians through the abuses they had both suffered at the hands of the Spaniards. . . .

Hidalgo Captured

After the sermon, [Hidalgo] continued moving north, perhaps with the intention of crossing into the United States. But he never reached the border. A royalist officer—learning that Hidalgo was advancing through his desert area with a small group of men—set a trap for him by closing all the water holes except one. With the sun and the sand as his allies (and including a pretended welcome among his weapons, as if he were going over to the Insurgents), the officer—Ignacio Elizondo—lured Hidalgo into an ambush and took him alive, along with Allende and other leaders of the Insurgency.

In the city of Chihuahua, he was tried both by a military court and then by the Inquisition. During the first trial, he recounted the details of his short-lived campaign. He declared himself "sincerely repentant." He took responsibility for the massacres of Spaniards in Valladolid and Guadalajara and claimed that it was because he had wanted to please "the Indians and the lowest rabble . . . the only ones who desired these scenes.". . .

Hidalgo had desired independence as if it were a vague utopia, something that would just happen, the fruit of a miracle as sudden and incomprehensible as the revolution he had unleashed with his preaching. That was why he never dared to declare himself openly in favor of independence. It would have been like substituting himself for Divine Providence. In his classic creole soul, resentment against the *gachupines* was counterbalanced by a traditional loyalty to the Crown. Hidalgo's perception of the state was in no way that of the later Liberals. He had no clear political alternatives on which to raise up anything new. He was a creole educated within the monarchy and trapped within the monarchy, although he resented the tyranny and despotism of the Spanish government. . . . Hidalgo wanted both monarchy and liberty, and when he realized that the two were incompatible, he abandoned himself to "regal pomp and ceremony." He lived out, with "frenzy," an imperial fantasy. . . .

On July 30, 1811, [Hidalgo] was executed (as were his closest aides—Allende, [Juan] Aldama, and Jiménez). Three lines, one after another, of nervous soldiers put bullets into Hidalgo's arm, belly, and spine but failed to kill him. Pedro Armendáriz, the commander of the firing squad, ordered two men to follow him as he approached the priest lying in agony. They were ordered to press their rifle muzzles to Hidalgo's heart. Armendáriz would remember that, as he gave the order to fire, Hidalgo "stared straight at us with those beautiful eyes."

The heads were displayed in cages on the four walls of the Alhóndiga de Granaditas, where the Spaniards of Guanajuato had been massacred. There they remained for ten years until Mexico won its independence in 1821.

For the War of Independence had not ended with the death of its first leader. It would go on, under the command of parish priests who were, unlike Hidalgo, mostly mestizos.

The Short-Lived Mexican Empire

By T.R. Fehrenbach

The uprising against Spanish rule begun by Miguel Hidalgo y Costilla in 1810 continued under independent guerrilla bands. The colonial government of New Spain regained control, however, and the independence movement seemed to stall. Many leading criollos (those of Spanish or European descent born in New Spain) opposed the violence carried out by the ragtag rebels and looked for a more orderly route to independence.

The following selection by historian T.R. Fehrenbach describes how Agustín de Iturbide (1783–1824) emerged as the unlikely architect of Mexico's independence from Spain. Iturbide, a criollo, was a general in the royalist army and had fought against rebel forces. When liberal reformers in Spain forced the king, Ferdinand VII, to sign a new constitution calling for self-rule for the Spanish people, Iturbide saw it as an opportunity for criollos to seize control in New Spain. Iturbide pressured the viceroy of New Spain (who governed in the name of the king) to resign and, in 1821, issued a declaration of Mexico's independence with himself as provisional head of a new government. In the following selection, historian T.R. Fehrenbach describes how Iturbide became Mexico's first monarch, Emperor Agustín I. This event, though brief, was a disaster for Mexico and marked the beginning of a tradition of rule by inept and corrupt despots.

T.R. Fehrenbach is a Texas-born journalist and historian. His most well-known work is Lone Star, *a history of his home state.*

I n the glittering air of its eternal spring, the capital [Mexico City] was brave in its bunting and grand expectations through all the fall of 1821. The bishops and those Mexicans who loved a *gran señor* [an impressive man] hourly expected the arrival of a king; the liberals had their quiet confidence that kings might come but a republic must evolve. The three guarantees [refers to the plan put forth by General [Agustín] Iturbide for Mexico's independence from Spain. His plan guaranteed (1) independence under King Ferdinand VII (2) continuation of Roman Catholicism as the state religion of Mexico, and (3) citizenship and equality for all Mexicans] satisfied no one completely, yet everyone to some extent. Even the down-to-earth Vicente Guerrero [a rebel leader who sided with Iturbide in declaring independence from Spain] professed hope. The one thing all Mexicans agreed on was that Mexico, free at last, would immediately take a rightful place among the great nations of the world. The capital was still the metropolis of the Americas, and it was destined in their eyes to become the seat of a great New World empire.

This empire already reached from the mountains of Guatemala, through the Great Plains and high sierras of the northern continent; its flag flew from the Sabine [River] to San Francisco.

The old imperialism was not quite dead. Almost all commerce was still in the hands of thousands of *gachupines* [European-born settlers]. The ousted Spanish army still clung to the fortress of San Juan de Ulua, commanding the vital port of Veracruz and collecting its customs revenues. Spanish prelates utterly dominated the national Church. Spanish officials and jurists, like Spanish merchants, carried on most public affairs. All this could be uprooted—but no one was sure how to begin.

In the magnificent National Palace the new management, the now Generalissimo and High Admiral Agustín de Iturbide, drawing a salary of one-hundred-and-twenty thousand pesos, appointed a Supreme Junta [small group ruling a country] of thirty-eight and a Regency Council of five to rule the kingdom. There were conspicuously no old insurgents among these men. Iturbide was the darling of the bishops and the turncoat royalist generals, who saw him as their tool, and he turned to where his support lay. He was also, not incongruously, the hero of the capital mob, because with his fine horse, plumed hat, handsome face, and charismatic tongue, he cut a fine appearance before the *léperos* [beggars]. The mob that tried to burn [Hernán] Cortés' bones cheered the generalissimo.

But the lower half of the *criollos* did not trust Iturbide, and the great men did not love him. He was an upstart, a dictator come from nowhere, and his very power provoked enormous jealousy.

As president of the Council of Regents, Iturbide presided over a euphoric but ruined country. Half the mines were flooded, their machinery wrecked; half the haciendas [estates] were idle, their tools and livestock looted. The national treasury was empty, and the government had no apparatus to collect new revenues. The national army, eighty thousand strong—half of them officers, commissioned and noncommissioned—fired off salutes and waited to be paid. Meanwhile, fully half the *criollo* population—according to one contemporary—had made application for public employment. *Empleomanía*, the madness for offices, reigned.

Iturbide's wits now deserted him. A wiser man would have remained with the army, letting others wrestle with the mounting problems, letting someone else absorb the discredit and disillusionment that was bound to come. But Iturbide saw himself as a new Napoleon [conqueror of Europe and, later, emperor of France], not recognizing that independent Mexico was not postrevolutionary France.

A Mexican Congress Is Elected

The junta supervised elections that produced a Mexican congress in February 1822. The elections were rigged. No Mexican had any experience with the electoral process, and almost none really believed in it; elections were an alien concept but too fashionable to be ignored. Their purpose was invariably assumed to be a ratification of the regime in power. The Anglo-Saxon process, by which men surrendered power and allowed principle to be turned around by a small, fickle plurality remained incomprehensible to the Hispanic mind. An overwhelmingly rich, conservative, royalist congress, sprinkled with a few intellectual gadflies like Carlos María de Bustamante was elected. The Congress arrived believing its purpose was to ratify the coming of a Bourbon [the ruling dynasty in Spain] king. However, Iturbide already had other plans.

Fernando VII was once again secure on the Spanish throne, supported by the so-called Holy Alliance. He had no intention of moving to Mexico, which he now claimed was still entirely subject to him, and his parliament forbade any Spanish prince to accept an American crown. The Mexican *borbonistas* [supporters of the Spanish King], in some confusion, began to debate the advantages of a centralist, aristocratic republic. The congress meanwhile neglected the duties of providing a viable constitution and assuring revenues.

There was neither governmental experience, or in fact, any useful public expertise among any of these men—or anywhere in Creole Mexico. Instead of attacking the pressing problems, the congress began to attack the generalissimo. Months now went by in futile deadlock and argument.

In April Iturbide charged eleven members with treasonous actions. The congress retaliated by removing three of his cronies from office. Bustamante [a member of Congress under Iturbide, he initially supported but then opposed Iturbide's rule] added erratic rhetoric to every session, comparing the deputies to Roman senators and Iturbide to [Roman general Julius] Caesar at the Rubicon. While nothing got done, the Trigarantine Army [the Army of the Three Guarantees; Iturbide's force] was eating the capital bare.

Iturbide, who shunned the old insurgents and new liberals, rapidly lost all their support. Nicolás Bravo and Guadalupe Victoria entered into a conspiracy and were briefly jailed. Afterward, Victoria returned to his old mountain hideouts.

In May the congress finally proposed to reduce the army to sixty thousand officers and men and to prevent any member of the Regency Council from holding a military command.

On May 18, 1822, there was a sergeants' revolt in barracks. The shout was raised: "¡Viva Agustín Primero!"

The regiments stationed in the capital and the volatile street mobs immediately took up the cry. Great throngs of soldiers and *léperos* massed in front of Iturbide's mansion, demanding that he take the throne of Mexico. Iturbide, who certainly planned and staged this coup, feigned reluctance to become emperor—a title his agents suggested—until the congress ratified the people's wish.

The congress was chivvied [harassed] into session. The deputies, who in this emergency possessed no traditional legitimacy and therefore no powers of any kind, were intimidated by the roaring mobs that filled their halls, and the massed regiments that impatiently awaited their verdict. They were not so much craven as divided, confused, and helpless. The deputies quickly bowed to the pressures of the hour, declaring Mexico an empire and Iturbide its emperor. Fifteen representatives, however, refused to acquiesce in this hysterical decision.

Emperor Agustín I

Agustín I was a prototype of a kind that would continue to plague the Hispanic world: leaders made by military success in a revolutionary milieu [setting]. Their success was as dazzling and pernicious as it was usually ephemeral. Men of this kind invariably had talent to plan and improvise and usually possessed great personal charm, but lacked entirely the qualities their societies most needed—and in fact, most despised: patience, firmness, discipline, moderation, a taste for hard work and self-sacrifice. Iturbide and his successors, risen from nothing to the heights, perhaps from an inherent inferiority complex had an uncontrollable appetite for pageantry and personal adulation; they loved appearances; they were frivolous, pretentious, dishonest, and surprisingly, even ignorant of the world. Iturbide and his more famous disciple, [Antonio Lopez de] Santa Anna, were paragons of all the vices of political figures in postcolonial societies.

Emperor Iturbide spent days designing chivalric orders and inventing titles for his court and planning his coronation, which was to be exactly like Napoleon's. He made princes of his family, and his clients ladies and gentlemen of the bedchamber. After the coronation, in which he appeared covered with borrowed decorations, he instituted the Order of Guadalupe, dispensing many grand crosses. Meanwhile, the imperial treasury was bare and the country still lacked a constitution. Expenses were met by confiscations from rich *gachupines*, who had no protection of laws.

All this apparently delighted the mob and imperial favorites, but it soon soured with the still-sitting congress. Iturbide knew how to organize coups, but he did not understand any true political process.

The Spanish, who intransigently refused to leave the fortress isle of San Juan de Ulua, artfully returned an old exile to Mexico. Fray Servando Teresa de Mier, the iconoclast and razor-tongued liberal who had roamed the world for thirty years, had been elected to the congress in absentia, and from this platform the old man who had ridiculed superstition and ignorance and tyranny in his youth began to slash through all Iturbide's ridiculous pomps and vanities. He had an immediate coterie—the fifteen men who had voted against the Mexican empire.

By August Fray Servando drew such blood that the emperor had him and fourteen deputies arrested. The remaining members, many of whom hated Mier but who asserted congressional immunity, caused so much trouble that Iturbide, emulating [Oliver] Cromwell [lord protector of England in the 1600s], forcibly dissolved the body with troops. He replaced it with forty-five new men, actually a hand-picked junta. But the congress-

junta refused to draft the kind of constitution Iturbide demanded, or even to legislate taxes. Upon this, the emperor declared a complete dictatorship and stated he would make his own
laws. He still had the army.

But he did not have the army, because the generals were not
getting paid. The army drank up all the enormous early coinage
Iturbide had issued stamped with his image and the crowned
"Aztec" eagle of the Mexican empire; running out of bullion,
the emperor printed paper money—the first in Mexican history—and made this worthless currency legal tender. Since generals and officials were paid in paper, their indignation was as
great as that of the general population.

In his high palace, bemused with his own grandeur, Agustín I
no longer smelled the wind. Young Antonio López de Santa
Anna did; he was a junior Iturbide with an uncanny nose and
sense of timing. Promised lavish promotions by Iturbide in 1821,
Santa Anna had fallen out of favor and had been banished to an
obscure command at Veracruz to watch the Spaniards. After he
had engaged in several schemes, including a defeat for which his
superior took the blame, Iturbide ordered him back to Mexico,
ostensibly for promotion. Santa Anna knew better, and he also
knew that the emperor's credit had run out.

Santa Anna Calls for a Republic

Santa Anna now issued a proclamation calling for a republic—the
meaning of which word, he admitted candidly, he did not understand. Guadalupe Victoria immediately came out of the hills and
joined him. The two led a small force toward the capital as a liberating army. Checked by a superior imperial army, Santa Anna
panicked; he was always a man of moods. He prepared to flee to
the United States, but Victoria drily informed him things were
not lost until the enemy sent him Victoria's own head.

The army failed to fight for Iturbide. Guerrero and Bravo,
moving to their old retreats to the south, were caught—and released—by an Iturbidist general. Then, General Eachávarri at Veracruz, with the main army, published his Plan de Casa Mata. Under this plan, the Mexican congress was to be allowed to meet
freely, without interference from the emperor. Most of the generals subscribed to it, and Iturbide's own imperial guards acclaimed Casa Mata with marches and band music.

Overwhelmed by this national ingratitude, the Liberator of

Mexico convened the old congress, but was only able to stammer a few suggestions to it. In March 1823, the stalemate ended, when the emperor sent a petulant message of abdication, saying he had been forced to accept the crown, and that furthermore, the nation was in arrears to him by one-hundred-and-fifty thousand pesos. Nicolás Bravo, the old guerrillero [guerrilla leader], made sure he embarked on a British ship, after congress accepted his resignation and sentenced him to perpetual exile.

Iturbide tried again, in the spring of 1824. He arrived in Tamaulipas with a packet of paper money and printed proclamations, unaware that the congress had voted a bill of attainder if he ever set foot again on Mexican soil. Petty local authorities seized him and shot him immediately. It was a sorry ending for the leader who after all, did at last achieve Mexican independence from Spain.

A Republic Is Established

By Robert Ryal Miller

Agustín de Iturbide's reign as Mexico's first emperor (1822–1823) was undone by economic failings and his arbitrary and dictatorial actions. Mexicans were soon discontented with the man who achieved their independence from Spain and looked to another military man to lead them. In December 1822, commander Antonio López de Santa Anna, a criollo (person of Spanish or European descent born in New Spain), rose up against Iturbide and proclaimed a republic. In the following selection, Robert Ryal Miller describes the early years of the republic of Mexico. During this period, titles of nobility created during the brief reign of Iturbide were abolished, as was slavery. Mexico's northern neighbor, the United States, extended recognition to the young republic. The early years of the republic were notable for the political divisions that emerged among Mexico's educated classes. Candidates from liberal and conservative camps vied for political office with military leaders called caudillos. Political factions often decided the outcome of an election by throwing their support to one candidate or another.

The most important military and political leader of the early republic was Antonio López de Santa Anna. Mexicans were strongly conflicted about Santa Anna, both idolizing him as the savior of Mexico and reviling him as one who aligned himself with any group in order to survive politically.

Robert Ryal Miller taught Mexican history at the college level and also authored several books on Mexico and Latin America, including For Science and National Glory: The Spanish Scientific Expedition to America, 1862–1866 *and* Arms Across the Border: United States Aid to Juárez During the French Intervention in Mexico.

Agustín's unscrupulous and arbitrary acts hastened his fall from "the cactus throne." Criticism of the emperor by journalists led to the suppression of several liberal newspapers, and an alleged conspiracy by congressmen resulted in the arrest of nineteen deputies. When other congressmen protested, Agustín [Iturbide] dissolved the Congress at the end of October, 1822. Thus he became a dictator—the first of many Mexican military *caudillos* who would suppress constitutions, dismiss congresses, and rule by fiat [decree].

A Republic Is Declared

Had the army remained loyal, the emperor could have continued his reign, but several dissatisfied commanders conspired to overthrow him. Many of the officers belonged to Freemasonry [a secret society called the Freemasons or Masons] lodges where they associated with civilian liberals who championed representative government. Some of the military leaders became outspoken republicans and opposed the autocratic monarch; others were disgusted with rising inflation and delays in receiving their pay or promotions. The revolt took definite form in December, 1822, when Antonio López de Santa Anna, the military commander of Veracruz, proclaimed a republic. This young *criollo* officer had fought with the Spanish infantry against the insurgents during the wars for independence until 1821, when he joined Iturbide's army. . . . Less than two years later he was instrumental in overturning the Mexican empire.

Santa Anna's revolt against Iturbide was supported by the heroic insurgent leaders [Vicente] Guerrero, [Guadalupe] Victoria, and [Nicolas] Bravo, who endorsed the Plan of Casa Mata. This plan, which called for a new congress and national representation, was first signed by Santa Anna and General [Jose Antonio] Echávarri, the imperial officer ordered to suppress the uprising. . . . In the capital, Iturbide resurrected the old Congress, but it was hostile. Finding himself abandoned and his situation hopeless, he abdicated on March 19, 1823. . . .

Upon the fall of the First Empire, a provisional government negotiated a loan of sixteen million pesos from Great Britain and encouraged a constituent congress to draft a new framework of government for the nation. In October, 1824, the Constitution of the United Mexican States was promulgated. Patterned after that of the United States, it made Mexico into a federal republic with a president, vice-president, two branches of legislature (Senate and Chamber of Deputies), and a judiciary. The country was divided into nineteen states, each with its own government, and five territories administered by the central government. Religious liberty was not guaranteed—indeed, the framers were true to Spanish tradition and the Plan of Iguala [the 1821 plan for independence from Spain] by permitting only the Roman Catholic religion to be practiced.

Historians call the subsequent era "The Early Republic." It was a period marked by political instability, financial chaos, and humiliation in dealing with foreign powers. Part of the trouble stemmed from lack of experience in self-government, the imposition of democratic institutions on a people inured to despotic leadership, and a national illiteracy rate of over 90 percent. Another factor was the preponderant role taken by military officers whose ambition exceeded their ability as statesmen and whose *fueros* [privileges] exempted them from civilian control. And the expulsion of all Spaniards (except some clergy), decreed in 1829, resulted in an exodus of many educated and talented persons.

Liberals and Conservatives

After independence, the members of the educated elite in Mexico soon were divided into liberal and conservative camps. For the next half-century, control of the government changed back and forth between representatives of these factions. Upon taking power, the new group not only changed key government personnel, it also rewrote laws and even the constitution to reflect its philosophy. Often the "outs" fled or were forced into temporary exile until their party regained office. The cleavage between "right and left" widened over the years. It split Mexican families, divided the clergy, and resulted in revolutions and civil war.

Most liberals supported federalism (which in Latin America means states' rights, not centralized control), freedom of the press, an egalitarian society, curtailment of privileges and titles, toleration of all religious sects, and public education rather than Church-controlled schools. Those liberals who favored moderate social reforms called themselves *moderados;* others who wanted a radical restructuring of society were known as *puros.* Liberals came from a variety of backgrounds, but many were middle-class intellectuals, journalists, teachers, lawyers, or small entrepreneurs. Three leading liberals were Valentín Gómez Farías, a physician and politician originally from Jalisco; Lorenzo de Zavala, a publisher and congressman from Yucatán; and José Luis Mora, an economist, doctor of theology, and lawyer from Guanajuato.

Opposing the liberals were the conservatives. They favored a centralized state, even a dictatorship; a certain amount of censorship; a class system with rule by an elite; preservation of privileges, *fueros* [privileges], and titles of nobility; monopoly of religion by Roman Catholicism; and Church control of education. Conservative membership came from the Church hierarchy, army officers, the landed elite, mineowners, and the great merchants. Peasants and Indians also generally supported conservative positions. Three prominent conservatives were Lucas Alamán, a mining engineer, statesman, and historian from Guanajuato; Nicolás Bravo, a general from Guerrero who had fought with [Father José María] Morelos in the independence war; and Carlos María Bustamante, a lawyer and publisher from Oaxaca.

The basic idealogical cleavage was also manifested in branches of Freemasonry to which many leaders, including Catholic priests, belonged. Conservatives were generally Scottish Rite Masons (*escoceses*); liberals tended to belong to the York Rite (*yorkinos*). As a secret society organized into lodges, Masonry provided meeting places and support for politicians and plotters during the earliest years of the Mexican republic.

Feuding Factions

In Mexico's first presidential election, in the fall of 1824, the state legislatures, acting as an electoral college, chose two men from opposing factions to become president and vice-president. Guadalupe Victoria, a *yorkino* and federalist, assumed the highest office; his vice-president was Nicolás Bravo, grand master of the *escoceses* and a centralist. Victoria was a national hero because of his valor and suffering during the independence wars, but he lacked the talent to run a nation. He was indecisive, showed poor judgment in picking cabinet and other officials, and was unable to address major domestic problems confronting the nation. Of utmost concern were the bankrupt treasury and a national debt that totaled over seventy-five million pesos.

Although Victoria lasted out his elected term—the only president to do so for the next forty years—in 1827 he had to put down a serious armed revolt led by his vice-president. Ultimately defeated by forces under General Guerrero, grand master of the *yorkinos*, Vice-president Bravo was captured, tried, and exiled. These internal struggles reduced the influence of Freemasonry on Mexican politics, but the strife continued in the form of bitter feuding between conservatives and liberals.

Factional rivalry marked Mexico's second presidential election in 1828, when the liberal, Vicente Guerrero, opposed the *moderado* ex-minister of war, Manuel Gómez Pedraza, who had conservative support. Although Guerrero apparently was the more popular candidate, he lost in a close election by the state legislatures, whereupon the liberals challenged the decision with arms. General Santa Anna "pronounced" in favor of Guerrero; so did General José Lobato in the capital, where his troops and a mob of five thousand *léparos* (vagabonds) provoked by *puro* Lorenzo de Zavala demonstrated in the main plaza. Their enthusiasm became a riot during which they sacked and destroyed the Parián Market, where many foreign traders sold their wares. Finally, the elected chief executive went into exile, and in April, 1829, Guerrero was installed as president, with a conservative vice-president, General Anastasio Bustamante. As a reward for his role in the uprising Santa Anna was promoted to major general, the highest rank in the army.

Guerrero's tenure as president was brief—he lasted only eight and a half months. During that period his administration abolished slavery by a law that was unopposed except in Texas, where Anglo-American colonists had been bringing in black slaves. The president also enforced the decree of March, 1829, expelling virtually all of the remaining Spaniards.

The Spanish Attack

The expulsion of Spaniards and reports of civil strife in Mexico prompted the Spanish government to launch an ill-conceived attempt to reconquer the former colony. In July, 1829, three thousand Spanish soldiers from Cuba landed at Tampico and soon occupied the principal fort, which had been abandoned by the Mexican defenders. But it was a quixotic [impractical] adventure. The landing site was too far from the center of population and government, the expeditionary troops could not move inland because they were beseiged by a Mexican army, yellow fever and tropical heat decimated their ranks, and their supply and retreat line had been cut when the Spanish transports returned to Cuba following a dispute between army and navy commanders. Finally,

on September 11, the Spanish general peacefully surrendered to
... General Santa Anna, who thereafter was known as the "Victor of Tampico."

At the end of 1829, Guerrero left the capital to put down a
revolt against him led by his conservative vice-president, Bustamante, who had the support of the army. One cause of the revolt was the liberal president's refusal to relinquish the extraordinary powers granted him at the time of the foreign invasion;
thus, Bustamanate posed as a champion of constitutionalism and
called Guerrero a dictator. Early in 1830 the vice-president took
over the president's office, and Congress disqualified Guerrero,
declaring him *imposibilitado* (unfit) to govern the republic.

Bustamante's administration improved government finances
and checked banditry in the countryside, but the conservative
president also created a dictatorship. He suppressed opposition
newspapers and intimidated the legislature and judiciary by the
threat of military force. With the aid of the army he replaced liberal governors and jailed, exiled, or executed liberal leaders. One
victim of the firing squad was Guerrero, who was captured
through treachery and bribery.... Guerrero's execution shocked
many Mexicans and triggered another military revolt.

The Emergence of Santa Anna

Santa Anna was one of the first military commanders who rebelled against Bustamante early in 1832. Uprisings also occurred
in Texas, Tamaulipas, Zacatecas, and the port of Acapulco. After
suffering an initial defeat, Santa Anna's forces eventually occupied the city of Puebla as they pushed on toward the capital. Finally, at the beginning of 1833, Bustamante went into exile, and
General Gómez Pedraza was recalled to serve out the last three
months of the term to which he had been elected five years earlier. A subsequent election resulted in the presidency of Santa
Anna, Mexico's latest *caudillo.*

Antonio López de Santa Anna was a principal historical figure
in Mexico for more than three decades. He helped topple Mexico's first empire and on eleven different occasions between 1833
and 1855 he served as chief executive of the nation. The Mexican general was a talented military commander revered as a hero
for his battle victories, and his personal magnetism could attract a
devoted following of soldiers or civilians. Santa Anna was intelligent and dynamic; he was also a clever politician who was able to

shift his policies when public opinion changed. Several times he was sent into "perpetual" exile, but when there were troubles in Mexico, he returned to be hailed as savior of the nation.

During Santa Anna's first presidency he retired to Manga de Clavo, his hacienda in the state of Veracruz, and permitted his more liberal (*puro*) vice-president, Valentín Gómez Farías, to act for him. Gómez Farías and his radical theoretician, Doctor José Maria Luis Mora, wanted to implement sweeping reforms such as: separation of Church and state; establishment of public education; an end to privileges held by the nobility, military, and clergy; suppression of monastic institutions; and transfer of surplus Church property to private individuals, preferably those with little or no land. Of course, they also favored freedom of the press and a guarantee of individual liberties.

Liberalization

Gómez Farías persuaded the national Congress and state legislatures to enact laws in the reform spirit. They abolished the death penalty for political crimes, reduced the size of the standing army, and eliminated the military *fuero* of trial in the special military courts for civil and criminal violations. Ecclesiastical changes were the most revolutionary: the right of *patronato* was granted to the central government, which meant that it had the power to name bishops and other Church officials; members of monastic orders—priests, nuns, and lay brothers—were permitted to retract their religious vows; payment of Church tithes was changed from compulsory to voluntary; the Franciscan missions of California were secularized and their funds and property sequestered; and the University of Mexico, where most of the professors were priests, was closed. A new office of public instruction was charged with organizing a system of government schools from primary to college level.

Rallying around the cry of "*Religión y Fueros*," the conservatives rose in revolt and called for annulment of the liberal-sponsored laws. During the second half of 1833, Santa Anna alternated between exercising the executive power and delegating it to his vice-president while he tried to put down the uprisings. The following year he succumbed to entreaties by the conservatives to become their leader and protect their prerogatives. Assuming absolute power in April, 1834, he ousted Gómez Farías, revoked the reforms, dissolved Congress, replaced liberal governors, and exiled the principal radicals. A new conservative Congress abolished the federal system and replaced it with a centralized one whereby the states became military departments headed by *caudillos* appointed by the president. This arrangement was eventually incorporated into the Constitution of 1836, sometimes called the *Siete Leyes* (Seven Laws). Meanwhile, opposition to this centralization was one of the causes of a revolt in the province of Texas—a revolt that proved disastrous to Mexican pride and to Santa Anna.

Problems in Texas

The difficulties in Texas arose from the presence of Anglo-American settlers who chafed under Mexican culture and laws. In the 1820s, Mexico had encouraged colonization of this northern province—proper settlement was seen as a barrier to future United States aggression. But more North Americans moved into Texas than did Mexicans from states farther south. Attracted by the abundance of arable land suitable for cotton cultivation, Stephen F. Austin and a few other entrepreneurs from the southern United States applied for colonization grants in Texas. Austin received a vast tract of land, the greater part of which he agreed to convey to immigrant families that he would bring to the state. Each family was permitted to purchase at least 640 acres at about ten cents an acre. The right to bring Negro slaves to Texas was a special inducement; so was the exemption from payment of general taxes for ten years and customs duties for seven years. All colonists were required to become Mexican citizens and to profess Roman Catholicism. . . .

By 1830 about nine thousand former United States citizens had migrated to Texas. Their part of the population was triple that of the Spanish-speaking component. For various reasons the two societies did not integrate. Anglo-Americans settled on rural estates remote from the old population centers, they continued to use English almost exclusively, most were Protestants, and they used black slave labor to grow cotton for export to England and the United States. In contrast, the Spanish-speaking residents of Texas lived in towns, much of their social life centered around the Catholic Church, ranching and small-scale farming was their major economic basis, and they did not own slaves or export surpluses abroad.

Serious conflicts developed between impetuous Anglos and

Mexican authorities in Texas. In 1826 Haden Edwards, claiming to have an *empresario* (entrepreneur) grant in eastern Texas, fortified his settlement and declared it to be the independent Republic of Fredonia. This ill-conceived revolt, which was opposed by Austin and the majority of American settlers, collapsed before Mexican troops arrived to quell it, but the uprising exacerbated the rift between the two cultures. Black slavery was another problem. When the Mexican Congress abolished all slavery in 1829, the Anglo-Texans protested vehemently and were allowed to keep their slaves but prohibited from further importation of bonded workers.

Belatedly, officials in Mexico City tried to remedy the problems in Texas. New regulations in 1830 closed the border to additional colonists from the United States (but not from Europe). Trade across the frontier was severely restricted, and new customs duties were levied on imports and exports. This affected the Anglos who regularly brought in American goods and shipped their cotton to Louisiana. Although additional Mexican revenue officials and army reinforcements were sent to implement these regulations, they could not patrol the long border—Americans continued to move westward across the Sabine River, thus becoming illegal aliens ("wetbacks") in Texas. By 1834, when the anti-Yankee immigration clause was set aside, the Anglo-Americans numbered 20,700 and the Spanish-speaking sector 4,000. Nevertheless, the Anglo majority was politically neutralized because in 1824 Texas had been combined with Coahuila, which had nine times the population of its northern neighbor. Another control factor was the distance to the state capital of Coahuila-Texas, which was located at Saltillo until 1833, when it moved to Monclova—both cities more than five hundred kilometers (three hundred miles) southwest of San Antonio.

Troubles in Texas escalated in the 1830s; as more Yankees arrived, so did more Mexican soldiers. Stephen Austin went to Mexico City on a futile mission to petition for separation from Coahuila, Mexican statehood for Texas, and a more convenient state capital. His demands were rejected. . . .

Meanwhile, Texans armed themselves, gathered in protest meetings, and debated what to do. Some advocated independence; others, who declared their allegiance to the defunct 1824 federal constitution, hoped for reforms and reconciliation; and a few talked of union with the United States or Great Britain. A number of Spanish-surnamed residents of Texas joined Anglos in opposing the Mexican dictatorship; foremost among these was Lorenzo de Zavala, an ousted liberal politician originally from Yucatán, who had held the posts of congressman, treasury minister, and diplomatic representative to France. Zavala was also a land speculator in Texas associated with David G. Burnet in the Galveston Bay & Texas Land Company. Reports that a Mexican centralist army would be sent to "occupy" Texas unified the war and peace parties and galvanized public opinion there.

When centralist forces under General Martín Perfecto de Cos, brother-in-law of President Santa Anna, moved into Texas in September, 1835, they met armed resistance. Hostilities erupted in October when colonists at Gonzales refused to surrender a small cannon to a detachment of soldiers—instead they opened fire on the troops. A week later, rebels captured the military post at Goliad. Then, late in the month, Stephen Austin led three hundred volunteers, half of them Spanish-surnamed, to San Antonio, where they laid siege to the invading army of more than seven hundred soldiers. Six weeks later General Cos surrendered; he and his soldiers were permitted (or obliged) to leave the province. Clearly, a war for separation had begun, and in March, 1836, delegates to a convention at Washington-on-the-Brazos declared independence and chose David Burnet as president and Lorenzo de Zavala as vice-president of the Republic of Texas.

Santa Anna on the March

Mexico's chief executive, General Santa Anna, who in April, 1835, had led a force that crushed an anti-centralist revolt in Zacatecas, determined to put down the Texas rebellion. Gathering an army of 6,000 men, he marched north in the winter of 1835–36. In late February as he approached San Antonio with half of his army, the Texans ordered the city evacuated and positioned 150 men under William Travis in an abandoned Franciscan mission known as the Alamo. Thirty-two volunteers arrived later to join Yankee frontiersmen Davy Crockett, Jim Bowie, and the other defenders. For ten days Santa Anna besieged the fortress and demanded unconditional surrender; when Travis refused, the Mexican commander signaled an all-out attack with no quarter or clemency. Santa Anna won the battle, his soldiers killed all the defenders, and Texas military units stationed elsewhere got a battle cry, "Remember the Alamo!"

The war lasted another six weeks. Late in March near the village of Goliad a unit of Texans under Colonel James Fannin was
surrounded and outnumbered by a Mexican army under General José Urrea. Fannin surrendered in the belief that he and his
men would be treated as prisoners of war, but Santa Anna enforced a recently-passed "piracy" law and ordered all 365 prisoners to be shot. They were. The situation looked bleak for the
remaining eight hundred Texas soldiers under General Sam
Houston. They were retreating toward the eastern border when
suddenly, on April 21, 1836, near the San Jacinto River, they attacked Santa Anna's army and won a stunning victory. Almost
the entire Mexican force of fourteen hundred men were captured or killed, and Santa Anna himself was taken prisoner.

Some Texans wanted to execute their distinguished prisoner,
but Houston realized that he could be very useful to the Lone
Star Republic. On May 14, as president of Mexico and general-
in-chief of the Mexican army, Santa Anna signed two treaties
with David Burnet, president of Texas. The first Treaty of Ve-
lasco was public; it specified that hostilities would cease, all Mexican troops would withdraw to the other side of the Rio Grande
without delay, there would be an exchange of prisoners, and
Santa Anna would not take up arms against Texas or cause others to do so.... At home, Santa Anna found himself in disgrace
for the Texas debacle, so he retired to his hacienda. In April,
1837, the Congress named General Bustamante president; his
government repudiated the treaty that Santa Anna had signed and
refused to recognize the independence of Texas. Moreover, various officials talked of reconquering the province, but internal
revolts and foreign threats precluded any such action.

Mexico at War with the United States

By Ramón Alcaraz

Mexico's conflict with Texas in 1836 and the resulting loss of that territory when Texas became an independent republic was a prelude to war with the United States. In 1845 Mexico cut off diplomatic relations with its northern neighbor after the U.S. Congress resolved to annex the Republic of Texas to the United States. In Mexico, the capitulation of President Antonio López de Santa Anna (1794–1876) to the Texans continued to rankle the Mexican congress, which had never approved his secret treaty recognizing Texas's independence. The border was another point of contention between Mexico and Texas. Mexico recognized the Nueces River as the border while the Texans claimed the Rio Bravo del Norte (Rio Grande) as their southern boundary. The Texan claim dramatically enlarged their republic.

The dispute heated up in 1845 when the American envoy James Slidell arrived in Mexico City to discuss payment of Mexico's debts to the United States and the U.S. purchase of California and New Mexico. The Mexicans refused to meet with Slidell. On April 25, 1846, some American soldiers who had been dispatched to protect the Texas border were killed in a fight with Mexican troops. U.S. president James Polk used the skirmish and Mexico's rejection of Slidell as proof of Mexico's aggression. His call for war was granted by Congress. In Mexico, Santa Anna, recently returned from exile in Cuba, took charge of Mexico's army.

The following eyewitness account describes the battle of Chapultepec fortress, the site of Mexico's national palace and the final campaign of U.S. general Winfield Scott's siege of Mexico City. It was written by Ramón Alcaraz, a soldier in the Mexican army. Chapultepec overlooked all the approaches to the city and was heavily fortified at its base and on its heights. After seizing the castle in 1847, American troops entered the city and remained there for nearly a year, during which time a peace treaty was drawn up and signed. Under the terms of the Treaty of

Ramón Alcaraz, *The Other Side: Or, Notes for the History of the War Between Mexico and the United States, Written in Mexico*, translated by Albert C. Ramsey. New York: J. Wiley, 1850.

*Guadalupe Hidalgo (1848) Mexico gave up California and New Mex-
ico to the United States and agreed to establish the boundary between
the two countries at the Rio Grande. In return, the United States paid
Mexico $15 million and assumed the claims of American citizens
against Mexico.*

We must give an idea of the situation held by the enemy around the city, before the storming of Chapultepec, and the position within guarded by our troops.
Their head-quarters were situated at Tacubaya. General [Win-
field] Scott resided in the Palace of the Archbishop. The brigade
of General [William J.] Worth was quartered in the houses of
the inhabitants.

The divisions of Generals [Gideon] Pillow and [John A.]
Quitman were found in cantonment [camps] in Coyoacan.

The general depot of wagons, munitions, and artillery was in
Mixcoac.

The rear-guard and reserve, composed of the brigades of
Generals [P.F.] Smith and [David E.] Twiggs, might be met with
in San Angel.

From the 9th to the 11th [of September] they made the following movements. The united divisions of Pillow and Quitman
moved silently in the night of the 11th to Tacubaya.

Before the eastern garitas [gates] of the city, that is to say, San
Antonio, the Candelaria, and the Niño Perdido, there remained
strong detachments of infantry and cavalry, and a battery of 12
pieces of cannon, one half light and the other siege ordnance.

Colonel [William S.] Harney, commander of the cavalry, with
a portion of it had charge of the depot and prisoners that were
in Mixcoac. Another part of the cavalry covered the American
flank and rear.

In the night of the 11th, four batteries were established, to operate against the castle. The first, composed of 2 sixteens and 1
eight-inch howitzer [cannon], was posted in the Hacienda of the
Condesa, to breach the south side of the castle, and to defend the
causeway running from Chapultepec to Tacubaya.

The second, formed of 1 24-pounder and 18-inch howitzer,
was situated in a point most commanding of the hills of Del Rey
and in front of the angle to the south-east of the castle.

The third, consisting of 1 gun, a sixteen, and 1 8-inch howitzer, was planted some 300 yards to the north-east of the buildings of the Molino.

The fourth, which was only 1 10-inch mortar, was imbedded within the mills, perfectly sheltered and concealed by a high wall of the aqueduct. Finally, 4 pieces of large calibre, 4 howitzers, and 1 mortar were ready to batter the castle.

On the 12th, at three in the afternoon, the division of General Pillow was moved from Tacubaya to the hills of Del Rey, and occupied the mill buildings.

With very slight difference these were the positions of the enemy. The forces of all arms came to 8,000 men with a numerous and well-served artillery, augmented considerably by the pieces lost by us in the fomer battles.

Mexico City on the Eve of the Siege

We must give a glance now at the city about to be stormed.

By a decree published on the 29th of July, at the moment the alarm was struck each one of the regidors [members of the city council] should direct himself to his respective quarter to attend in good order to whatever the occasion required. The regidors who then occupied their positions, and D. Manuel Reyes Veramendi, first Alcalde [Mayor], remained in the consistorial houses, receiving all the orders of the General-in-chief. The fortifications of the menaced garitas were strengthened as far as possible by working incessantly in them, in which they were assisted by a multitude of peasants who came with others, to be spectators of the works and military operations. Justice requires us to say that the greater part of the capitularies worked with much energy and patriotism, and that Sr. Reyes Veramendi was indefatigable in the performance of his duties as first Alcalde.

On the other part, the aspect of the city, saving the frequent passing movement of troops through the streets, was truly sad and frightful. The emigration of many families from the beginning of hostilities by the enemy in the valley of Mexico, had deprived this city of the bustle and life which are observed ordinarily, a circumstance which was increased by the seclusion to which others had resorted either from excessive selfishness or pusillanimity [cowardice].

We will speak in the first place of Chapultepec, the key of Mexico, as then was commonly said, and whose reminiscences and traditions made it doubly important for the enemy, and

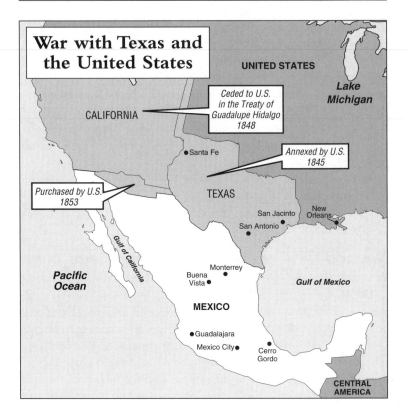

War with Texas and the United States

UNITED STATES

Lake Michigan

CALIFORNIA

Ceded to U.S. in the Treaty of Guadalupe Hidalgo 1848

Santa Fe

Annexed by U.S. 1845

Purchased by U.S. 1853

TEXAS

San Jacinto
New Orleans
San Antonio

Pacific Ocean

Gulf of California

Monterrey
Buena Vista

Gulf of Mexico

MEXICO

Guadalajara
Mexico City
Cerro Gordo

CENTRAL AMERICA

moreover for the military projects they had conceived.

On the exterior it had the following fortifications. A horn-work in the road which leads to Tacubaya. A parapet in the gate at the entrance. Within the inclosure which surrounds the woods to the south side a breast-work was constructed, and a ditch eight yards wide and three in depth.

Within there were the following defences, many of them in-complete. In the circuit of the botanical garden, was a stand sup-ported by a wall serving for a parapet. For some 250 yards there was a scaffold which ran round the inclosure of the woods, from which the soldiers could fire from under cover. A breast-work at the south enfiladed the entrance. Another was at the east and the last at the summer house at the foot of the hill. Moreover at the point where it was supposed the enemy would pass six mines were dug, of which three were charged.

On the first level landing-place to the south a parapet was built, and another at the glorieta between the two entrances.

Ascending to the building it was met protected with blinds in that part called the dormitories, and the circuit of the edifice was surrounded with sacks of earth.

The artillery defending this fortification were 2 pieces of twenty-fours, 1 of eight, 3 field of fours, and 1 howitzer of 68, in all 7 pieces.

The chief of the castle was General D. Nicolas Bravo and the second General D. Mariano Monterde.

The chief of the section of engineers who had labored with indefatigable energy was D. Juan Cano, and the commandante of artillery D. Manuel Gamboa. Generals Noriega, Dosamantes and Perez were likewise sent afterwards to the fortress.

The troops on the 12th were some 200 men at the foot of the hill, distributed in groups, assisted by the students of the military college, and some more forces, who in all did not amount to 800 men.... General Santa Anna distributed his disposable forces at the posts that he believed would be attacked, varying each moment the situations of the corps, and remaining with a force in reserve to send and to assist in person with it at the point requisite.

This was then, in brief, the situation which the two armies preserved. We will now return to the transactions of war that followed....

At dawn on the 12th, the enemy's battery, situated in the hermitage, opened its fire on the garita of the Niño Perdido, without any other object, as we can learn from the documents published by the American chiefs, than to call attention, and to properly be able to plant the ordnance [bombs] which should batter Chapultepec in the places which we have mentioned.

In effect, in a few minutes, these batteries began to fire upon Chapultepec. At first they caused no destruction. But rectifying their aim, the walls of the building commenced to be pierced by balls in all directions, experiencing great ravages also in the roofs, caused by the bombs which the mortar threw, that, as we have said, was concealed in the court of the Molino. The artillery of Chapultepec answered with much precision and accuracy. The engineers worked incessantly to repair the damage done by the enemy's projectiles, and the troops quite behind the parapets suffered from this storm of balls. The most intelligent in military art judge that the troops could have been placed at the foot of the hill, to avoid the useless loss, leaving in the building only the artillerymen and the requisite engineers. This was not done, and the carcasses of the bombs and hollow balls killed and wounded many soldiers, who had not even the pleasure of discharging their muskets. . . .

The bombardment had been horrible. It commenced a little after five in the morning, and did not cease until seven in the evening. In these fourteen hours the American batteries, perfectly served, had maintained a projectile in the air, and the greater part of their discharges taking effect. In the corridor, converted into a surgical hospital, were found mixed up the putrid bodies, the wounded breathing mournful groans and the young boys of the college; and, singular fact! the assistance and requisite medicines were wanting. General Bravo had resisted with valor and calmness this storm of fire; but knowing he would soon be assaulted, he demanded reinforcements of General Santa Anna, who answered . . . that he did not think of sending more troops until the hour of the storming.

In the balance of the night General Monterde labored with assiduity to repair the damage caused by the bombs, and to replace the blinds and strengthen the fortifications. But the time was very limited and peremptory. Nevertheless all hope was not lost. . . .

On the 13th at daybreak the enemy's batteries returned to open their fire upon Chapultepec much more vividly than on the day before.

General Santa Anna having in the preceding night caused all the reserve to enter Mexico, leaving only about 800 men in Chapultepec; many of whom deserted shamefully. Some were visible at six in the morning on the causeway of Belen. . . . As soon as General Bravo observed the movement of the enemy's troops he sent to advise General Santa Anna that he was going to be attacked, demanding . . . reinforcements. He likewise placed Lieutenant Alaman ready to spring the mines. General Santa Anna unfortunately, who in the whole of this had neither comprehended the vulnerable point of the enemy nor his own, nor the time when to attack decisively, judged that Chapultepec was not about to be stormed, and therefore did not reinforce. . . .

The U.S. Army Seizes the Chapultepec Fortress

The enemy, who had formed three strong columns, under the orders of Pillow, Quitman, and Worth, occupied the woods with the rifles, and sallying out of the Molino, overturned our few skirmishers, who defended at the foot. The column of General Worth, leaping the position and feigning an attack by the causeway of Anzures, called the attention of General Santa Anna. A cloud of skirmishers, advancing rapidly over the bridge of the causeway of the Condesa, sheltered themselves among the stocks of the magueys that had been cut down, and in the unevenness of the ground, and in the huts in the vicinity. The enemy, seeing their plan take effect and that the false attacks were resisted with vigor, directed the bulk of their columns that entered by the Molino to storming the hill. These, flanked and preceded by skirmishers, began to climb up, some by the opening, and others at that part accessible from the north-west. In the meanwhile a cloud of skirmishers ascended, and appropriating the rocks, bushes, dead angles, and the unfortunate ground for our fortifications, destroyed with their sure shots the defenders, or distracted them from attending to the storming columns. These encountered no more formal resistance than what the entrance afforded and the foot of the hill, with the brave and distinguished Lieut.-Colonel D. Santiago Xicoténcal's battalion of San Blas. But this chief being flanked, pushed back, and killed, along with the greater part of his officers and soldiers, the Americans advanced to the second landing in the road leading up the hill, with a banner displayed, which sometimes fell from the one bearing it being killed, and the columns slightly giving way. Another, however, taking the colors, the advance continued to the rampart, where our defenders, astounded by the bombardment, fatigued, wanting sleep, and hungry, were hurled over the rocks by the bayonet or taken prisoners. A company of the New York regiment ascended to the top of the building, where some of the students still fired, and who were the last defenders of that Mexican flag which was quickly replaced by the American.

THE HISTORY OF NATIONS
Chapter 4

Reform and Revolution, 1855–1920

Juárez's Plan for Reforming Mexico

By Walter V. Scholes

Benito Juárez (1806–1872), a Zapotec Indian and lawyer, was deeply influenced by the liberal views of European philosophers and theorists such as Jean-Jacques Rousseau (1712–1778), John Stuart Mill (1806–1873), and Pierre-Joseph Proudhon (1809–1865). Juárez and other like-minded men, working in the safety of exile in the United States, plotted to overthrow Antonio López de Santa Anna, who had seized power in 1853 and ruled Mexico as a dictator. When their plan became known in Mexico and gained the support of the Mexican people, Santa Anna bowed to pressure for his resignation and left office (for the last time) in 1855. Liberals, headed by Juárez, took charge of Mexico's government and set about instituting a series of reform laws, ushering in the period in Mexico's history known as La Reforma *(the Reform).*

Conservatives, represented by the military, the Roman Catholic Church, aristocrats, and large landowners, opposed Juárez's plan and the loss of their privileges. The main point of contention between conservatives and liberals was the Constitution of 1857, a staunchly liberal document guaranteeing a bill of rights, suffrage, the abolition of titles of nobility, and freedom of worship. A bloody civil war, the War of the Reform (1858–1860), followed, during which Mexicans killed one another over property as well as ideology. Juárez fled arrest by conservatives and established a government in exile in the city of Veracruz. When liberal armies triumphed, Juárez returned to Mexico City in 1861 to rule the country.

The following selection by Walter V. Scholes is from his history of politics in Mexico during Juárez's rule. It describes the government's program for reform with an emphasis on the most controversial and wide-ranging aspect of that program: the abolition of the privileges of the church and the nationalization of church property.

Walter V. Scholes, "The Government's Program and the Reform Laws," *Mexican Politics During the Juárez Regime, 1855–1872.* Columbia: University of Missouri Press, 1957. Copyright © 1957 by the Curators of the University of Missouri. Renewed in 1985 by Marie V. Scholes. Reproduced by permission.

On July 7, 1859, the Juárez government in Veracruz issued a manifesto outlining in broad terms its program of aims and objectives. It summarized the government's thinking not only on military aspects of the war [War of the Reform] but also on the administrative changes to be carried through when peace was restored. In view of the revolt it had originally been intended to postpone publication of the program, but the war had lasted longer than had been anticipated and the fighting had become extremely bitter. Under the circumstances, the government finally concluded that it would be shirking a duty which the situation demanded were it to withhold any longer its plans for correcting the basic defects of Mexican society. The affairs of the nation had reached a crisis, declared the manifesto, for on the outcome of the bloody struggle which the conservatives were waging against the principles of liberty and social progress depended the future of the nation. The government felt itself bound to make known to the people their rights and interests, not only to unify public opinion but also that the people could then better understand the reasons for their great sacrifices and that the civilized world would know the true objective of the struggle in Mexico.

Basic Ideas

Since the [Juárez] government derived from the Constitution of 1857, it naturally subscribed to the doctrines of that charter; equal rights and guarantees for all citizens, administration within the clearly defined limits of the law, and the principle of state autonomy as long as the states did not interfere with the rights and general interests of the republic. Although these basic ideas had formed a part of almost every liberal code written since independence, they had not yet been able to take root in the nation. Nor would they do so as long as social and administrative institutions retained various elements of despotism, hypocrisy, immorality, and disorder which all worked together to prevent the establishment of good principles of government. The Juárez administration pledged itself to eliminate these vicious elements, for it believed that as long as they persisted order and liberty would be impossible.

To achieve its twin aims of stability and freedom the government intended to unify opinion on the question of social reform through a series of measures which would produce a complete

and durable triumph of desirable principles. Specifically the program listed the following: separation of church and state; suppression of monasteries and secularization of clergy living in
those institutions; abolition of brotherhoods and other organizations of a similar nature; abolition of novitiates [novices] in convents; nationalization of all the wealth administered by the secular and regular clergy; and elimination of the civil authority in
the matter of payment of church fees.

The government believed that only by enacting these measures could the clergy be made to submit to the civil authority
in temporal matters and still be left free to carry on their sacred
calling. In addition the government also considered it indispensable to protect religious liberty throughout the nation, for freedom of choice in this regard was essential to the country's prosperity and growth.

The general statement of the government's program thus included an outline of the Reform Laws which were to be issued
shortly, but that was only the beginning of what its liberal rulers
envisioned doing for the improvement of Mexico. They also intended to overhaul the administration of justice; and their plans
included the formulation of civil and criminal codes, the introduction of the jury system, and the elimination of court fees.
The country would have more free primary schools, and a new
plan of studies for secondary schools and colleges would be
drawn up. Attention would be given to aiding the states in order to strengthen the ties which should exist between the states
and the federal government. The government believed that one
of the best ways to attain this unity was through establishing better internal security, not only because the highwaymen were a
plague to the inhabitants but also because it felt that the insecurity kept out of the country much capital and many industrious
people who would otherwise come. The constitutional provision eliminating passports would be implemented as part of the
government's program to clear away all obstacles to free movement within the country. A free press and a civil register would
be established.

The last half of the program was devoted primarily to fiscal
and financial matters. In the field of public finances the government believed radical changes were needed, and leading the list
was reform of the national treasury. The government planned to
abolish all domestic taxes collected on the movement of money

and persons. Similarly, although its effects were not quite as injurious to the nation's economic health, the tax on the transfer of rural and urban property was also slated for repeal. In the same category came the removal of restricting and unfair taxes on mining. The government promised to do its best to stimulate foreign commerce by simplifying the commercial regulations established under existing laws and by reducing taxes.

In the government's opinion, the various laws promulgated to regulate the division of revenues between the national and state governments had failed to establish a clear distinction in sources of income. To clarify the situation the government proposed that revenues from direct taxes on persons, properties, commercial and industrial establishments, and professions be kept by the states; revenues from indirect taxes would go to the national government.

The Problem of Pensioners

One of the great burdens on the government, a problem inherited from Spain, was the many pensioners classified variously as retired officers and government officials, old age pensioners, widows, and others. The situation called for prompt attention, and the government felt that the only solution was to capitalize these claims once and for all. Whether they were acquired justly or unjustly, the government believed that in all fairness they could not be disavowed if they had been granted in accordance with the laws and by competent authorities. The revenue to settle these claims would be raised by a special series of so-called capitalization bonds which would be issued upon the basis and under the circumstances to be fixed by law.

The plan to clear up pension payments would have an added advantage. As the system had functioned, the government took deductions from the salaries of government employees and men in the army with the view to providing them with a pension, but the promised security had almost always proved illusory. In the future no deduction would be made, and the individual could invest the extra money to provide for his old age. He could put it in savings banks and in mutual assistance societies whose establishment the government favored and which it assumed would spring up in all parts of the country. Mutual assistance societies, in addition to being a very effective means of insuring the savings of government employees as well as those of all people with scanty resources, would also produce immense advantages for society in other ways, because their regular accumulations of capital would serve to carry out many undertakings both useful and profitable for the whole country.

Reducing Debt and Building Infrastructure

The government also intended to reduce the public debt. One method of achieving this objective would be provided in the law, soon to be issued, nationalizing church holdings. The law would require new owners to pay part of the purchase price in currency and the remainder in government bonds. A similar arrangement applied to the sale of public lands would also help reduce the debt. The government expressed confidence that if these two methods of amortization were used to pay off the outstanding government indebtedness, a great part of both the capitalization bonds and the foreign debt would be retired. If these revenues were not sufficient to pay off foreign commitments, the government pledged itself to continue to respect the agreements it had made regarding payments.

The government was anxious to encourage immigration, but before any success could be expected two things were essential. Jobs had to be available when the immigrants arrived, and to help meet this need the government envisioned projects such as roads and canals. In addition, the newcomers must feel secure in their person and property. The latter objective would be only one of several advantages anticipated from the improvement of the army and the creation of a national militia, proposed elsewhere in the program. To give impetus to immigration, large landholders in the interior would be urged, in their own interest and that of the country, to make arrangements to sell or rent lands on reasonable terms to the newcomers. Disposition of public lands would also be linked to plans for colonization.

In considering the problem of improving transportation facilities, the program declared that the government ought to abandon the custom of building roads itself. Instead contracts should be given to private enterprises with government inspection to see that the work was properly done. A new law regulating railroad construction would be passed which would contain ample and generous concessions in order to stimulate both domestic and foreign capital to enter this field of investment.

But important as the program was in indicating the government's stand on various matters, it was completely overshadowed by specific laws affecting the status of the church. The effect of this body of decrees, generally known as the Reform Laws, would be felt for many years. Obviously the Reform Laws were only one part of the general program, but it was natural that attention, both at that time and ever since, should be focused on them.

The Law of July 12, 1859

While subsequent decrees were of significance in their effect upon the church, the law promulgated on July 12, 1859, was the real bombshell. The first article provided for the confiscation of all the wealth administered by the regular and secular clergy. To prevent a repetition of mortmain [perpetual ownership] holdings the law stipulated that while the clergy would be free in the future to accept offerings for the religious services which they performed, under no circumstances could such gifts take the form of real property. The law also decreed the separation of church and state and promised state protection of public worship to all religions, whether Catholic or any other denomination.

The articles dealing with the regular clergy abolished all the brotherhoods and regular orders and prohibited the establishment of new monasteries. The regulars were to join the secular clergy and as such would thereafter be subject to the proper ecclesiastical authority. Every regular who accepted the government's decree was to receive a gift of 1,500 pesos, but any monks who reassembled in an effort to continue their communal way of life would be expelled from the country. Upon petition from the archbishop and bishop of the diocese, the civil authorities would designate the churches of the suppressed orders which would continue to serve as houses of worship, and the sacred objects from all others would be turned over to the bishop. The books, antiques, and works of art would be transferred to public libraries and museums.

Convents which were in existence when the decree appeared were to continue without interference, but no novices were ever to be admitted in the future. In addition, nuns were encouraged to leave their convents by the promise of financial assistance.

Another decree issued the following day established the procedure for an inventory of the nationalized property by civilian authorities, and outlined the procedure by which individuals could acquire ownership. The groups of buildings formerly occupied by the regular orders were to be subdivided and a price put on each piece of property by an official appraiser. These properties were then to be offered at public auction, but they would be sold only if the bid were equivalent to two-thirds of the appraised value. Of this amount, one-third had to be in cash and another one-third was to be paid in securities of the national debt. If more than one bid were received the property would go to the individual offering the largest amount in government securities. . . .

Any person who brought to the attention of treasury officials church property of whose existence that department was unaware would have the right to acquire title to it. In such cases the buyer would have to pay seventy per cent of the property's value in government bonds and the remainder in forty monthly cash installments. If such a person did not take up his option to buy within twenty days, the government would sell the property at public auction.

Twenty per cent of the money, both cash and time payments, collected as a result of this law was to remain in the states. They were to use this money for the improvement of roads and other means of communication and for the projects which promoted the general welfare.

Other decrees followed in 1859 and 1860 which secularized cemeteries, made marriage a civil contract, and recognized legal separation, although absolute divorce was prohibited. Additional laws reduced the number of religious feast days and spelled out the regulations governing religious toleration.

The law nationalizing church property did not embody an idea that was completely novel to Mexican thinking; as far back as the 1830's, and particularly during the time Gómez Farías was in power, demands were made that such a decree be issued. The same situation repeated itself in 1846–1847 during the war with the United States and in 1856–1857 at the time of the constitutional convention. As a matter of fact, before the national government issued the Reform decree of July 12, some of the states on their own initiative had already taken rather drastic action against the church. In the north, Vidaurri had confiscated church property, as had Ortega in Zacatecas. In Michoacán a beginning had been made toward the eventual suppression of all monasteries. In a sense, therefore, the national government was legalizing actions which some states had already undertaken.

The Porfirio Díaz Era

By Anita Brenner

In 1871 Mexico held its presidential elections. Among the candidates were incumbent Benito Juárez and José de la Cruz Porfirio Díaz (1830–1915). When the election resulted in no clear majority for any of the candidates, the congress chose Juárez. Díaz responded by staging a revolt against Juárez in late 1871. As political factions struggled for power, Juárez died on July 18, 1872. Four years later, Díaz staged another revolt against the sitting president and seized Mexico City. Thus began the thirty-four-year rule of Porfirio Díaz, a period known in Mexican history as the "Porfiriato."

In the following selection, Anita Brenner describes the character of Díaz's presidency, during which Mexico was modernized and its economy revived due largely to investment by foreign companies and individuals. In order to maintain law and order and keep Mexico attractive to foreign companies and investors, Díaz suppressed political opponents and appointed only those who were loyal to him and supportive of his regime. These men maintained strict control of political life at all levels. Most of the economic growth that occurred during the Díaz era, however, failed to benefit the lowest rungs of Mexican society. The peasants remained poor and subservient to wealthy foreigners and well-to-do landowners. Urban workers in factories and mines who were toiling for ten hours a day for meager wages were forbidden to organize to express their discontent with wages and working conditions. Eventually, opposition to Díaz's dictatorship fomented into revolution. In 1910 a group of revolutionaries led by Francisco Madero rose up against Díaz and eventually forced him to resign. In the following year, Madero became president of Mexico. However, the country remained in revolutionary turmoil for the next decade.

Anita Brenner was born in Mexico in 1905. During the Mexican Revolution (1910–1920), her family moved back and forth between Mexico and Texas and eventually settled in Texas. Brenner's other works include Idols Behind Altars, *a book about Mexican art and culture. She died in 1974.*

Anita Brenner, *The Wind That Swept Mexico: The History of the Mexican Revolution, 1910–1942.* Austin: University of Texas Press, 1971. Copyright © 1971 by Anita Brenner. Reproduced by permission of the publisher.

I n the year 1910 there was a Strong Man of the Americas advertised in all the world, and his name was Porfirio Díaz of Mexico. Each time he reassumed his dictatorial position the Kaiser the Mikado all important potentates flashed messages of joy. Financiers, industrialists, illustrious public men congratulated the Mexican people regularly on his existence. Elihu Root [a U.S. senator and former secretary of state] advised them to render Don Porfirio reverence. Writers and speakers multilingually raised him up as the salvation of his country, the stern wise parent of his people. A genius. A colossus. Inscrutable. Incomparable. Irreplaceable.

The aged man had been sitting for thirty-four years—with one brief interim—in the presidential chair. Round him, like cherubim and seraphim in a religious picture, there was a group of courtly elderly men who had long since done away with politics, devoting themselves to nourishing business.

At his right hand—pale, scrupulous, and faultless as a tailor's dream—hovered Don José Yves Limantour, primate of the holy of holies, Secretary of the Treasury. Respectfully close to the chair there knelt, bringing gifts and testimonials, a select little group of men of affairs, named the Circle of Friends of Porfirio Díaz. Near Limantour there was another little group, select too, consisting chiefly of foreigners, and nicknamed, by Americans, The Full Car. Beyond, on all sides, landowners, high Church dignitaries, heads of foreign houses, concessionaires and their prosperous Mexican advocates praised without end the blessings that flowed from *la paz porfiriana*—the Porfirian Peace.

The revolutions that had boiled for three-quarters of a century (since 1810, when Mexicans declared their independence from Spain) and that had wasted the country's substance needlessly (said the Porfirian intellectuals) were now entombed in historical volumes, printed on fine paper at the government's expense. The army's old Spanish custom of plotting to change the government had only one successful living exponent, General Díaz himself, who had practiced it on [Benito] Juárez [the late president and opponent of Díaz]. The last try against Díaz, made in the eighties, had been picked off when the General sent a list of names to the commanding officer, wiring, "Catch in the act, kill on the spot."

Thrift, too, had clipped the military talons. Limantour controlled expenditures for arms and munitions strictly, these being expensive imports. Army bigwigs, except of course General Díaz, had been edged to the fringes of state business. As for the soldiers, they were peasants, thinking little, wanting less, living on minimal wages, and why give them more to waste on drink? Many had been recruited on personal word of some local authority—by seizure at night. Troublemakers, safely and cheaply garrisoned.

The wars for power between Church totalitarians and liberal democrats that had torn the people from 1810 to the 1870's were now appeased. The Juárez Constitution and reform laws, which had expropriated the Church, and forbidden it henceforth to own property, and closed all monasteries and convents, and reduced the clergy to the status of citizens, and even required all priests and religious to appear in public only in lay clothing, had not been abrogated. They were still the law of the land and no one had dared attempt to change it. But the President's young second wife, Doña Carmelita Romero Rubio, was a pious lady; and the President's advisers valued the resignation that the Church reinforced, teaching "Render unto Caesar . . ." So appearances were preserved, and the old Spanish maxim regarding inconvenient laws was practiced: Observe, do not fulfill.

The perfect formula for the perfect stability that money seeks had been found. It was a Strong Man with a constellation of grayed experts in business and finance, revolving around the Treasurer, and governing according to the maxim, "Little politics, much administration."

Limantour and His Views

The bankers had confidence in Limantour. From time to time through the years they had stipulated, in arranging loans, that he remain in place, as guarantor of the status quo. The Limantour group, known as *los científicos* [the scientists] and in that name execrated by everybody locked out of the profitable circuit, had a doctrine, "Let us be scientific, let us be realistic." It was ground out solemnly in the academies, the University, the press, raisined with scholarly arguments quoted from the French physiocrats [advocates of opening the nation to foreign investors] and positivists [eighteenth-century economists who advocated laissez-faire practices], in French, of course. It was taught in practice to the bright apprentices being groomed against the day when time, alas, should foreclose on General Díaz, and their Science would inherit full control. Democracy, the official philosophers recited, was a utopian dream, an anachronism, a plaything for rich countries. "Its bad government," Limantour remarked of the United States, "is the best proof of its greatness."

But in a land where not even fifteen per cent could read, how absurd to spend money on open elections! How visionary among a people more than ninety per cent mixed breed, dominantly Indian, racially inferior! The conquerors had indeed made a mistake—influenced by religious sentimentalisms—in allowing the creatures to live and propagate. They should have been handled as in the United States [where wars against Native Americans killed great numbers of the population]. It was now Mexico's misfortune to try to progress with such a burden upon it: more than three-fourths of the population nearly pure Indian, practically subhuman, degenerate, apathetic, irresponsible, lazy, treacherous, superstitious—destined to be a slave race. Such beings could never perform, surely could not claim participation in the acts of government. Let them work, and keep the peace. For them the standard, *pan y palo*—Bread and Club. The government must be an aristocracy, an aristocracy of brains, technicians, wise and upright elders, scientists.

How Díaz Ruled

The intricacies of financial arithmetic were dull to Díaz; he left all that to Limantour, and himself ran the political machinery. He chose the governors, each one of whom—usually the biggest landowner or businessman, or an old military friend from the Juárez days—enjoyed dictatorial powers. Each one, like Díaz, had his right-hand man, the chief of police, whose organization worked smoothly toward the disappearance of malcontents and people suspected of dangerous thoughts. The methods: *pan*—a job, a few pesos, social flatteries; *palo*—blackmail; and the final alternative of the *ley fuga* (fugitive law)—"shot while attempting to escape."

A lower hierarchy, the *jefes políticos* (political chiefs), ruled the small towns. They were chosen by the governors and okayed by Díaz, and their job was to guide the municipal "authorities," operate the elections, cooperate with the secret police, and nudge the courts.

It was a safe land in which to do business. Justice was carried out according to an unwritten, unbreakable law which required that a case be settled in rigid observance of who the attorney was, who the client. Cases involving a foreigner against a Mexican were decided according to the principle that the foreigner must be right, unless word came from Don Porfirio, exceptionally, to discover otherwise. In the remotest places judges understood the fine points of these usages, and could interpret skilfully the precept taught by the U.S. State Department, that Americans were guests and must be spared the judicial annoyances unavoidable to Mexicans; that every American living and working in Mexico, from plant manager to gang foreman and oil driller, and every company that had American money in it—even if it were only one red cent, said the Embassy—had the right to this same kind of extraterritorial immunity.

Order reigned. Bullion [gold and silver coins or bars] could be transported with dozing guards, and travelers could jog along through the sun-drenched landscape, fearing no disturbance of their right of way. The peasants abased themselves before men on horseback, murmuring, hat in hand, "Go with God." The roads were patrolled by *rurales*, well-mounted active men in dove-gray uniforms, tightly buttoned with silver. They knew the trails and hideouts as well as the Indians, for many had been smugglers and ambushers, and had been persuaded into the handsome uniform by exercise of the Díaz methods. Plantation owners and the prosperous people in small communities loved them as Texas does its Rangers and Canada its Mounties. Village and hacienda workers had other emotions, since it was the *rurales* who kidnaped recruits for the army, or tied suitable prospects into the gangs shipped to the tropics—where labor was short-lived and plantation owners were willing to pay for able-bodied men at twenty-five pesos a head. Or, in general, dispense justice among the cacti according to the precepts laid down in Díaz' famous telegram.

Men of Influence

There was music on the plazas in the evenings, and the small-towners came out to sit among the palms and listen to the waltzes and military airs. The young people promenaded, males clockwise, females in pastel muslins counter-clockwise, exchanging at the intersections meaningful silences and wadded notes of undying love. One of the benches on the plaza was always occupied by the municipal president, the judge, and the *jefe político*. As a rule he was also the local money-lender, only source of credit for small farmers, at twelve per cent and up. Most of the marketable corn and beans accumulated in his warehouse, and in combination with other *acaparadores* (monopolizers, their name in common usage) he kept supply, demand, and prices under comfortable control. This little group of solid men was sometimes joined by the parish priest, and perhaps too by a neighboring *hacendado* [large landowner], who might take the pleasant occasion to transact some little business, while they sat in the incense of good cigars, and smoothed their mustaches grown plump and pointed in the Díaz fashion.

On the opposite side of the plaza there was another bench occupied by the heterodox: the doctor, the pharmacist, a lawyer maybe, the newspaper editor if there was one, the schoolteacher if any, the local telegrapher, and perhaps the barber. In some towns the priest might be the kind of man who gravitated in their direction too. Not usually, however, as it was taken for granted that these were the town's Freemasons, as well as its dreamers and odd fellows, collectors of botanical specimens and curious rocks, delvers in old papers, mouthers of obsolescent political ideas. People of no importance visited their bench. One-horse ranchers, marginal miners, shopkeepers pushed by the big-store Spaniards, ex-artisans ousted by factory goods, and spindly boys who had studied in the capital. There they sat, talking low, the old ones chewing over the Juárez days, the young ones repeating futilities heard from their fathers and teachers: democracy, free elections, municipal self-rule, lay education, independent courts, equal opportunities, citizens' rights. . . . It was evident from the way they dressed, in severe worn black, that such preoccupations led nowhere.

As far back as 1896, the last belligerently independent liberal paper, *El Monitor Republicano*, had committed suicide. Its editor had written in farewell: "Since there is no longer a liberal party, but only a very few men of political faith, and many degenerates, we lack a point of reference . . . Our paper, faithful observer of constitutional law, has managed to give some service defending it against the Power . . . We look for some base on which to resist, and find a vacuum . . . We furl, therefore, the remaining shred of constitutionalist flag . . . and wrapping ourselves in it go down to the grave of oblivion." The *Monitor* was, from a business viewpoint, a going concern. But it closed refusing to sell its name and following.

Mexico—a "Bonanza" Land?

There was no open challenger henceforth to the self-perpetuating Power. It was unthinkable to anyone except the shabby talkers in low key that the country would ever again hear the word "revolution," once its most common noun. Revolutions, it had been announced by Francisco Bulnes, the brilliant orator and intellectual [Alessandro, count of] Cagliostro [an eighteenth-century occultist and healer] of the regime, "occur according to natural social law. And that law is that governments break down when they cannot pay their bills."

Of this condition there was not the slightest portent. The Treasury had a surplus of 62,483,119 pesos, gold. Revenues were comfortably over expenditures. From the time the Treasury had come into his hands, fourteen years earlier, Limantour had administered it like a business in receivership, which essentially it then was. The army appropriations had been whittled; interest payments on the foreign debt came first. Many measures had been taken to free business from feudalistic and other restraints. Internal customs were abolished, taxes reapportioned. The currency, to benefit the export trade, had been put on a gold basis.

The national credit was such that smiles flowered on the faces of bankers floating new bonds. Through Limantour and his friend Hugo Scherer [a banker] and their mutual friends in German and other European banks, Mexico had been encouraged to borrow on better and better terms. The debt had rolled from eighty million pesos to four hundred and forty million, held chiefly in Germany, and about to be consolidated at four per cent, as the crowning achievement of Limantour's career.

Railroads, to which Juárez (and Díaz when he had been a Juárez general) had once objected, fearing easy invasion from the United States, now cut important export routes, carrying ore and other raw materials free from interstate tolls. Built with government subsidies, perennially unprofitable because they served so little of the national market, the main lines had been merged through a Limantour maneuver into a national company, stock-controlled by the government, run by American management. And other industries, subsidized too, had developed by leaps and bounds. In every money market of the world investors were accustomed to regard Mexico as a bonanza land.

A dazzling future was prophesied, a golden era had arrived already, and the stock phrase was that Mexico had abandoned her turbulent, unproductive past and begun to take her rightful place among the sisterhood of modern industrial nations. Gentlefolk lived fittingly, in stone mansions, lace-hung and furnished in

Louis Quinze or Directoire [styles popular in France]. They relaxed abroad in fashionable resorts; visited, with gay, exquisitely
dressed parties of friends, their immense haciendas, where the
manor house surrounded perhaps a half-acre of polished corri-
dors and patios blooming with Castilian roses. Their families were
intermarried with the nobilities of France and Spain. Their finances were integrated with the enterprises of German, French,
British, American concerns. Their transactions were carried on
elegantly, over long lunches prepared by French chefs, consum-
mated with Rhine wines, Havana cigars, Napoleon brandy, accompanied by light Italian operatic airs.

Foreign investors, the Aladdins of expanding industry—from
which would emanate all the benefits of modern civilization—
were cherished. Their capital, secured by the gold standard and
multiplied by government-stabilized rates of exchange, enjoyed
every guarantee: tax-free concessions for ample years; customs-
free machinery and supplies; subsidies; right of way in the courts;
useful laws, such as those suspending the constitutional provisions
(inherited from colonial days and from the Juárez charter) that
had reserved subsoil resources to the nation; and above all the essential, the quintessential, guarantee, cheap and docile labor.

A Celebration

These were the achievements that the government of General
Porfirio Díaz prepared to celebrate in the fall of 1910, as a patriotic apotheosis of one hundred years of national independence.
The whole month of September was set aside as a holiday, and
provision was made in the budget to make the days and nights a
blazing processional of gaiety for the distinguished guests invited,
all expenses paid, from every powerful nation on earth. The Plaza
of the Constitution, the Cathedral, the National Palace, the avenues and boulevards [of Mexico City] were radiantly illumi-
nated. Indians, peasants, all who showed poverty, were forbidden
the central thoroughfares. The waiters who served the banquets
were Europeans, or hand-picked Mexicans who could be taken
for foreigners. Little girls strewed flowers in the streets, floats
rolled conveying damsels in Greek draperies, holding scrolled
wonderful words: *patria, progreso, industria, ciencia* [country, progress,
industry, science]. The loveliest women were brought in from the
provinces. Champagne was imported in carloads for the President's Ball alone, which seven thousand guests attended.

All the evidences of culture and prosperity were displayed: the monster drainage tunnel that had freed the capital of valley floods, at enormous cost in pesos and uncounted Indian lives ... the Renaissance post office and many other imposing government buildings ... the electric lights in the principal cities ... the streetcars, the telephones, the national telegraph system, the punctual railways ... the four ports dredged and fitted up for maritime commerce ... the industries—textiles, smelters, steel, paper ... the Italian marble opera house begun to commemorate this anniversary, with its fabulous glass curtain already in place, a curtain made by Tiffany at the cost of—but why count the cost? ... Envoys presented trophies. The American Ambassador unveiled a pedestal for a statue of George Washington, counseling the Mexicans there assembled to respect and admire his spirit. But the peak—the golden brooch, as society reporters said in Spanish—of the public solemnities was the inauguration of three superb buildings, three models of Porfirian progress: a hospital, a jail, and an insane asylum.

It was a cumulative picture, dramatically unrolled, to give to foreign eyes a splendid panorama. Land of promise, exploding in bloom wherever water reached it. Land where men of imagination and money could be as Midas [a character from Greek mythology whose touch turned everything to gold], and live in a paradise of natural beauties. Behold the works of some pioneers. There was the Englishman Weetman Pearson, who had built the railway connecting the two oceans, amply helped by the government; had dredged the ports, had secured the drainage-tunnel concession, and was enjoying and carrying out many other contracts. He had found oil and signed a concession, in generous partnership with the government, over the vastest rich deposits—and was now Lord Cowdray.

There was the German Hugo Scherer, intimate of Limantour. He had become connected with money in many countries and, with much pomp, embraced the Catholic faith. Through his hands had passed much of the European capital that had gone into government loans. (Church money, some believed, directed from Germany through its powerful Catholic party, with the encouragement of the Kaiser, and funneled into Mexico for reasons of *realpolitik*.)

As for Americans, the invasion dreams of the nineteenth century were no longer necessary, for American industrial and agricultural enterprises were spread peacefully over the whole north and ran deep southward along both coasts. The golden tide and appetites of the [eighteen] eighties had jumped the Rio Grande [river]. Guggenheim and U.S. Smelting dominated the mines, holding over ninety per cent of Mexico's most important industry. In railroads, American money far outcounted any other, and American management ran all lines except Cowdray's and a few unimportant narrow-gauge concerns. [Edward] Doheny, helped by the railroaders, had energetically ridden through jungles looking for fuel, and had found it. Waters-Pierce, [Oil Company] and Standard Oil with that early start were crowding Cowdray's Dutch Shell-Eagle Oil combine. American money had absorbed plantations and ranches—cotton, sugar, timber, cattle—had developed the most profitable agricultural enterprise in the country, and now nudged for first place in this field even the Spanish, who had for generations been the lords of land. Indeed, though European money was still first in public finance and the retail trade, the dollar had long since submerged the pound and franc and peseta. The value of American holdings, virtually nothing in 1877, was gauged at $500,000,000 in 1902, and had tripled to a billion and a half dollars by 1910.

Limantour, it was true, was none too friendly to the march of the dollar, and followed a calculated policy of checks and balances, whereby dollars invested were offset by better concessions for Europeans. He practiced financially the traditional strategy by which Mexico tried to fence each hungry power, playing it off against another. Church money, forbidden by Juárez laws to accumulate in earthly property, could under his benevolent eye take cover in securities and corporations, and help dam back the dreaded liberal influences that might spread with American domination.

Still, to capital of every nationality Limantour was unquestionably a sound man, a gilt-edged guarantor of the *status quo.* And some of his best friends and even business partners were Americans, who in turn were friends of the new Ambassador, Henry Lane Wilson, who in turn had friends and relatives in the Guggenheim, [John D.] Rockefeller, and Aldrich [family related to the Rockefeller family by marriage] interests; while President [William Howard] Taft's brother was the counsel for, and a director of, the Cowdray oil concern.

On the whole it was a cozy little *status quo.* There was only one flaw in it. Díaz was eighty years old, and not immortal.

A Call for Revolt: The Plan of San Luis Potosi, 1910

President Porfirio Díaz, who ruled from 1876 to 1911, resorted to dictatorial methods to carry through his promise of "order and progress," as his plan for the modernization of Mexico was called. The press was controlled, attempts to form labor unions were squashed, and the army was used to suppress political discontent wherever it appeared. Opponents eventually rose up against the Díaz regime and began to demand change. Francisco Madero (1873–1913), a landowner, industrialist, and candidate for president in the election of 1910, was arrested by Díaz, who feared the Partido Liberal Mexicano (PLM), the party that backed Madero. Rather than submit, Madero escaped across the border into Texas, where he issued the Plan of San Luis Potosi in October 1910. In this document, Madero declares the election null and void and calls on the Mexican people to rise up on November 20 and demand the restoration of democracy as embodied in the Constitution of 1857. The plan also calls for the replacement of Díaz with a provisional government.

The Plan of San Luis Potosi made no recommendations for curing Mexico's diverse political, economic, and social ills, but it did energize the disparate elements in Mexico's states who stood prepared to rebel against their local, Díaz-dominated governments. When Madero crossed over into Mexico with a small band of supporters, the mass uprising he envisioned failed to ignite. Madero returned to the United States to watch and wait. By January 1911 events took a dramatic turn in the northern state of Chihuahua. There, a local businessman, Pascual Orozco, and sometime bandit Francisco "Pancho" Villa led a revolt. Madero, sensing the outbreak of revolution, hurriedly returned to Mexico to lead it. The success of the uprising in Chihuahua inspired rebels in other states to do the same, marking the beginning of the Mexican Revolution.

Francisco Madero, "The Plan of San Luis Potosi," document submitted to the U.S. Senate Subcommittee on Foreign Relations, Washington, D.C., November 20, 1910.

The following selection is taken from Madero's Plan of San Luis Po-tosi. In it, Madero describes how the conduct of Díaz has led to the trampling of democracy. Speaking with outrage on behalf of the Mexican people whose rights have been violated, Madero declares himself the law-ful president and demands the ouster of those he calls "the audacious usurpers."

Peoples, in their constant efforts for the triumph of the ideal of liberty and justice, are forced, at precise historical mo-ments, to make their greatest sacrifices.

Our beloved country has reached one of those moments. A force of tyranny which we Mexicans were not accustomed to suffer after we won our independence oppresses us in such a manner that it has become intolerable. In exchange for that tyranny we are offered peace, but peace full of shame for the Mexican nation, because its basis is not law, but force; because its object is not the aggrandizement and prosperity of the country, but to enrich a small group who, abusing their influence, have converted the public charges into fountains of exclusively per-sonal benefit, unscrupulously exploiting the manner of lucrative concessions and contracts.

Rule by Caprice

The legislative and judicial powers are completely subordinated to the executive; the division of powers, the sovereignty of the States, the liberty of the common councils, and the rights of the citizens exist only in writing in our great charter; but, as a fact, it may almost be said that martial law constantly exists in Mexico; the administration of justice, instead of imparting protection to the weak, merely serves to legalize the plunderings committed by the strong; the judges instead of being the representatives of justice, are the agents of the executive, whose interests they faith-fully serve; the chambers of the union have no other will than that of the dictator; the governors of the States are designated by him and they in their turn designate and impose in like manner the municipal authorities.

From this it results that the whole administrative, judicial, and legislative machinery obeys a single will, the caprice of General Porfirio Diaz, who during his long administration has shown that the principal motive that guides him is to maintain himself in power and at any cost.

For many years profound discontent has been felt throughout the Republic, due to such a system of government, but General Diaz with great cunning and perseverance, has succeeded in annihilating all independent elements, so that it was not possible to organize any sort of movement to take from him the power of which he made such bad use. The evil constantly became worse, and the decided eagerness of General Diaz to impose a successor upon the nations in the person of Mr. Ramon Corral carried that evil to its limit and caused many of us Mexicans, although lacking recognized political standing, since it had been impossible to acquire it during the 36 years of dictatorship, to throw ourselves into the struggle to recover the sovereignty of the people and their rights on purely democratic grounds. . . .

In Mexico, as a democratic Republic, the public power can have no other origin nor other basis than the will of the people, and the latter can not be subordinated to formulas to be executed in a fraudulent manner. . . .

The People Protest

For this reason the Mexican people have protested against the illegality of the last election and, desiring to use successively all the recourses offered by the laws of the Republic, in due form asked for the nullification of the election by the Chamber of Deputies, notwithstanding they recognized no legal origin in said body and knew beforehand that, as its members were not the representatives of the people, they would carry out the will of General Diaz, to whom exclusively they owe their investiture.

In such a state of affairs the people, who are the only sovereign, also protested energetically against the election in imposing manifestations in different parts of the Republic; and if the latter were not general throughout the national territory, it was due to the terrible pressure exercised by the Government, which always quenches in blood any democratic manifestation, as happened in Puebla, Vera Cruz, Tlaxcala, and in other places.

But this violent and illegal system can no longer subsist.

I have very well realized that if the people have designated me as their candidate for the Presidency it is not because they have had an opportunity to discover in me the qualities of a statesman or of a ruler, but the virility of the patriot determined to sacrifice himself, if need be, to obtain liberty and to help the people free themselves from the odious tyranny that oppresses them.

From the moment I threw myself into the democratic struggle I very well knew that General Diaz would not bow to the will of the nation, and the noble Mexican people, in following me to the polls, also knew perfectly the outrage that awaited them; but in spite of it, the people gave the cause of liberty a numerous contingent of martyrs when they were necessary and with wonderful stoicism went to the polls and received every sort of molestation.

But such conduct was indispensable to show to the whole world that the Mexican people are fit for democracy, that they are thirsty for liberty, and that their present rulers do not measure up to their aspirations.

Besides, the attitude of the people before and during the election, as well as afterwards, shows clearly that they reject with energy the Government of General Diaz and that, if those electoral rights had been respected, I would have been elected for President of the Republic.

Therefore, and in echo of the national will, I declare the late election illegal and, the Republic being accordingly without rulers, provisionally assume the Presidency of the Republic until the people designate their rulers pursuant to the law. In order to attain this end, it is necessary to eject from power the audacious usurpers whose only title of legality involves a scandalous and immoral fraud.

With all honesty I declare that it would be a weakness on my part and treason to the people, who have placed their confidence in me, not to put myself at the front of my fellow citizens, who anxiously call me from all parts of the country, to compel General Diaz by force of arms, to respect the national will.

Pancho Villa: Portrait of a Revolutionary

By John Reed

Francisco Madero inspired Mexican peasants and workers to mobilize against the Porfirio Díaz regime. In 1911 uprisings took place in states across Mexico. Local leaders such as Pascual Orozco, Francisco "Pancho" Villa, and Emiliano Zapata took charge of rebels in their respective states. Villa (ca. 1877–1923), a sometime cowboy and cattle thief, and his followers (called Villistas) fought for Madero's cause in northern Mexico. There, the guerrilla band and its leader came to the attention of the American reporter John Reed.

Born in 1887 in Portland, Oregon, John Reed came from a well-to-do, socially prominent family. He pursued a career as a journalist in New York City and had articles published in the leading magazines of the day. In 1913 Reed was hired by Metropolitan *magazine to report on the revolution in Mexico. His lack of knowledge of Mexico's history or culture was not considered a drawback and Reed eagerly accepted the assignment.*

Reed, like many Americans, regarded Pancho Villa as a Mexican Robin Hood fighting for the poor and oppressed against the forces of greed and political corruption. Villa, one of the most colorful and controversial personalities of the Mexican Revolution, was not easy to categorize. Born into poverty and ignorance, he learned to read while imprisoned and never forgot the value of education in bringing about change in a society. He continued to expound on the importance of education even while killing those he regarded as enemies. A charismatic leader, Villa lacked the diplomatic and analytical skills required of a successful revolutionary.

In the following excerpt taken from Reed's account of his meeting with Villa in 1914, the Mexican leader was still in the good graces of the

John Reed, *Insurgent Mexico*. New York: Simon and Schuster, 1969.

American president, Woodrow Wilson, who gave unofficial aid to the guerrilla leader. Their friendly relationship changed in 1915 when Wilson threw his support to Villa's rival, Venustiano Carranza. Villa responded by turning against the United States. In 1916, Villistas crossed into New Mexico and raided the town of Columbus. Once held up as a hero by Americans and the American media, Villa was now viewed as a bloodthirsty bandit and attacker of the United States. Reed's opinion of Villa, however, did not waver. Despite his subject's cruelty and violence, Reed continued to esteem Villa as one who rose from poverty and idealistically fought to better the lives of the Mexican people.

I t was while Villa was in Chihuahua City, two weeks before the advance on Torreón, that the artillery corps of his army decided to present him with a gold medal for personal heroism on the field.

In the audience hall of the Governor's palace in Chihuahua, a place of ceremonial, great luster chandeliers, heavy crimson portières and gaudy American wallpaper, there is a throne for the governor. It is a gilded chair with lion's claws for arms, placed upon a dais under a canopy of crimson velvet, surmounted by a heavy, gilded, wooden cap which tapers up to a crown.

The officers of artillery, in smart blue uniforms faced with black velvet and gold, were solidly banked across one end of the audience hall, with flashing new swords and their gilt-braided hats stiffly held under their arms. From the door of that chamber, around the gallery, down the state staircase, across the grandiose inner court of the palace and out through the imposing gates to the street, stood a double line of soldiers with their rifles at present arms. Four regimental bands grouped in one wedged in the crowd. The people of the capital were massed in solid thousands on the Plaza de Armas before the palace.

"Ya viene!" "Here he comes!" "Viva Villa!" "Viva Madero!" "Villa, the Friend of the Poor!"

The roar began at the back of the crowd and swept like fire in heavy growing crescendo until it seemed to toss thousands of hats above their heads. The band in the courtyard struck up the Mexican national air, and Villa came walking down the street.

He was dressed in an old plain khaki uniform, with several buttons lacking. He hadn't recently shaved, wore no hat, and his hair had not been brushed. He walked a little pigeon-toed, humped over, with his hands in his trouser pockets. As he entered the aisle between the rigid lines of soldiers he seemed slightly embarrassed, and grinned and nodded to a *compadre* here and there in the ranks. At the foot of the grand staircase, Governor [Manuel] Chao and Secretary of State [Silvestre] Terrazas joined him in full-dress uniform. The band threw off all restraint, and, as Villa entered the audience chamber, at a signal from someone in the balcony of the palace, the great throng in the Plaza de Armas uncovered, and all the brilliant crowd of officers in the room saluted stiffly.

It was Napoleonic!

Villa hesitated for a minute, pulling his mustache and looking very uncomfortable, finally gravitated toward the throne, which he tested by shaking the arms, and then sat down, with the Governor on his right and the Secretary of State on his left.

Señor Bauche Alcalde stepped forward, raised his right hand to the exact position which Cicero took when denouncing Catiline, and pronounced a short discourse, indicting Villa for personal bravery on the field on six counts, which he mentioned in florid detail. He was followed by the Chief of Artillery, who said: "The army adores you. We will follow you wherever you lead. You can be what you desire in Mexico." Then three other officers spoke in the high-flung, extravagant periods necessary to Mexican oratory. They called him "The Friend of the Poor," "The Invincible General," "The Inspirer of Courage and Patriotism," "The Hope of the Indian Republic." And through it all Villa slouched on the throne, his mouth hanging open, his little shrewd eyes playing around the room. Once or twice he yawned, but for the most part he seemed to be speculating, with some intense interior amusement. . . .

Finally, with an impressive gesture, Colonel Servín stepped forward with the small pasteboard box which held the medal. General Chao nudged Villa, who stood up. The officers applauded violently; the crowd outside cheered; the band in the court burst into a triumphant march.

Villa put out both hands eagerly, like a child for a new toy. He could hardly wait to open the box and see what was inside. An expectant hush fell upon everyone, even the crowd in the square. Villa looked at the medal, scratching his head, and, in a reverent silence, said clearly: "This is a hell of a little thing to give a man for all that heroism you are talking about!" And the bubble of Empire was pricked then and there with a great shout of laughter.

They waited for him to speak—to make a conventional address of acceptance. But as he looked around the room at those brilliant, educated men, who said that they would die for Villa, the peon, and meant it, and as he caught sight through the door of the ragged soldiers, who had forgotten their rigidity and were crowding eagerly into the corridor with eyes fixed eagerly on the *compañero* [buddy] that they loved, he realized something of what the Revolution signified.

Puckering up his face, as he did always when he concentrated intensely, he leaned across the table in front of him and poured out, in a voice so low that people could hardly hear: "There is no word to speak. All I can say is my heart is all to you.". . .

Villa's Background

Villa was an outlaw for twenty-two years. When he was only a boy of sixteen, delivering milk in the streets of Chihuahua, he killed a government official and had to take to the mountains. The story is that the official had violated his sister, but it seems probable that Villa killed him on account of his insufferable insolence. That in itself would not have outlawed him long in Mexico, where human life is cheap; but once a refugee he committed the unpardonable crime of stealing cattle from the rich *hacendados* [landowners]. And from that time to the outbreak of the Madero revolution [1911] the Mexican government had a price on his head.

Villa was the son of ignorant peons. He had never been to school. He hadn't the slightest conception of the complexity of civilization, and when he finally came back to it, a mature man of extraordinary native shrewdness, he encountered the twentieth century with the naïve simplicity of a savage.

It is almost impossible to procure accurate information about his career as a bandit. There are accounts of outrages he committed in old files of local newspapers and government reports, but those sources are prejudiced, and his name became so prominent as a bandit that every train robbery and holdup and murder in northern Mexico was attributed to Villa. . . .

His reckless and romantic bravery is the subject of countless poems. They tell, for example, how one of his band named Reza was captured by the *rurales* [rural police] and bribed to betray Villa. Villa heard of it and sent word into the city of Chihuahua that he was coming for Reza. In broad daylight he entered the city on horseback, took ice cream on the Plaza—the ballad is very explicit on this point—and rode up and down the streets until he found Reza strolling with his sweetheart in the Sunday crowd on the Paseo Bolívar, where he shot him and escaped. In time of famine he fed whole districts, and took care of entire villages evicted by the soldiers under Porfirio Díaz's outrageous land law. Everywhere he was known as The Friend of the Poor. He was the Mexican Robin Hood.

In all these years he learned to trust nobody. Often in his secret journeys across the country with one faithful companion he camped in some desolate spot and dismissed his guide; then, leaving a fire burning, he rode all night to get away from the faithful companion. That is how Villa learned the art of war, and in the field today, when the army comes into camp at night, Villa flings the bridle of his horse to an orderly, takes a sarape over his shoulder, and sets out for the hills alone. He never seems to sleep. In the dead of night he will appear somewhere along the line of outposts to see if the sentries are on the job; and in the morning he returns from a totally different direction. No one, not even the

WOMEN IN THE REVOLUTION

Mexican women were essential to the revolution in a number of ways. They were involved in politics, were strong advocates for the causes they believed in, and participated in life on the battlefields [as *soldaderas*, female soldiers]. The female political figures [such as Dolores Jimenez y Muro and Hermila Galindo] were probably the most important and influential women in the Mexican Revolution. They were prominent political activists, thinkers, writers, role models, and were fearless in their pursuit of their goals. . . . Both upper and lower class women managed to [rise] high in the ranks of politics despite the inequalities they had to face, and gained the respect of men and women alike.

Tereza Jandura, *Revolutionary Mexican Women*. www.u.arizona.edu/ic/mcbride/ws200/mex-jand.htm.

most trusted officer of his staff, knows the least of his plans until he is ready for action.

When [Francisco] Madero [initiator of the Mexican Revolution] took the field in 1910, Villa was still an outlaw. Perhaps, as his enemies say, he saw a chance to whitewash himself; perhaps, as seems probable, he was inspired by the Revolution of the peons [uprising of peasants during the early days of the revolution]. Anyway, about three months after they rose in arms, Villa suddenly appeared in El Paso [Texas] and put himself, his band, his knowledge of the country and all his fortune at the command of Madero. The vast wealth that people said he must have accumulated during his twenty years of robbery turned out to be three hundred sixty-three silver *pesos*, badly worn. Villa became a Captain in the Maderista army, and as such went to Mexico City with Madero and was made honorary general of the new *rurales*. He was attached to [General Victoriano] Huerta's army when it was sent north to put down the Orozco Revolution. Villa commanded the garrison of Parral, and defeated [Pascual] Orozco [a hero of the early phase of the revolution] with an inferior force in the only decisive battle of the war.

Huerta put Villa in command of the advance, and let him and the veterans of Madero's army do the dangerous and dirty work while the old line Federal regiments lay back under the protection of their artillery. In Jiménez, Huerta suddenly summoned Villa before a court-martial and charged him with insubordination—claiming to have wired an order to Villa in Parral, which order Villa said he never received. The court-martial lasted fifteen minutes, and Huerta's most powerful future antagonist was sentenced to be shot.

Alfonso Madero, who was on Huerta's staff, stayed the execution, but President Madero, forced to back up the orders of his commander in the field, imprisoned Villa in the Penitentiary of the capital. During all this time Villa never wavered in his loyalty to Madero—an unheard-of thing in Mexican history. For a long time he had passionately wanted an education. Now he wasted no time in regrets or political intrigue. He set himself with all his force to learn to read and write. Villa hadn't the slightest foundation to work upon. He spoke the crude Spanish of the very poor—what is called *pelado.* He knew nothing of the rudiments or philosophy of language; and he started out to learn those first, because he always must know the *why* of things. In nine months he could write a very fair hand and read the newspapers. It is interesting now to see him read, or, rather, hear him, for he has to drone the words aloud like a small child. Finally, the Madero government connived at his escape from prison, either to save Huerta's face because Villa's friends had demanded an investigation, or because Madero was convinced of his innocence and didn't dare openly to release him.

From that time to the outbreak of the last revolution, Villa lived in El Paso, Texas, and it was from there that he set out, in April, 1913, to conquer Mexico with four companions, three led horses, two pounds of sugar and coffee, and a pound of salt. . . . He recruited in the mountains near San Andrés, and so great was his popularity that within one month he had raised an army of three thousand men; in two months he had driven the Federal garrisons all over the State of Chihuahua back into Chihuahua City; in six months he had taken Torreón; and in seven and a half Juárez had fallen to him, Mercado's Federal army had evacuated Chihuahua, and Northern Mexico was almost free.

Villa in Politics

Villa proclaimed himself military governor of the State of Chihuahua, and began the extraordinary experiment—extraordinary because he knew nothing about it—of creating a government for 300,000 people out of his head.

It has often been said that Villa succeeded because he had educated advisers. As a matter of fact, he was almost alone. What advisers he had spent most of their time answering his eager questions and doing what he told them. I sometimes used to go to the Governor's palace early in the morning and wait for him in the Governor's chamber. About eight o'clock Silvestre Terrazas, the Secretary of State, Sebastián Vargas, the State Treasurer, and Manuel Chao, the Interventor, would arrive, very bustling and busy, with huge piles of reports, suggestions and decrees which they had drawn up. Villa himself came in about eight-thirty, threw himself into a chair, and made them read out loud to him. Every minute he would interject a remark, correction or suggestion. . . . When they were all through he began rapidly and without a halt to outline the policy of the State of Chihuahua, legislative, financial, judicial, and even educational. When he came to a place that bothered him, he said: "How do they do that?" And then, after it was carefully explained to him: "Why?" Most of the acts and usages of government seemed to him extraordinarily unnecessary and snarled up. . . .

Schools

Villa's great passion was schools. He believed that land for the people and schools would settle every question of civilization. Schools were an obsession with him. Often I have heard him say: "When I passed such and such a street this morning I saw a lot of kids. Let's put a school there." Chihuahua has a population of under 40,000 people. At different times Villa established over fifty schools there. The great dream of his life has been to send his son to school in the United States, but at the opening of the term in February he had to abandon it because he didn't have money enough to pay for a half year's tuition.

No sooner had he taken over the government of Chihuahua than he put his army to work running the electric light plant, the street railways, the telephone, the water works and the Terrazas flour mill. He delegated soldiers to administer the great haciendas which he had confiscated. He manned the slaughterhouse with soldiers, and sold Terrazas's beef to the people for the government. A thousand of them he put in the streets of the city as civil police, prohibiting on pain of death stealing, or the sale of liquor to the army. A soldier who got drunk was shot. He even tried to run the brewery with soldiers, but failed because he couldn't find an expert maltster. "The only thing to do with soldiers in time of peace," said Villa, "is to put them to work. An idle soldier is always thinking of war."

Expelling the Spanish

In the matter of the political enemies of the Revolution he was just as simple, just as effective. Two hours after he entered the Governor's palace the foreign consuls came in a body to ask his protection for two hundred Federal soldiers who had been left as a police force at the request of the foreigners. Before answering them, Villa said suddenly: "Which is the Spanish consul?" Scobell, the British vice-consul, said: "I represent the Spaniards." "All right!" snapped Villa. "Tell them to begin to pack. Any Spaniard caught within the boundaries of this State after five days will be escorted to the nearest wall by a firing squad."

The consuls gave a gasp of horror. Scobell began a violent protest, but Villa cut him short.

"This is not a sudden determination on my part," he said; "I have been thinking about this since 1910. The Spaniards must go."

Letcher, the American consul, said: "General, I don't question your motives, but I think you are making a grave political mistake in expelling the Spaniards. The government at Washington will hesitate a long time before becoming friendly to a party which makes use of such barbarous measures."

"Señor Consul," answered Villa, "we Mexicans have had three hundred years of the Spaniards. They have not changed in character since the *conquistadores*. They disrupted the Indian empire and enslaved the people. We did not ask them to mingle their blood with ours. Twice we drove them out of Mexico and allowed them to return to steal away our land, to make the people slaves, and to take up arms against the cause of liberty. They supported Porfirio Díaz. They were perniciously active in politics. It was the Spaniards who framed the plot that put Huerta in the palace. When Madero was murdered the Spaniards in every State in the Republic held banquets of rejoicing. They thrust on us the greatest superstition the world has ever known—the Catholic Church. They ought to be killed for that alone. I consider we are being very generous with them."

Scobell insisted vehemently that five days was too short a time, that he couldn't possibly reach all the Spaniards in the State by that time; so Villa extended the time to ten days.

The rich Mexicans who had oppressed the people and opposed the Revolution, he expelled promptly from the State and confiscated their vast holdings. By a simple stroke of the pen the 17,000,000 acres and innumerable business enterprises of the Terrazas family became the property of the Constitutionalist government, as well as the great lands of the Creel family and the magnificent palaces which were their town houses. Remembering, however, how the Terrazas exiles had once financed the Orozco Revolution, he imprisoned Don Luis Terrazas, Jr. as a hostage in his own house in Chihuahua. Some particularly obnoxious political enemies were promptly executed in the penitentiary. The Revolution possesses a black book in which are set down the names, offenses, and property of those who have oppressed and robbed the people. . . .

Villa knew that the reserve of the Banco Minero, amounting to about $500,000 gold, was hidden somewhere in Chihuahua. Don Luis Terrazas, Jr. was a director of that bank. When he refused to divulge the hiding place of the money, Villa and a squad of soldiers took him out of his house one night, rode him on a mule out into the desert, and strung him up to a tree by the neck. He was cut down just in time to save his life, and led Villa to an old forge in the Terrazas iron works, under which was discovered the reserve of the Banco Minero. Terrazas went back to prison badly shaken, and Villa sent word to his father in El Paso that he would release the son upon payment of $500,000 ransom. . . .

As a Guerrilla Leader

On the field, too, Villa had to invent an entirely original method of warfare, because he never had a chance to learn anything of accepted military strategy. In that he is without the possibility of any doubt the greatest leader Mexico has ever had. His method of fighting is astonishingly like Napoleon's. Secrecy, quickness of movement, the adaptation of his plans to the character of the country and of his soldiers, the value of intimate relations with the rank and file, and of building up a tradition among the enemy that his army is invincible, and that he himself bears a charmed life—these are his characteristics. He knew nothing of accepted European standards of strategy or of discipline. One of the troubles of the Mexican Federal army is that its officers are thoroughly saturated with conventional military theory. The Mexican soldier is still mentally at the end of the eighteenth century. He is, above all, a loose, individual, guerrilla fighter. Red tape simply paralyzes the machine. When Villa's army goes into battle he is not hampered by salutes, or rigid respect for officers, or trigonometrical calculations of the trajectories of projectiles, or theories of the percentage of hits in a thousand rounds of rifle fire, or the function of cavalry, infantry and artillery in any particular position, or rigid obedience to the secret knowledge of its superiors. It reminds one of the ragged Republican army that Napoleon led into Italy. It is probable that Villa doesn't know much about those things himself. But he does know that guerrilla fighters cannot be driven blindly in platoons around the field in perfect step, that men fighting individually and of their own free will are braver than long volleying rows in the trenches, lashed to it by officers with the flat of their swords. And where the fighting is fiercest— when a ragged mob of fierce brown men with hand bombs and rifles rush the bullet-swept streets of an ambushed town—Villa is among them, like any common soldier.

Up to his day, Mexican armies had always carried with them hundreds of the women and children of the soldiers; Villa was the first man to think of swift forced marches of bodies of cavalry, leaving their women behind. Up to his time no Mexican army had ever abandoned its base; it had always stuck closely to the railroad and the supply trains. But Villa struck terror into the enemy by abandoning his trains and throwing his entire effective army upon the field, as he did at Gómez Palacio. He invented in Mexico that most demoralizing form of battle—the night attack. . . .

Villa on Armies, Work, and His Future

It might not be uninteresting to know the passionate dream—the vision which animates this ignorant fighter, "not educated enough to be President of Mexico." He told it to me once in these words: "When the new Republic is established there will never be any more army in Mexico. Armies are the greatest support of tyranny. There can be no dictator without an army.

"We will put the army to work. In all parts of the Republic we will establish military colonies composed of the veterans of the Revolution. The State will give them grants of agricultural lands and establish big industrial enterprises to give them work. Three days a week they will work and work hard, because honest work is more important than fighting, and only honest work makes good citizens. And the other three days they will receive military instruction and go out and teach all the people how to fight. Then, when the *patria* [the nation] is invaded, we will just have to telephone from the palace at Mexico City, and in half a day all the Mexican people will rise from their fields and factories, fully armed, equipped and organized to defend their children and their homes.

"My ambition is to live my life in one of those military colonies among my *compañeros* whom I love, who have suffered so long and so deeply with me. I think I would like the government to establish a leather factory there where we could make good saddles and bridles, because I know how to do that; and the rest of the time I would like to work on my little farm, raising cattle and corn. It would be fine, I think, to help make Mexico a happy place."

THE HISTORY OF NATIONS
Chapter 5

Mexico from Postrevolution to Modernization, 1920s–1990s

Rebuilding Mexico

By Thomas Benjamin

Francisco Madero, the man who set the Mexican Revolution (1910–1920) into motion, was elected president in 1911 but was soon beset by enemies within and outside his administration. Madero failed to win over revolutionaries who demanded drastic social and economic reforms. One of these leaders was Emiliano Zapata, who led an armed peasant revolt against government armies. Counterrevolutionaries in Madero's government conspired against him and staged a coup. In 1913, Madero was toppled from the presidency by General Victoriano Huerta and was murdered shortly thereafter. Huerta tried to end civil upheaval by waging war against the rebels and ruthlessly suppressing their supporters. He failed to restore calm, however, and was forced to resign.

In the following selection, Thomas Benjamin, professor of history at Central Michigan University, describes the diverse personalities of Mexico's revolutionary political leadership and their attempts to rebuild the nation after the military phase of the revolution ended in 1920. He examines the accomplishments of Presidents Álvaro Obregón, Plutarco Calles, Lázaro Cárdenas, and Manuel Ávila Camacho as they expanded the power of the presidency and reformed Mexican society from the 1920s to the 1940s. As Benjamin points out, change came slowly and haltingly to Mexico and with considerable controversy and violence. One of the most important changes involved the breakup of haciendas (large estates) and the redistribution of land to peasants in the form of ejidos (land held communally by peasant farmers who share the work and the profits). Industrial workers also achieved important rights during the 1920s and 1930s. In addition, women gained access to the workplace and to education, which became a key factor in the nation's development.

The idealistic and the hardheaded revolutionaries in power during the 1920s and 1930s worked with multitudes of everyday Mexicans to rebuild the country. Their objective was not simply to repair the damage left from nearly ten years of political upheaval and civil war but to reconstruct the nation on a new basis, to regenerate Mexico and its people. Their many and varied efforts to rebuild Mexico constitute one of the most extraordinary episodes not only in that nation's history but also in the world upheavals of the 20th century. A nation organized for the benefit of peasants and workers was under construction; a fundamental change in spirit and structure was taking place. Then, in the 1940s, Mexicans chose a different course and abandoned their remarkable experiment in social democracy.

The very fluidity of the power and interests that existed at every political level in the 1920s and 1930s made the reform process uncertain and imperfect, conflicted and often violent, uneven across the country, and subject to slowdowns. In retrospect we can detect an unfolding process. At the state and local levels, revolutionary leaders nurtured radicalism, encouraged popular mobilization, attacked the Catholic Church, built schools, and redistributed land. In the 1920s, national leaders too were pushed into reform by popular politics more than they wished. During the early 1930s, under the pressure of the Great Depression a revolutionary momentum seeking radical reconstruction emerged from localities, the provinces, and mass organizations and captured the leadership of the ruling "revolutionary family," a fractious coalition of self-made generals, provincial strongmen, and agrarian and labor leaders. With strong presidential leadership supported by a new official revolutionary party from above, and mass mobilization from below, reformers sought to consummate the Mexican Revolution. . . .

The Effects of Revolution

For the ten years from 1910 to 1920, Mexicans devoted most of their energy to war and destruction. When the officially proclaimed era of peace and reconstruction began in 1920, the nation's population was smaller and poorer. By any measure the cost of those ten years was enormous. The 1921 census counted more than 800,000 fewer people than the country had had 11 years before. Most of the missing, however, were émigrés in the United States, whose number would increase during the 1920s as well. The largest number of deaths came as the result of two epidemics. Famine also took many lives during the worst mid-decade years. The decline in population naturally reduced the working population, perhaps by as much as half a million farmworkers, factory workers, and miners.

The national system of railroads, the proudest accomplishment of those known as *científicos*, supporters of the dictator Porfirio Díaz, was bankrupt and in ruins. More than a thousand miles of telegraph lines were destroyed out of a total of only some 20,000 miles in a nation more than twice as large as Texas. It would take more than a decade to repair the damages and losses, especially since military uprisings in the 1920s only added to the problem.

During the decade, agricultural and mining production had fallen by half. The hacienda system, an economic sector composed of agricultural estates, survived the armed revolution, but thousands of estates were destroyed or simply disappeared. The only sector of the economy to experience growth in this decade was petroleum, which had succeeded to the degree that by the early 1920s Mexico was one of the largest producers in the world. The foreign debt was an astonishing $1 billion, and interest payments were overdue. Foreign governments, the United States in particular, were demanding compensation for damages incurred by their citizens. However, the bloated revolutionary army took more than 60 percent of the national budget. As a result of all these factors, Mexico's economy did not experience sustained growth until the 1940s.

National reconstruction, to say nothing of meaningful reform, would require an enormous investment and years of effort under the best of conditions. Yet favorable conditions were hard to find in the 1920s and 1930s. Nationally, military rebellions and popular uprisings consumed scarce resources. Violence persisted at the local level throughout the country for the entire period. The world economic depression of the 1930s hit Mexico hard and was compounded by the forced repatriation of 300,000 to 400,000 migrant workers from the United States.

These tremendous costs of revolution were the price the nation paid for the Constitution of 1917, arguably the most progressive charter in the world. This document provided the basic plan for the rebuilding project. Its designated articles became revolutionary symbols. Yet in 1920, the provisions of the constitution were, with only a few exceptions, little more than promises on paper. No enabling legislation had been passed by Congress. It seemed that the cost had been great, the result pitifully small.

The constitution nevertheless proved to be a powerful goal and instrument. It was the bridge between the popular mobilization of the decade after 1910 and the revolutionary reforms of the

1920s and 1930s. The victorious revolutionary generals used it to justify a new political order that included organized peasants and workers. Ordinary people allied with populist political leaders used the constitution to rebuild the nation. It was the Revolution in law, but it meant little until the Revolution became government.

The armed struggle of the second decade of the [twentieth] century progressively destroyed the national state. Congress was dissolved by General Victoriano Huerta in 1913, the federal army was defeated and extinguished by the summer of 1914, the courts of law simply disappeared as revolutionary justice was dispensed by new generals, and the various states and localities became the fiefdoms of strongmen. President Venustiano Carranza (1917–20), the first president elected under the new Constitution of 1917, attempted to restore order, recentralize authority and rebuild the state. But his regime practically ignored the constitution and the new political reality of postrevolutionary Mexico: the entry of peasants and workers into local and regional politics. When most of the revolutionary army rebelled in 1920 in support of General Alvaro Obregón (president, 1920–24), Carranza had no popular support to draw upon. Future leaders learned this lesson, for Carranza's government was the last government to fall to armed rebellion in the 20th century. . . .

President Obregón

The new president was the undisputed caudillo (political boss) of the Revolution. He was undefeated in battle, fiercely anticlerical, and a friend of peasants and workers. Obregón's reputation was formidable, untainted as he was by the mistakes and corruption of the last years of the Carranza regime. He was, in fact, more the pragmatic politician and capitalist than the social revolutionary. He did recognize the need for redistribution of land here and there in order to pacify those in the countryside. And he made an alliance with organized labor to offset the political power of ambitious generals. Yet beneath these poses Obregón was nothing if not practical. He believed that Mexico desperately needed economic recovery and growth, to be based on commercial agriculture and a small industrial sector. Government's role, for Obregón, was important. But what was central, he believed, was the conciliation of class interests that would bring peace and progress. . . .

During the 1920s, the most fertile political experimentation took place in the states. With Carranza out of the way, reformers and, in a few states, determined radicals ascended to the governor's palace. The president needed their political support, and they needed his. These governors began to create agrarian and labor organizations (in some states arming them) and to form mass-based political parties. With this backing they started to implement reforms and further encourage and consolidate popular mobilization. In 1923, the American journalist Carleton Beals praised these "experimental laboratories" where "for the first time in Mexican history, a fundamentally new method of social control has been evolved."

Governor Adalberto Tejeda of Veracruz encouraged the organization of labor unions, agrarian leagues, and socialist parties. He made an alliance with the local Communist Party to establish the League of Agrarian Communities and Peasant Syndicates of the State of Veracruz. Similar official agrarian leagues were organized in Michoacán, Aguascalientes, Chiapas, and many other states. The Veracruz league provided the nucleus of the National Peasant League, which was formed in 1926 with a membership of 300,000. In the southeastern state of Yucatán, Governor Felipe Carrillo Puerto took office in 1922, proclaiming the "first socialist government in the Americas." His Leagues of Resistance recruited and organized Maya peasants to advance land reform and the unionization of agricultural workers. . . .

Governor Tomás Garrido Canabal in the state of Tabasco organized a labor-peasant federation that provided a mass base for his radical Socialist Party of Tabasco. Garrido's radicalism leaned more in the direction of cultural than economic restructuring. In particular, his government sought to break the hold of the Catholic Church on the minds and souls of Tabascans. In the northeastern state of Tamaulipas, Governor Emilio Portes Gil built his Border Socialist Party on a foundation of local agrarian leagues and labor unions. Like many official revolutionaries at the state level, Portes Gil pursued a moral offensive to mold a new Mexican citizen. Through prohibitions and regulations this governor attempted to reduce gambling, blood sports, drinking and drunkenness, prostitution, and other "counterrevolutionary" vices. . . .

President and Strongman: Calles

Alvaro Obregón, as the self-proclaimed heir to Francisco Madero (who campaigned and ultimately rebelled for "Effective suffrage and no reelection"), and because of the constitutional restriction against it, could not stand for reelection in 1924. An election, however, as 1920 had certainly revealed, was an invitation for political intrigue leading to a military uprising. Although the caudillo was prepared, conflict was unavoidable. The Sonorans patched up relations with the United States during the Bucareli Conference, so named after a street in Mexico City, in the spring of 1923. Then in July the unpredictable Pancho Villa was gunned down near his hacienda in Parral, Chihuahua, which prevented any rebellion or interference on his part. The United States extended formal diplomatic recognition in August. Within days, Plutarco Elías Calles, the minister of the interior, declared his candidacy for the presidency. Obregón had chosen his successor. . . . In July the 47-year-old Calles, reputedly more radical and nationalist than Obregón, was elected president for the term 1924–28. He traveled to Europe before his inauguration to study industry and cooperatives in social democratic Germany. Obregón returned to his farm in Sonora, declaring proudly, "I am going to leave by the front door of the National Palace, bathed in the esteem and affection of my people." . . .

New president Calles built upon the accomplishments of his predecessor. His regime's alliance with labor was solidified by the appointment of CROM [Regional Confederation of Mexican Workers] boss Luis Morones as minister of industry, commerce, and labor. Under him, land redistribution was accelerated, more rural schools built, the railroad system aggressively expanded. Reflecting the temper of the times, Calles expanded the economic role of the national state. A central bank, the Bank of Mexico, was created in 1925. The following year a new National Bank of Agricultural Credit began to finance local and regional cooperative societies. The government built irrigation projects around the country, a new system of highways, and agricultural colleges to modernize that sector.

Presidential power under Calles expanded at the expense of a more professionalized military and increasingly dependent state governments. During Calles's term the army was reduced to 40,000 soldiers, and 25 governors were deposed in 15 different states. There were also fewer radical leaders at the state and local level, although by now all the state governments practiced some form of mass politics through labor and agrarian alliances.

Two powers, the United States and the Catholic Church, resisted the expansion of the revolutionary state. Washington began to see the Calles regime as Bolshevik [the party that seized power in Russia in 1917], to the degree that hysteria over "Soviet Mexico" produced a war scare in 1927. As before, the real issue was oil regulation. The church suspended the hearing of mass in 1926 when provocative anticlerical laws were enacted. As a result, militant Catholics rose in The Cristero rebellion in west-central Mexico. By 1927, a savage war was under way that would kill tens of thousands of Mexicans before it ended in 1929.

Reelection of Obregón

The return of the caudillo was predictable, though controversial. No revolutionary principle was more sacred than *no reelección*. Supporters argued, however, that the choice was between "Obregón or chaos." In 1927, the constitution was amended to permit one nonconsecutive reelection, and in early 1928 the presidential term was extended to six years. Obregón began his campaign with the support of the National Agrarian Party but without the backing of the CROM and its disappointed boss, who had been a presidential aspirant. Two opposing candidates, both generals, rebelled in the fall of 1927 and were shot to death. The uprising provided an excuse for a murderous purge of political enemies, from Sonora to Chiapas. Obregón survived two attempts on his life before being reelected president in July 1928. "I have proved," he told Calles, tempting fate, "that the presidential palace is not necessarily the antechamber to the tomb." A little more than two weeks later this "indispensable man" was assassinated by a religious zealot during an open-air banquet.

Obregón, as had Porfirio Díaz decades before, knew how to play politics: how to balance interests and rivalries, and how to conciliate and intimidate regional and national political factions. His abrupt disappearance from the scene led to the sharpening of knives. Supporters of Obregón suspected Calles and his closest ally, Morones. Another revolutionary schism of historic proportions, in the midst of the continuing Cristero rebellion, threatened to erupt. To try to head off disaster, President Calles attempted to unite all the revolutionaries in one common political front: a national revolutionary party.

The most immediate concern was presidential succession. In what would be his last annual Informe, or address to Congress, in September 1928, President Calles declared the end of personalist rule in Mexico and the creation of a "nation of institutions and laws." He prudently resisted the temptation of reelection, stepped down at the end of his term of office in December, and handed the presidency to a politician acceptable to both Obregonistas and Callistas, Emilio Portes Gil. The following year both factions created a federation of all the revolutionary parties, the National Revolutionary Party (PNR), and nominated the rather obscure ambassador to Brazil, Pascual Ortiz Rubio to be its presidential candidate. His opponent, the Maderista true believer José Vasconcelos, may have actually garnered the most votes. Nevertheless, Ortiz Rubio was the winner and occupied the presidential office. But Calles, now the Jefe Máximo (Supreme Chief) of the Revolution, exercised the greater power and authority.

The Maximato

During the period from 1928 to 1934, known as the Maximato, the country saw three presidents wrestle politically with the strongman Calles. Mexico City's residents sometimes wisecracked, when they passed Chapultepec Castle, the president's residence, that "the president lives here, but the man who gives the orders lives across the street." Emilio Portes Gil (1928–30) negotiated an end to the Cristero rebellion, improved relations with the United States, and repressed the last serious military revolt against the national government. Pascual Ortiz Rubio (1930–32) got off to a bad start when he was wounded in an assassination attempt on his inaugural day. He had difficulty accepting the political direction of the Jefe Máximo's men and finally was forced to resign. His successor, Abelardo Rodríguez (1932–34), "the Country Club President," served the remaining two years of Obregón's term and knew how to take orders, even if he did not like it.

During the period of the Maximato, during the Great Depression [1929–1938], Calles became increasingly conservative, while the nation's peasants and workers became more radical and assertive. In 1930, in the midst of growing economic crisis, the Jefe Máximo declared agrarian reform a failure and ordered it terminated. Certain governors, Lázaro Cárdenas of Michoacán being one, continued to distribute land and keep the dream alive. But elsewhere the agrarian slowdown and hard times in the countryside produced more militant agrarian leagues and parties.

A revitalized agrarian movement from the states grew to become particularly influential within the new revolutionary party.

The PNR was formed of state and regional revolutionary parties that were largely agrarian in their makeup. CROM was not
invited into the party (because of Morones's close alliance with
Calles and his opposition to Obregón's reelection), so Calles had
no counterweight to the agrarian influence within the PNR. In
the spring of 1933, the agrarian forces from the provinces and
within the party made their move. Led by Portes Gil, they established the National Peasant Confederation and issued a manifesto
calling for the renewal of agrarian reform and the nomination of
their own Lázaro Cárdenas as the party's candidate for president
in the 1934 election. The Jefe Máximo chose not to oppose public opinion and the party he'd created, reversed his position on
agrarian reform, and went along with the nomination of Cárdenas—his friend and loyal supporter—during the party convention in December 1933.

President Cárdenas Continues the Revolution

Although Cárdenas as the official party candidate faced no opposition, he campaigned across the length and breadth of Mexico with an intensity not seen since Madero's aborted campaign
in 1909–10. Cárdenas sought more than votes: He wanted a popular mandate for revolution. In July 1934, "the Boy Scout"—so
nicknamed by political insiders because of his personal honesty
and austerity—was elected president. He took office in December and set about to advance the rebuilding of Mexico. . . .

Rebuilding the nation meant, before anything else, "saving"
Mexicans: reforming, improving, and liberating men and women,
peasants and workers, families and communities, native peoples,
and—above all—children, the future of the nation. . . .

The new Mexican citizen would be formed in the government school. "To educate is to redeem," a slogan of the time
stated. Educators sought to redeem the child, the adult, the Indian, the woman, the peasant and the worker, the nation. The
program of redemption included not only the three Rs [reading,
writing, and arithmetic] but also hygiene and nutrition, sports
and physical fitness, morality and self-control, the fine arts and
useful crafts. Agricultural and industrial knowledge and skills,
community activism, patriotism, and citizenship were also
stressed. This program was called integral or functional education
(creating "Action Schools") by its original proponent, the pro-

gressive U.S. reformer John Dewey. . . .

Congress amended the constitution to include socialist education in December 1934. President Cárdenas gave the job of implementing it to Ignacio García Téllez, the new SEP [education] minister. The new so-called socialist schools were in fact the old Action Schools, but now with an ideological mission. "Our socialistic education attempts to inculcate in our children a true sympathy for the working classes and for the ideals of the Revolution," Ramón Beteta [a member of Cárdenas's think tank] wrote in 1937. "We want to convince them of the benefits of land distribution and the protection of labor; we want them to realize the necessity of protecting the country's natural resources and to appreciate the dignity of work." New textbooks emphasized agrarianism and the dignity of labor, a materialist approach to history, and the new Mexicanized national identity. Building on the efforts of the 1920s, teachers put particular emphasis on replacing the traditional religious calendar with a new patriotic and revolutionary calendar of national holidays celebrating the great men and women—revolutionaries all—of Mexican history. . . .

Women's Rights and the Education of Indians

The deep and apparent religiosity of Mexican women convinced many male revolutionaries in the 1920s and 1930s that instituting woman suffrage would advance "reactionary" interests. A small but persistent women's movement that had emerged from the Revolution was campaigning for the right to vote. However, from 1920 to 1934, only four states granted women the vote—Yucatán in 1922, San Luis Potosí in 1923, Chiapas in 1925, and Tabasco in 1934—two of which later revoked it.

"Women must organize," Lázaro Cárdenas stated in a campaign speech, "so that the home shall cease to be looked upon as a prison for them." And organize they did. In 1934, the Revolutionary Feminist Party supported Cárdenas; a year later the new president incorporated the party into the PNR. This step started things moving. Several states then granted woman suffrage, and the PNR granted women full membership as well as the vote in party primaries.

Pressured by a hunger strike staged outside his home, Cárdenas agreed in 1937 to send an amendment to Congress providing women the vote. The amendment passed both chambers in

1938 and was sent to the states for ratification. After all 28 states approved it late in the year, the constitutional amendment and a new national election law were placed before Congress for final approval in 1939. But there the initiative languished. By 1939, a growing conservative opposition to the government and the official party, and the start of the next presidential campaign, combined to produce second thoughts within the ranks of the revolutionaries. The influence of President Cárdenas, now a lame duck [political leader who is not up for reelection], was fading fast. The old concern about Mexican women's supposed innate conservatism in the middle of a crucial tight election led to legislative inaction.

Less controversial than socialist education and woman suffrage was the Cárdenista policy and ideology regarding Indians called *indigenismo*, or indigenism. The folk and cultural nationalism that became more influential in the 1920s flew in the face of the earlier Mexican objective of "civilizing" the Indians and turning them into Mexicans. "Revolutionary Mexico," Moisés Sáenz noted, "has developed a new conscience about the Indian." Yet old prejudices faded slowly. In Chiapas, one of the states with the largest native populations, the state Department of Indigenous Protection initiated in 1934 a "pants campaign" to force the Indians to abandon their traditional costume and wear trousers. Despite regional holdouts such as Chiapas, by the 1930s revolutionary intellectuals believed that government policy should promote the social, economic, and spiritual emancipation of the Indians while preserving the best characteristics and habits of native culture. . . .

Indigenous education programs remained with the Ministry of Public Education. In the early 1930s, SEP established regional Centers of Indigenous Education, in effect residential colleges, to educate boys and girls in the mid- to late-teen years. In 1937, the ministry created the Department of Indigenous Education, which supervised 33 regional centers. As in the rural primary schools, integral education—learning by doing—was the preferred method in these centers. There students built their own houses, tended a garden, formed cooperatives, learned different arts and crafts, dances, songs, and games, and used machinery and modern tools. Graduates were expected to return to their villages and put in practice the lessons learned. . . .

Agrarian reform was not simply a legal, bureaucratic, and political process but a violent struggle that continued in many localities for years on end. In the 1920s and 1930s, rural society remained a battlefield of the Mexican Revolution. Landowners in defense of the "sacred" principle of private property frequently had agrarian leaders murdered. Haciendas [large estates] organized armed "white guards" in the name of defense, and peasants involved in agrarian organizations were sometimes hanged from roadside trees as a warning. The peasants fought back, burning haciendas and killing landowners. In several states radical governors armed peasant militias. The opposing forces often met at election time to fight for control of local voting stations. . . .

In early 1934, President Abelardo Rodríguez created a new, autonomous Agrarian Department, which immediately accelerated land distribution. In March a new agrarian code was approved that revolutionized the [land] reform process. For the first time, resident hacienda workers were given the right to petition for land, while lands producing export crops were brought under the purview of agrarian reform. Reform was simplified and centralized as well, giving the president new powers to push reform. Two years later Congress gave the president the authority to expropriate private property and enterprises.

During 1935, Cárdenas's first year in office, land grants quadrupled. His most dramatic agrarian actions came after the termination of the Maximato in 1936. Starting with the Laguna region in northern Mexico, an area of large cotton estates, the president began to expropriate the richest zones of commercial agriculture in the country. Three hundred communal ejidos [farms] on 600,000 acres were established in the Laguna, benefiting 30,000 peasants. Once they had organized cooperative societies, the new National Ejidal Credit Bank extended financing for hundreds of tractors and other farm implements. Similar actions followed in the henequen plantation zone of Yucatán (August 1937), in the Yaqui Valley in the state of Sonora (December 1937), on the Cusi family haciendas in Michoacán and the sugar plantations of Sinaloa (1938), and in the coffee plantation zone of Chiapas (April 1940).

"We have chosen the ejido," Ramón Beteta, one of Cárdenas's ideologues, stated in 1935, "as the center of our rural economy." During the course of the Cárdenas administration some 50 million acres were distributed to nearly 800,000 peasants. More than 11,000 new ejidos came into being. Land grants were accompanied by the formation of producers' and consumers' cooperatives and the extension of agricultural credit. By 1940, nearly half of Mexico's cultivated land was held by 20,000 ejidos, the number of whose peasant members exceeded 1.6 million. Nine hundred of these were communal ejidos. The great hacienda, an institution that had evolved over four centuries, no longer existed. The basis of a new rural economy was in place, with a new ethic: "We must always keep in mind," wrote Beteta, "that it is people and their happiness and not the production of wealth that matters.".

Labor

Empowering workers through unionization and putting the state on the side of labor provided nationalists with a less directly confrontational—and therefore less dangerous—approach to undermining the power of foreign enterprise. Thus, in a country that had had only a small working class and an even smaller labor movement in 1917, the position of labor in politics and the economy would change dramatically. . . .

During the 1920s, unions became free to organize and strike without government opposition or repression for the first time. With government backing and favorable appointments in relevant offices, CROM's membership rapidly expanded. Pro-labor conciliation and arbitration boards helped solidify the position of CROM unions by favorable settlements with employers and let them thereby raise wages. In 1925, CROM obtained the first collective labor contract in Mexican history. By 1926, the zenith of its influence, more than 2,000 individual unions and 75 labor federations (representing two-thirds of Mexican workers) were following Luis Morones and his "official" labor movement. No labor movement in any other country, noted Samuel Gompers, head of the American Federation of Labor, has been able to strike an equilibrium between capital and labor as quickly as in Mexico. . . .

With a nearly united labor movement and a supportive government, labor activism began to show real gains after 1936. Wages rose as new contracts were signed and the government implemented the constitutional guarantee of a mandatory Sunday wage. Strikes became the wedge for Cárdenas to undermine foreign economic power. A general strike of farmworkers and employer obstinacy in the Laguna region gave him an opportunity to expropriate the lands of the three large foreign companies dominating the region. The same thing took place later in the

U.S.-dominated Mexicali Valley of Baja California. Then labor problems led to the nationalization of the railroads in 1937 and, nearly a year after that, the establishment of worker management. In other cases around the country, whether in sugar mills, mines, or factories, the government instituted worker control through cooperatives.

The most momentous labor dispute occurred in 1938 in the petroleum industry. Repeated strikes in that sector put the issue in the hands of a local federal arbitration board, which ruled in favor of a significant raise in wages and improved social bene-fits. But the oil companies refused to pay the increased wages and appealed to the Federal Conciliation and Arbitration Board. When that board ruled in favor of the workers and the compa-nies still balked, Cárdenas acted. The president announced to the nation on March 18, 1938, the expropriation of the single most powerful and valuable foreign sector in Mexico. The oil prop-erties were turned over to worker control. At a mass rally in Mexico City placards hailed "the economic independence of Mexico." This moment was, unquestionably, the high point of the Mexican Revolution. . . .

Turning Away from Revolution

In 1938, the political nation began to look toward the 1940 elec-tion. The power of lame-duck president Cárdenas was slowly dis-solving. He did not help himself by declaring that he would not intervene in the electoral process. His opponents started to orga-nize, politics took center stage, and the reform momentum slowed. By the late 1930s, Mexicans realized that the nation was coming to a critical juncture. . . .

The Avila Camacho government (1940–46), though publicly committed to consolidating the gains of the Cárdenas regime, in fact guided Mexico in a different direction. "The Gentleman Pres-ident," so called because he was courteous and well dressed, in the name of national unity and class conciliation, ended "rational ed-ucation" and the socialist schools where it was practiced, looked the other way as church schools multiplied, and shifted school construction to the cities. In 1943, however, Jaime Torres Bodet took over as education minister and embarked upon a new liter-acy campaign that included bilingual education in Indian learn-ing centers, funding for state instruction centers, and new cultural missions to remote villages. By 1946, the nation's commitment to the principle of education for all Mexicans was undisputed.

On the other hand, the nation's commitment to landless peasants wavered. By 1943, the distribution of land was reduced by 50 percent; by 1945, it was reduced by more than 90 percent, compared with Cárdenas's last year in office. The collective ejidos were starved of necessary financing, and wherever possible, the land was divided into individual parcels. Public policy, investment needs, and changing technology all favored private farms and commercial agriculture.

In 1943, the Rockefeller Foundation and the Mexican Ministry of Agriculture established the Mexican Agricultural Project, which promoted hybrid grains and modern technology. The resulting "Green Revolution" dramatically favored commercial farmers (whose wheat yields, in time, became the highest in Latin America), but the project essentially bypassed Mexico's peasant farmers (whose average corn yields remained the lowest).

The Cárdenista vision of a rural Mexico of prosperous ejidos was replaced by a new government policy favoring industrialization. The entry of the United States into World War II in late 1941, followed by Mexico's entry in 1942, greatly stimulated Mexican industry and expanded the industrial labor force. Lombardo Toledano and other labor leaders who were behind the push for industry suspended strike activity during the war. Mexico's industrialists organized powerful business associations to represent their interests and shape official economic policy. The U.S. government helped with an Export-Import Bank loan to develop a steel- and tinplate rolling mill. Mexico's industrial sector grew on average 10 percent a year from 1940 to 1945.

Mexico's large industrial unions had watched inflation eat up wages during the war and with the coming of peace wanted a fair share of the national income. Government and business, on the other hand, feared that strikes and higher wages would slow capital accumulation, discourage foreign investment, and thus undermine industrialization. . . .

At the end of Avila Camacho's term in late 1946, the noted economist Daniel Cosío Villegas wrote an article called "The Crisis of Mexico," published the following year in Mexico's most prestigious intellectual review, announcing the "death" of the Mexican Revolution. Cosío Villegas maintained in it that the great principles of the Revolution had been corrupted or abandoned. . . .

Beginning in the 1940s, a different Mexico was envisioned—and created. The ejidos became increasingly marginal in national agriculture, and growing rural poverty pushed the peasants into shantytowns. A relatively small number of business groups came to own and control industry, commerce, communications, and finance. An increasing portion of the national economy was owned by foreign companies and investors, mainly with U.S. capital. Private farmlands became concentrated in the hands of a few landowners and agricultural companies. Wages for most workers lagged behind inflation. From the 1940s to the present, decade by decade, as the publication of each succeeding census demonstrated, income inequality increased, with the rich becoming richer and the poor poorer.

Mexico Industrializes

By Robert Ryal Miller

Mexico entered a new phase of economic development in the 1940s. The government began to abandon the old revolutionary commitment to land reform in favor of building a broad industrial base powered by urban workers. Despite various crises, Mexico's industrialization continued unabated for the remainder of the twentieth century.

The story of the nation's industrialization and modernization from the 1940s to the early 1980s is the topic of the following selection by historian Robert Ryal Miller. Miller's survey begins with Mexico's industrial expansion during World War II. Factories churned out war materials, and Mexican workers migrated north to take jobs left open by Americans fighting the war. The economic growth experienced during the war continued into the postwar era. Miller describes how Mexico's presidents invested heavily in mineral and oil exploitation and improved and expanded the nation's infrastructure. This involvement increased during the 1960s as land distribution was revived and foreign-owned utility companies were nationalized. The explosive economic growth of three decades slowed down in the 1970s. Because of decisions made during boom times, Mexico gradually fell into debt and overreliance on oil. As the nation entered the decade of the 1980s, the goals of the Mexican Revolution (1910–1920) appeared to have faded and the divide between rural and urban, poor and rich, "modern" and traditional appeared greater than ever.

Robert Ryal Miller is a retired professor of history and has authored books and articles on Mexican and Latin American history. He is the author of Arms Across the Border: United States Aid to Juarez During the French Intervention in Mexico *and the editor and translator of* Chronicle of Colonial Lima: The Diary of Josephe and Francisco Mugaburu, 1640–1697.

Robert Ryal Miller, *Mexico: A History*. Norman: University of Oklahoma Press, 1985. Copyright © 1985 by Robert Ryal Miller. Reproduced by permission.

Beginning in 1940, Mexico entered a new phase of its history. One author termed the transition "from Revolution to evolution"; another said the Revolution had not ended, it merely had been "institutionalized." Although revolutionary rhetoric continued to be used, there was a move to the right, evidenced by a shift from radical socialism to industrial capitalism. The government played a major role in converting the economy from a backward agrarian type to one with a modern industrial base. . . .

Mexico and the War

World War II, which roughly coincided with Avila Camacho's presidency, projected Mexico into an active role in international relations. Within a few days after the Japanese attack on Pearl Harbor in December, 1941, Mexico broke diplomatic relations with Japan, Germany, and Italy. . . . The Mexican Congress declared war on the Axis powers on May 28, 1942, after German submarines in the Caribbean torpedoed two Mexican tankers, with the loss of twenty-three Mexican lives. The government seized German-held property including ships, coffee plantations, and retail stores; it arrested dozens of enemy agents and interned them in a fortress in Perote for the duration of the war; it instituted compulsory military service for able-bodied men over eighteen; and it recalled former president [Lázaro] Cárdenas, who became secretary of defense. One Mexican air squadron of three hundred men participated in active combat in the Philippine Islands. (About fifteen thousand Mexican citizens who resided in the United States served in that country's armed forces during the war.)

Mexico's close cooperation with its northern neighbor during the war was an abrupt change from its traditional xenophobic attitude. The new *amigo* policy was highlighted when Ávila Camacho and Franklin Roosevelt met in Monterrey, Mexico, in April, 1943. That was the first time a United States president had entered Mexico ([U.S. president William] Taft met with [Mexican president Porfirio] Díaz on the border in 1909). An agreement between the two executives initiated the important *bracero* (hired hand) program of contract paid laborers who went north to alleviate the wartime manpower shortage in the United States. About 200,000 Mexican *braceros* worked in railroad maintenance and agriculture during World War II. (Although the program was terminated in 1964, it continued to fulfill contracts until 1967. During the quarter-century this program was in effect, 4,712,866 Mexicans participated, and bank records show they sent back home $749,900,000 through official channels, plus an unknown amount through the mails.)

Mexico's chief contribution to the Allied war effort was supplying strategic materials. During those years, production of the following was rapidly increased: copper, antimony, cadmium, graphite, lead, zinc, mercury, petroleum, rubber, agricultural products, and pharmaceutical drugs. A reciprocal trade treaty in 1942 lowered duties on raw materials sent north across the border and on a long list of manufactured goods exported south.

Because many formerly imported items were unavailable to Mexicans, new businesses were established and others expanded to fill the domestic need for such things as cement, steel, textiles, glass, and processed foods. This wartime expansion dovetailed with the administration's policy of fomenting industrialization. . . .

World War II stimulated Mexico's economic development, but it also produced economic dislocation. High profits to certain producers, amplified by profiteering and corruption in some cases, accentuated the unequal distribution of wealth. Soaring inflation—the cost of living more than doubled during the war—complicated matters for workers, as did wartime government regulations. Because the population increase outpaced the growth of agricultural production, there were food shortages that resulted in food riots in 1943 and 1944. . . .

Growth in the 1950s

During the presidential term of Miguel Alemán (1946–52) Mexican agriculture continued to expand. Candidate of the official party, renamed the *Partido Revolucionario Institucional* (PRI), Alemán had been governor of Veracruz, a national senator, and Ávila Camacho's secretary of the interior. He promised to eliminate corruption in the state and local party organizations, but as time went on his own national regime became tarnished by extravagance and graft. Doubtless some of the corruption resulted from the government's inexperience in supporting a number of massive construction schemes. Vast irrigation projects involving government-financed dams brought hundreds of thousands of hectares of land into cultivation and tripled the output of electrical energy. Morelos Dam on the Colorado River near Mexicali, Baja California, made the desert bloom. Álvaro Obregón Dam in northern Sonora had the same effect for its region, and there were other new water reservoirs in Nayarit and Michoacán. The most ambitious project was on the Papaloapan River in the states of Veracruz and Oaxaca, where four dams were built to control flooding, provide electricity, and reclaim agricultural land.

Alemán's government also focused new attention on the subsoil industries of mining and petroleum exploitation. The management of Pemex [the national petroleum company] was reorganized; new refineries, pipelines, and wells were completed; and production of crude oil doubled. In 1947, Alemán became the first Mexican president to visit the United States as head of state. During that visit he arranged loans from the Export-Import Bank and invited American investment capital to participate in the off-shore petroleum explorations of Veracruz and Tabasco—their pay would be in oil rather than cash.

The regime allocated considerable funds for improvements in transportation. The mileage of paved roads quadrupled, the final link in the Pan-American Highway to Guatemala was completed in 1951, a new freeway connected Mexico City and Acapulco, and a highway across the Isthmus of Tehuantepec was built. The government also acquired the last foreign-owned railroad, the Southern Pacific of Mexico, thereby extending its national rail network. New airports were constructed and older ones modernized to allow expansion of air service, which was vital in attracting the important tourist dollars. In 1953 more than half a million foreigners visited Mexico (84 percent of them were from the United States); they spent $313 million for goods and services. . . .

President Cortines

Adolfo Ruiz Cortines, a fellow Veracruzano and protégé of Alemán, became the PRI candidate for the presidency in 1952. After his military service during the Great Revolution he had become a functionary in the federal bureaucracy; then he served as governor of Veracruz from 1944 to 1948, when he was appointed secretary of the interior in Alemán's cabinet. In the 1952 election he easily defeated his principal challenger for the presidency.

Almost immediately the new president, who had a longstanding reputation for honesty, sought to eliminate corruption that had crept into the central government. He instituted a complete audit of the previous administration and warned civil servants that the public expected and deserved an honest government. Concurrently the Congress passed a law against "illegal enrichment," according to which all federal officials were required to file a declaration of their own and spouse's wealth at the time they took office and to be liable to an accounting on leaving their posts. However, only modest headway was made against the well-established custom of the *mordida* ("bite" or bribe) demanded by minor bureaucrats and the larger payoffs expected by those officials who awarded lucrative government contracts.

Another "clean-up campaign" involved the coastal areas, where the government launched a vast program to drain the swamps and eradicate malaria. Focusing attention on the nation's maritime resources, the president's "March to the Sea" project embraced improvements in port facilities for seventy Gulf and Pacific harbors, new interoceanic communications, creation of additional links between the highlands and littoral, and a program to resettle families in newly-developed areas of the lowlands. . . .

Land to Peasants, Votes to Women

Although the total amount of land granted to peasants, 3.5 million hectares (8.65 million acres), was lower than under either of his two immediate predecessors, Ruiz Cortines did continue that revolutionary program. The most notable redistributions followed expropriation (with compensation) of three latifundia located in northern Mexico and owned by foreigners; these haciendas were named: Cananea, San José Cloete, and Babícora (the latter belonged to the Hearst family). Because of the regime's measures, agricultural production showed improved results. In 1954 the nation did not have to import maize or wheat, and sugar became an export commodity. When set alongside the rapidly increasing population—it doubled between 1934 and 1958—the progress appeared to be significant.

Agricultural production was outmatched by industrial output, which rose at an annual rate of 8 percent in the 1950s. The dozen automobile assembly plants were a major component of the manufacturing sector, and in 1952 the government helped to establish a new factory at Sahagún, Hidalgo, to build railroad cars. Labor unrest was at a minimum during these years. Hundreds of disputes were settled by arbitration or by mediation of the secretary of labor; there were only thirteen industrial strikes in the Ruiz Cortines years. A general strike was narrowly averted in

April, 1954, when the government devalued the peso; it went from 8.65 to 12.50 to the American dollar.

Culminating years of protest and hard work by many people, in 1953 the president pushed through a constitutional change that gave women the right to vote and to hold elective offices. Like men, they were enfranchised at age eighteen if married, or age twenty-one if not. Within the next two years five women legislators had been elected; others were appointed as ambassadors, magistrates, and high-level bureaucrats.

In 1958, when women voted for the first time in a presidential election, it was conjectured that they might support the Church-endorsed PAN [Partido de Acción National] conservative candidate, but the results showed an overwhelming preference for the PRI nominee, Adolfo López Mateos. Comparatively young and energetic, he became one of the most popular Mexican presidents both at home and abroad. His modest family background—orphaned at five, he had worked his way through school—and his previous experience as a professor, senator, diplomat, and secretary of labor, gave him broad training for the difficult position as chief executive. . . .

State Control Is Extended

State control of the nation's economy increased in the 1960s. Early in that decade the government nationalized all foreign power companies and touted the new slogan, *"La electricidad es nuestra"* (The electricity is ours). Intervention in the automobile industry took the form of an executive decree of 1962 that required car and truck manufacturers to use at least 60 percent Mexican-made components. The decree also restricted motor vehicle imports, regulated the price of vehicles and fixed annual production quotas for each firm on the basis of prior sales and the amount of Mexican capital participation in each company. The Mexican government itself owned 60 percent of two of the principal firms: Diesel Nacional (Renault), and Vehículos Automotores Mexicanos (American Motors).

Labor unrest in 1959 and 1960 resulted in a series of strikes by workers who protested the inflationary rise of prices. When the National Railroad employees joined the strike, the president ordered the arrest of Demetrio Vallejo, head of that Communist-dominated union, and used the army to end the walkout. He also expelled two members of the Soviet embassy for their alleged role in the strike and arrested a former secretary of the Mexican Communist Party, the famous painter David Siqueiros, who was imprisoned on the charge of "social dissolution" (equated with subversion). As a benefit to labor the government expanded social security coverage and instituted a profit-sharing plan for Mexican industrial workers.

Education was also emphasized by the López Mateos regime, which allocated more for it than any other component of the national budget. Jaime Torres Bodet, who had served Ávila Camacho as secretary of education, was recalled to that post, where he launched a series of programs to build schools, train additional teachers, and provide teaching materials. During just one year, 1963, a dozen new classrooms were constructed each day, and 82 million free textbooks were distributed. . . .

In a familiar pattern the outgoing president nominated his secretary of the interior, Gustavo Díaz Ordaz, as his successor, and when the PRI concurred, it assured his victory in the election of 1964. But PRI candidates did not win all the congressional posts, because a constitutional amendment of 1964 guaranteed minority parties representation based on their percentage of the national vote. Thus in 1964 the *Partido de Acción National* (PAN) received twenty congressional seats and the *Partido Popular Socialista* (PPS) got ten out of the total of 210 seats. The revision only partially alleviated criticism of the official party's monopoly of government. . . .

Relations with Central America and the United States

Relations with Central America were improved when Díaz Ordaz became the first Mexican president to visit that neighboring region. Problems had developed—Central Americans were agitating against Mexican commercial imperialism and were referring to Mexico, not the United States, as the "Colossus of the North." Furthermore, Mexico's relative prosperity had attracted illegal or undocumented immigrants; 30,000 Guatemalan *braceros* crossed the border each year to compete with Mexican workers, and others arrived from countries farther south. The president's diplomatic tour alleviated friction and opened avenues of communication to resolve regional controversies.

Interrelations with the United States were very cordial under Díaz Ordaz. An enthusiastic welcome was given to President

Lyndon Johnson when he visited Mexico City in 1966 to attend the unveiling of a statue of Abraham Lincoln. A year later the Mexican president traveled to Washington, where he spoke before the Organization of American States and conferred with President Johnson; and in 1970 he met with President Richard Nixon at Puerto Vallarta. During those visits two issues were of special concern: illicit drug traffic across the border and high unemployment along the Mexican side of the frontier. The executives pledged to cooperate in seeking solutions to the problems.

After bilateral negotiations the Mexican government established the Border Industrialization Program in 1965. A twenty-kilometer (12.4-mile) strip south of the boundary was designated as a special zone where American (or any foreign) companies could import parts and components, have them assembled by Mexican labor, and then export the finished items without payment of duties on either side except for the value-added tax. Within ten years these assembly plants, called *maquiladoras*, which produced chiefly television sets, electronic devices, and toys, employed about a hundred thousand people in the nine Mexican border cities where they were located. . . .

Mexico: A Leader of Developing Countries

When Luis Echeverría won the 1970 presidential election, it was the first time he had ever run for office, despite a political career of twenty-eight years. . . . Proclaiming that Mexico followed a path between capitalism and socialism, Echeverría hoped to establish his country as a leader of the Third World with himself as chief spokesman. He said that Mexico was a developing country with problems of international commerce, balance of payments, technological backwardness, and strong social contrasts similar to the other hundred *tercermundista* (Third World) nations. In various world forums the Mexican president deplored the growing imbalance between rich and poor nations, and he asked for a new international economic order. In 1976, Echeverría proposed, and the legislature approved, a constitutional amendment that extended Mexico's maritime claim over an economic zone two hundred miles (322 kilometers) offshore. This action greatly increased the nation's fishing and petroleum potential, but it conflicted with United States policy.

Echeverría tried to lessen Mexico's economic and cultural dependence on the United States and asked his countrymen to stop emulating Yankee styles, customs, and business endeavors. "We ought to be profoundly independent in economy, in technology, in spirit, in the education of our children," he said. Concerned that three-fourths of the foreign investment in Mexico was American and two-thirds of his nation's foreign trade was with its northern neighbor, the president sought alternate sources of financing and commerce. His success was minimal, though he attracted a few Japanese investors. . . .

At home the chief executive lambasted transnational corporations and private enterprise, which he charged with "betrayal of Mexico's national needs." To curb foreign or multinational companies a landmark law of 1971 required all new business ventures to have a majority of Mexican ownership and local management control. Increased regulation of licensing and patent agreements was another aspect of this Mexicanization of business. At the same time, the government expanded its role in business—it provided more than half of the new investment capital, and state-owned corporations increased from 86 to 740. During Echeverría's tenure, Mexico more than doubled its production of petroleum, electrical energy, and steel—but this was accomplished through heavy government borrowing.

After thirty years of sustained economic growth, sometimes called "the Mexican Miracle," the economy cooled in the early 1970s, and the nation was in serious financial difficulty. The foreign debt had doubled to more than $20 billion; government expenditures—triple those of the previous administration—greatly exceeded income, and the shortfall required further borrowing. To offset huge budget deficits the government increased taxes and fees; it raised prices for gasoline, electric and telephone services; and it increased the amount of money in circulation. These factors contributed to an inflation rate of 20 to 30 percent a year. Finally, Mexico's economic problems resulted in devaluation of the peso in 1976, the first time the dollar-peso relationship had changed in twenty-two years. The peso fell from 12.5 to more than 20 to the dollar. This was a blow to national pride but more important, it caused an outflow of Mexican capital. . . .

Aiding Growth into the 1980s

José López Portillo, who had been secretary of the treasury, was inaugurated as president on December 1, 1976. His election had been unopposed. . . . Based on his recent experience with monetary matters and international financing, López Portillo reorganized the administration of the federal bureaucracy. Some secretariats were consolidated, centralized control of the budget was instituted, and the position of the proliferated government agencies and institutes was clarified. After consultation with the governors, the president transferred to the states certain responsibilities including maintenance of local highways, provision of potable water, improvement of housing, and establishment of regional cultural centers. His appointees to high-level positions represented a broad cross-section of society: labor chiefs, scholars, peasant leaders, businessmen, and politicians. One appointee, Rosa Luz Alegría, minister of tourism, became Mexico's first female cabinet officer.

To aid the nation's economy the administration offered tax credits to entrepreneurs who would create jobs by starting new businesses or expanding older ones. Four family-linked holding companies based in the industrial city of Monterrey took maximum advantage of the tax credits and cheap energy provided by the government. . . .

While industrial growth was notable, the agricultural sector performed poorly, with the consequent need to import food. Grain imports from the United States in 1980 totaled 8.2 million tons, and sugar, formerly an export product, was purchased from Cuba. Drought and climatic conditions only partially explained the lagging farm productivity; other factors were low prices, inadequate credit, lack of storage facilities, and poor transportation. Hoping to increase food production, the administration launched the Mexican Food System (SAM) in 1980. It was a program of government subsidies to producers, processors, and consumers—growers were given a boost in price guarantees, and the government agreed to compensate farmers in case of crop failure. Although the government "mulched the plants with 1,000 peso notes," the program fell far short of its goal, to make Mexico self-sufficient in agriculture. Grain imports continued to be paid for with petrodollars.

The Impact of Oil on the Economy

After the discovery of vast new oil fields in the southeastern states of Tabasco and Campeche, petroleum was perceived as a panacea for all of Mexico's problems. Between 1977 and 1980 the nation's estimated petroleum reserves tripled from 20 to 60 billion barrels. (Four years later the government decreased the estimates by half.) Although not a member of the Organization of Petroleum Exporting Countries (OPEC), Mexico benefitted when the tactics of that cartel increased the world price of crude oil. By 1980, Mexico, with an output of 2,300,000 barrels a day, was the world's fifth largest oil producer.

Capitalizing on the oil gushers, the government built new refineries, pipelines, railroad sidings, tanker facilities, and petrochemical plants. In the private sector factories converted from coal to diesel fuel or natural gas supplied by the government at very low rates. After two years of negotiations, Mexico agreed in 1979 to sell natural gas to the United States—300 million cubic feet a day. Contracts to sell oil were signed with the United States and a number of countries, several of which bartered goods or services for "black gold." But there were serious problems with the oil bonanza. It created a scant number of jobs compared with other industries; careless drilling and escaping gases caused ecological problems; a blowout of the Ixtoc well fouled Gulf waters for ten months in 1979–80; and in order to exploit the offshore oil, Mexico had to import machinery and technology and borrow billions of dollars from international lenders. . . .

During López Portillo's final year as president, Mexico experienced one of the most severe economic crises of its history, the worst in fifty years. It began in 1981 when a worldwide oil glut forced Mexico to curtail production of crude oil and cut its price, which resulted in a fall of revenue that triggered spending cutbacks. To keep its many enterprises going, the government borrowed billions of dollars at high interest rates until finally, in 1982, it announced that it would have to postpone payments on its foreign debt, which had risen to $80 billion (dollars), one-fourth of which was private—one of the highest in the world. The crisis had international implications that caused major world banks to tremble as they reconsidered their indulgent policy of making loans to developing countries. Behind Mexico's troubles was a legacy of government mismanagement, overextended spending, padded budgets, gross overstaffing, excessive political patronage, and massive corruption. . . .

López Portillo's popularity plummeted in 1982—he called himself "a devalued president,"—but the alienation seemed not to affect his hand-picked presidential candidate, Miguel de la

Madrid Hurtado, who won the July election with 74 percent of the vote.... [President de la Madrid] had served in the cabinet as secretary of budget and planning. Although he had designed Mexico's long-range Global Development Plan, that plan had to be shelved as Mexico sought to remedy the economic crisis. On taking office in December, 1982, the new president acknowledged that Mexico was in serious trouble, but he expressed confidence in the nation's ability to recover.

Part of the prescription for economic recovery was dictated by the International Monetary Fund (IMF) which offered a bailout loan of $4 billion provided the government would slash public spending, raise taxes, and curb imports. Besides accepting the IMF conditions, President de la Madrid initiated a strong campaign against government graft and corruption. Jailed and charged with fraud were several officials including Senator Jorge Díaz Serrano, head of Pemex from 1976 to 1981. The new administration also raised prices for public goods and services (utilities, gasoline, permits); doubled the value-added tax (IVA); lifted subsidies for food and transportation; abolished price controls on 4,700 items; began phasing out free-trade zones along the border (to curb luxury imports); offered to sell more than three hundred government-controlled companies; and inaugurated a program to create 700,000 jobs in road construction and public works. The new direction had positive results: inflation in 1983 was reduced to 80 percent, and the trade balance showed a surplus of approximately 12 billion dollars. Like his predecessor, the new president was a technocrat rather than a politician, and some observers suggested that Mexico's problems required a politician's skills.

NAFTA Goes into Effect

By Carlos Salinas de Gortari,
interviewed by Nathan Gardels

The economic crisis of the 1980s, characterized by plummeting oil prices and corruption and the subsequent government nationalization of banks, forced Mexico's leaders to consider new ways to achieve growth. President Carlos Salinas de Gortari, elected in 1988, made divestment of government control of business a key aspect of his presidency. With the goals of boosting economic growth and reducing foreign debt, Salinas ended government restrictions on businesses and encouraged foreign companies to invest in Mexican industry. In 1993, the president continued to pursue his goals when he signed the North American Free Trade Agreement (NAFTA) with the United States and Canada. The treaty went into effect on January 1, 1994, and provided for the removal of most barriers to cross-border trade and investment among the three neighbors. Industries affected included farm products, automobile parts, textiles, energy, financial services, telecommunications, and trucking. Under the terms of NAFTA, many tariffs (such as those on agricultural goods) were eliminated at once while others were scheduled to be phased out over a five- to fifteen-year period.

The following selection is taken from a 1991 interview with President Salinas in which the interviewer, Nathan Gardels of the New Perspectives Quarterly (NPQ), *explores NAFTA's potential effects on Mexico's place in the hierarchy of the world's economies. Gardels poses questions of deep concern to Americans and Mexicans: environmental safety, the movement of workers from Mexico to the United States, national sovereignty, the transfer of jobs from north to south, and access to markets.*

Nathan Gardels has edited the global viewpoint service of the Los Angeles Times *syndicate and* NPQ *since 1985. He is a member of*

Nathan Gardels, "North American Free Trade: Mexico's Route to Upward Mobility," *New Perspectives Quarterly*, vol. 8, Winter 1991, pp. 4–6. Copyright © 1991 by *New Perspectives Quarterly*. Reproduced by permission.

the board of directors at the Center for the Study of Democratic Institutions and a member of the Council on Foreign Relations. His articles and interviews have appeared in the Washington Post, *the* Los Angeles Times, *the* New York Times, *and many other newspapers.*

N*ew Perspectives Quarterly (NPQ):* The Mexican poet Octavio Paz . . . has said "the precedent of European integration is very important for the future of our region." Having a common market and political community like the Europeans in 1992, he suggests, would be good for the Americas. Do you share this vision?

Carlos Salinas de Gortari: No. My vision stops at the free-trade area. . . . It is . . . clear that world trade is concentrating in three-huge blocs: the US and Canada; Europe; Japan and the Pacific Asian countries. Either you have access to the huge trading blocs or you are left out of the dynamics of development and growth. And, for a country of 82 million people, to which 10 million more will be added during my administration, growth is a necessity. So, I decided that it was time for Mexico to recognize this reality and belong to this future by building on the already very strong trade relations we have with the US. Along with Canada, we can create the biggest free-trading area in the world. . . . We shall keep our autonomy in other areas intact.

NPQ: Not long ago, even the idea of free trade with the US was unspeakable, conjuring up images in Mexico of imperialism and the loss of Mexican sovereignty. Is the kind of nationalism associated with such attitudes anachronistic in the 21st century?

Salinas: We can be close to our neighbors without endangering our sovereignty. Indeed, one of the best ways to strengthen our sovereignty is to improve the standard of living through an influx of investment to Mexico.

NPQ: Mexico has already unilaterally gone a long way toward free trade. . . . 100 percent foreign ownership is now allowed in almost every area except in the extraction and trade of petroleum. Is Mexico more open to trade and investment than the US?

Salinas: That is absolutely true. Mexico is open at the border. The US is closed at the border. Goods coming from the US that arrive at our border can enter almost freely, but Mexican exporters do not have certainty of access to the American market and sometimes not even the possibility of access.

This is true in a range of areas, from textiles to cement to vegetables. . . . Let me take a specific example: brooms. We used to export brooms, which are manufactured by very poor people in the center of Mexico. Suddenly, the shipment of brooms was stopped by US Customs. Why? They said it was because brooms are manufactured in the US by the blind. So, we did some research and found out that two percent of brooms manufactured in the US are manufactured by the blind while 98 percent are manufactured by machines. . . . What we want instead of this is a relationship that gives us certainty of access to the biggest market in the world. . . .

NPQ: What are the advantages for the US in this free-trade agreement?

Salinas: First, US goods would have access to a growing Mexican market. Can you imagine a growing market of 82 million people? That would mean the creation of additional jobs in the US through expanding exports. Second, Mexicans would be able to find jobs in Mexico and wouldn't have to look for them in the United States. Migration could be reduced substantially, and Mexicans wouldn't compete with Americans for US jobs. . . .

NPQ: How do you respond to the fears in the US that free trade will mean de-industrialization and the loss of manufacturing jobs to Mexico because US companies will simply locate where wages are cheapest? This isn't a problem for the US in the free-trade pact with Canada because their average hourly manufacturing wage is $12, compared to $10 an hour in the US. In Mexico, that average wage is 84 cents an hour.

Salinas: First, those are jobs that would be lost in the US anyway, if not to Mexico then to the Asian Tigers (Singapore, Hong Kong, South Korea, Taiwan) or other newly industrializing countries. So, it is better that these jobs are created in a country where the nationals might be tempted to compete for jobs in the United States. Second, our perspective is not to have such low wages forever. On the contrary, we want not only more jobs, but better paying jobs. That means wages in Mexico will have to go up, but as a reflection of productivity. We must have the capacity to pay for higher wages by becoming competitive. And, of course, the higher the wages and the larger the employment in Mexico, the bigger the purchasing power for US goods.

NPQ: It appears jobs might also flee the US as firms seek to locate in Mexico where environmental standards are less strict.

For example, since the air quality authorities in Los Angeles introduced strict control of paint solvents in firms that make furniture, some 40 firms have moved or are planning to move across the border.

Salinas: We do not want dirty growth in Mexico. We don't want polluters here. And, along the border, we are introducing strict penalties for polluting companies. In this, we are acting decisively. SEDUE, the Mexican equivalent of the US Environmental Protection Agency, already has regulations that say any firm in Mexico within 100 kilometers of the US border must abide by the federal US-EPA standards as well as the environmental regulations of the US state near which they are located—California, Arizona, New Mexico or Texas....

NPQ: After years of protectionism, won't many Mexican firms be unable to withstand the winds of competition and be forced to close down, causing people to lose their jobs?

Salinas: We have already paid the cost of opening our economy. When we began to open a couple of years ago, we heard this complaint, yet we didn't witness a massive bankruptcy of firms in Mexico nor massive new unemployment. I think this showed there was plenty of room among Mexican manufacturers for improvement. On the whole, they adjusted very rapidly and introduced the most modern technology. This was particularly apparent in textiles and domestic appliances. In fact, Mexico is about to become the biggest world exporter of kitchen stoves. So, the Mexican businessman has demonstrated the capacity to change, not as a result of exhortations and speeches, but as a result of strong competition from imports.

NPQ: If a free-trade pact is really to be fair for Mexico, don't workers have to be able to move as freely across the border as goods?

Salinas: During the current negotiations, we are dealing mainly with trade. But sooner or later we will have to sit down and look at labor mobility. The sooner the better. I am for the free movement of labor.

NPQ: With such a large wage differential, won't such free movement of workers mean more immigrants moving to the US?

Salinas: I believe Mexicans go to the US looking for jobs, but they want to return. If we provide job opportunities for them here, they will remain. They are very attached to the land and their nation. Therefore, when I speak of free mobility of labor, it is not for Mexicans to become immigrants to the US, but merely migrants—temporarily moving for a job to the US, but returning to Mexico. . . .

NPQ: You have said that "eliminating extreme poverty" is one of your highest priorities. But you are also eliminating [government] subsidies on staples such as tortillas. How do you square those two objectives?

Salinas: It is true that we have decided to cut general subsidies because we were subsidizing the rich as well as the poor. Take the case of the price of tortillas. The richest Mexican would pay the same price as the poorest Mexican. Tortilla subsidies cost us one billion dollars a year! So we decided to eliminate the subsidies for the rich and even middle-income groups by substantially increasing the price by 137 percent. But at the same time, we determined, after about ten months of detailed research, that any family that earned twice the minimum wage or less deserved a subsidy. That means five million families in Mexico will get a card with magnetically taped information that will enable them to get every third day one kilo of tortillas at no cost at all. At the same time, we have reduced subsidies by half. A similar program applies for almost two million children who get subsidized milk while everyone else must pay the market price. Also, some two million children who previously didn't finish their primary education, because they had to quit to help their families earn additional income, now receive a cash subsidy to finish primary school. . . .

NPQ: What have you done to improve political freedoms? What more do you plan to do?

Salinas: First, freedom of speech has been here for decades in Mexico. You can open the newspapers and read whatever you want; people can write whatever they want to write. . . .

NPQ: . . . But the critics always charge that the government subtly censors the media, for example, through the control of newsprint. . . .

Salinas: Oh—ha—just read the papers and make a decision yourself. You know, I have proposed the privatization of PIPSA, the state-owned newsprint monopoly that was considered to be the source of this supposed censorship. I have also decreed the free import of newsprint at market prices. And, we are also privatizing four state-owned television networks, leaving only one nationwide television [network] in the hands of the state.

Please, in Mexico you have the freedom of movement, freedom of commerce and industry. . . . What hasn't existed is the freedom of productive activity, because the government owned so many enterprises. So, actually, we have been more rapidly transforming the economic structure while striving along many paths of reform on the political side.

The Zapatistas Declare War

BY THE ZAPATISTA NATIONAL LIBERATION ARMY

On January 1, 1994, the day the North American Free Trade Agreement (NAFTA) went into effect, the Zapatista National Liberation Army (EZLN) issued a declaration of war. The following selection is that declaration. The Zapatistas, who take their name from the Mexican revolutionary Emiliano Zapata, represent the native Maya of the state of Chiapas. In their declaration they demand that the people of Chiapas be given the right to control their own lives, their own land, and their own natural resources. The Zapatistas are opposed to global free trade (as envisioned by the framers of NAFTA) and being "developed" in any way by outside forces, namely the political leaders in Mexico City and multinational corporations. The Zapatistas see free trade as yet another way for the land to be taken over by the wealthy. They also reject economic development without social development.

Chiapas lies along Mexico's southern boundary with Guatemala. It is a region of heavily forested highlands, tropical rain forests, and coastal coffee and banana plantations. It is also rich in oil. The Indians of Chiapas eke out a living by subsistence farming, harvesting, and some tourism. Native land was and continues to be held communally but is cultivated without technology or investment of capital. During the 1940s and 1950s, the Mexican government began to develop Chiapas by building hydroelectric dams. The electricity produced helped develop other regions of the nation, however. Large-scale coffee and banana growers increased production for the export market and cut their costs by hiring migrant workers from Guatemala. Wealth became overwhelmingly concentrated in the hands of an agricultural elite while the Indians remained illiterate and poorly paid.

During the administration of President Carlos Salinas de Gortari (1988–1994), the federal government ended the redistribution of land to the poor—a fundamental goal of the 1910 revolution—and also made it possible for foreign buyers to purchase communal lands. Tensions over own-

Zapatista National Liberation Army, "Enough! The Zapatista Declaration of War, January 1, 1994," *Rebellion in Chiapas: An Historical Reader*, edited and translated by John Womack Jr., *The New Press*, 1999. Copyright © 1999 by The New Press. (800) 233-4830. Reproduced by permission.

ership and use of land increased in the 1980s and 1990s and led to the formation of armed resistance on the part of the native people. In January 1994, the EZLN occupied towns in Chiapas and seized government buildings. It then embarked on repossessing Indian lands. A cease-fire between the EZLN and government forces was later declared and was still in effect in 2003. Despite the federal government's insistence that the uprising in Chiapas is over, EZLN leaders maintain otherwise. They are especially angered by evictions of indigenous peoples from the land as carried out by paramilitaries sympathetic to the government.

To the people of Mexico:
        Mexican Brothers:
        We are a product of 500 years of struggle: first against slavery, during the War of Independence against Spain led by the insurgents; afterward to avoid being absorbed by American imperialism; then to promulgate our constitution and expel the French Empire from our soil; and later the Porfirista dictatorship denied us just application of the Reform laws, and the people rebelled, forming their own leaders; [Pancho] Villa and [Emiliano] Zapata emerged, poor men like us, who have been denied the most elemental preparation so as to be able to use us as cannon fodder and pillage the wealth of our country, without it mattering to them that we have nothing, absolutely nothing, not even a decent roof over our heads, no land, no work, no health care, no food, or education; without the right to freely and democratically elect our authorities; without independence from foreigners, without peace or justice for ourselves and our children.

But TODAY WE SAY, ENOUGH! We are the heirs of those who truly forged our nationality. We the dispossessed are millions, and we call on our brothers to join in this call as the only path in order not to die of hunger in the face of the insatiable ambition of a dictatorship for more than 70 years led by a clique of traitors who represent the most conservative and sell-out groups in the country. They are the same as those who opposed [Father Miguel] Hidalgo [who began Mexico's war for independence from Spain in 1810] and [Jose Maria] Morelos [a leader of Mexico's insurgents against Spain in the early 1800s], who betrayed Vicent Guerrero [leader of the anti-Spanish rebel armies], the same as those who sold over half our territory to the foreign invader, the same as those who brought a European prince to rule us, the same as those who formed the dictatorship of the Porfirista "scientists," the same as those who opposed the Oil Expropriation, the same as those who massacred the railroad workers in 1958 and the students in 1968, the same as those who today take everything from us, absolutely everything.

To prevent this, and as our last hope, after having tried everything to put into practice the legality based on our Magna Carta, we resort to it, to our Constitution, to apply Constitutional Article 39, which says:

"National sovereignty resides essentially and originally in the people. All public power emanates from the people and is instituted for the people's benefit. The people have, at all times, the unalienable right to alter or modify the form of their government."

Therefore, according to our Constitution, we issue this statement to the Mexican federal army, the basic pillar of the Mexican dictatorship that we suffer, monopolized as it is by the party in power and led by the federal executive that is presently held by its highest and illegitimate chief, Carlos Salinas de Gortari.

In conformity with this Declaration of War, we ask the other branches of the Nation's government to meet to restore the legality and the stability of the Nation by deposing the dictator.

We also ask that international organizations and the International Red Cross keep watch over and regulate the battles that our forces fight, in order to protect the civilian population, for we declare now and forever that we are subject to the stipulations of the Geneva Convention's Laws on War, the EZLN forming a belligerent force in our struggle for liberation. We have the Mexican people on our side, we have a Fatherland, and the tri-color Flag is loved and respected by the INSURGENT fighters. We use the colors red and black on our uniforms, symbols of the working people in their struggles on strike. Our flag bears the letters, "EZLN," ZAPATISTA ARMY OF NATIONAL LIBERATION, and under our flag we will always go into battle.

We reject in advance any attempt to diminish the just cause of our struggle by accusing us of narco-traffic, narco-guerrilla war, banditry, or any other term our enemies may use. Our struggle sticks to constitutional law, and justice and equality are its banners.

Therefore, and in conformity with this Declaration of War, we give our military forces of the Zapatista Army of National Liberation the following orders:

First: Advance to the capital of the country, conquering the Mexican federal army, and in the course of your liberating advance protecting the civilian population and permitting liberated peoples to elect their own administrative authorities freely and democratically.

Second: Respect the lives of prisoners and turn over the wounded to the International Red Cross for their medical attention.

Third: Initiate summary judgments against soldiers of the Mexican federal army and political police who have taken courses or have been advised, trained, or paid by foreigners, either in our country or outside it, under accusation of treason to the Fatherland, and against all those who repress and mistreat the civilian population and rob or transgress against the people's goods.

Fourth: Form new ranks with all those Mexicans who declare their enlistment in our just struggle, including those who, being enemy soldiers, surrender without fighting our forces and swear to follow the orders of this General Command of the Zapatista Army of National Liberation.

Fifth: Request the unconditional surrender of enemy garrisons before engaging in combat.

Sixth: Suspend the plunder of our natural resources in the places controlled by the EZLN.

PEOPLE OF MEXICO: We, upright and free men and women, are conscious that the war we declare is a last resort, but it is just. The dictators have been applying an undeclared genocidal war against our people for many years. Therefore we ask for your decided participation in support of this plan of the Mexican people in their struggle for work, land, housing, food, health care, education, independence, liberty, democracy, justice, and peace. We declare that we will not cease fighting until we achieve the fulfillment of these basic demands of our people by forming a free and democratic government in our country.

JOIN THE INSURGENT FORCES OF THE ZAPATISTA ARMY OF NATIONAL LIBERATION.

General Command of the EZLN, 1993

THE HISTORY OF NATIONS
Chapter 6

Mexico in the Twenty–First Century

Kidnapping and Police Corruption

By Kevin Sullivan

Upon taking office in December 2000, Mexico's president Vicente Fox Quesada vowed to deal with a variety of issues, including economic development, the establishment of an independent judiciary, the enactment of labor laws, the raising of the standard of living, and an end to decades-old police and political corruption. For too long Mexicans have regarded lawlessness and corruption among law enforcement officers and the judicial system as a fact of life.

In the following selection from the Washington Post, *writer Kevin Sullivan focuses on one aspect of the problem of lawlessness and police corruption: the widespread practice of kidnapping for ransom. As he describes in a series of interviews with the families of victims, kidnapping for ransom is a recent development in Mexico, growing out of the economic hard times of the 1990s. Kidnappers are not ordinary bandits; rather, they use the latest technology and methods to target victims and extract money from their families or their corporations. Businessmen, both Mexican and foreign, are frequent targets of kidnappers, which thus makes doing business in Mexico extremely hazardous. However, not all victims of kidnapping are rich or corporate executives. Maids and schoolchildren are also taken and held for smaller fees. And as Sullivan's informants are quick to point out, seeking justice for the crime of kidnapping is nearly impossible since the Mexican police are often directly involved in the activities of the criminals.*

Kevin Sullivan frequently writes about Mexico for the Washington Post. *He was awarded the 2003 Pulitzer Prize for international reporting for his writing on the conditions in Mexico's criminal justice system and how they affect the lives of ordinary people.*

MEXICO CITY—The videotapes and photos arrived every few days. They showed a young woman, bound and scared, crying out as her kidnappers slapped her face and beat her. The pictures, the sounds of pain, tore at her uncle Gerardo like a dull razor. "When do you want us to stop?" the kidnappers asked on the tapes, and in phone calls that always came between 2 and 4 in the morning. They threatened that the next time they would send her tongue, her eye, her ears, her fingers. They wanted $5 million in ransom, and they offered specific suggestions about which of Gerardo's properties and businesses he could sell to raise it.

He didn't call the police. The kidnappers said they would kill his niece, his mother, his children if he did. From the extent of the kidnappers' information about him, he suspected that the police were involved anyway, as they are in so many cases here. Police cars parked outside his office and his mother's house seemed like a warning he didn't dare ignore.

Gerardo said he considers himself brave, a steel-spined businessman, tough as his Lebanese grandparents who moved to Mexico at the turn of the [twentieth] century. But the cries of his 19-year-old niece, kidnapped at the point of a machine gun as she walked to school, were more than he could take. And, he said, the words—"When do you want us to stop?"—haunted him.

"They get one of your kids and they finish you," he said.

A Part of Life

At least once a day in Mexico, someone is kidnapped for ransom, ruining lives and extracting a punishing economic cost from the victims and their companies. It has become so common here that being abducted at gunpoint and held for weeks or months has become part of the fabric of life, an accepted risk, a simple cost of doing business.

Mexican businessmen are overwhelmingly the victims, largely because Mexico has developed a culture in which ransoms are quickly paid and the police are rarely notified. According to court records and interviews with victims and security specialists, police are often involved in kidnappings, and a weak and corrupt judicial system often means they won't be caught.

This article is another in an occasional series about how Mexico remains a nation lacking rule of law. President Vicente Fox took office [in 2000] promising to tackle the legacy of corruption that developed during seven decades of authoritarian one-party rule. But as he struggles against these deeply entrenched forces, Mexico is still a place where criminals carry out the cruelest of acts knowing they are safely beyond the law.

"Criminals do risk analysis," said Jorge Septien, a private security specialist. "They know that less than 1 percent of criminals end up in jail because there's so much corruption and impunity. The government is giving the message to criminals that crime is a good business."

Fifteen years ago, kidnapping barely existed here. But crime began increasing here in the 1980s and an economic crash in 1994–95 seemed to make fundamental changes in Mexico, turning kidnapping—and crime generally—into a growth industry. Kidnappings decreased some in the late 1990s, but analysts said they are again increasing in a society where people feel the authorities do not protect them.

Last year, businessman Eduardo Gallo conducted his own investigation into the kidnapping and murder of his 25-year-old daughter, Paola. Furious with police inaction, Gallo began a private probe that eventually nabbed the killers. He recently published a book on his travails called *Paola: Denunciation of a Kidnapping and of a Corrupt Society.*

Officials at Coparmex, the country's largest and most influential employers' association, said they know of at least 360 kidnappings last year [2001], and that has jumped sharply to 331 in the first eight months of this year [2002]. There are no reliable and complete statistics available. But security firms say the actual numbers are many times higher than what Coparmex has recorded, leaving Mexico and Colombia in a league of their own in Latin American kidnappings.

Kidnapping has become such an industry in Mexico that no one is immune: Maids are held for $500 in ransom; a 12-year-old Tijuana girl was kidnapped this year by college students trying to raise money for school; people fake their own kidnappings to collect from their own families or businesses.

Executives are still the most lucrative target, including foreigners. The daughter of the local head of a Japanese tire manufacturer was kidnapped in 2000, and the company paid more than $1 million in ransom. The chief of a German car manufacturer's Mexican operation left the country about 18 months ago after his wife was kidnapped and a $1 million ransom was paid. A Spanish banker left this summer after he was kidnapped and released.

"It's not unusual for people to take their whole families and leave the country," said the president of Coparmex, Jorge Espina

Reyes. "Once someone suffers a kidnapping in their family, it affects them for the rest of their lives. They're willing to do anything, leave their country and their business, so that they won't ever have to live through that experience again."

Forced into Ruin

Six months after the kidnapping, Gerardo said he is still too frightened of the kidnappers to allow his last name to be used in this article. He said his niece, an architecture student, was held for more than a month in a small, dark room with the television turned up loud day and night. She told him four of her captors slept in the room with her. They never sexually assaulted her, but their presence in the flickering light of the TV every night added to her terror.

Another kidnapping victim, a teenage boy, was being held in the same house. The niece told Gerardo that she never saw him, but she could hear him, listening through the wall as the kidnappers stripped him and beat him until he cried, and videotaped it all for his parents. As they hit the boy, over and over, she heard them say the words her own family had come to dread: "When do you want it to stop?"

As the patriarch of an extended family, and as the clear target of the kidnappers' demands, it fell to Gerardo to negotiate. He said he eventually paid hundreds of thousands of dollars in ransom, but he would not say exactly how much.

He got his niece back in March, but the ordeal didn't end. He said the kidnappers kept calling him, threatening to kill his children if he made trouble for them, if he called the police. Once, he said, they called to let him know they were sitting outside his mother's house. They described the place to him, told him what his mother was doing just then. And they said they were going to kill her.

"You go crazy," Gerardo said. He said he bought a gun.

Then a few weeks ago he sold his Mercedes, put his house on the market and moved his family permanently to Boca Raton, Fla., unable to endure the insecurity he felt constantly in the country where he was born. His niece is now studying architecture in Florida and his children are in school there.

"I can't live here anymore," said Gerardo, 45, a fit and trim marathon runner, as he sat among boxes in his Mexico City office on the day before he left. "We have to change our lives. I have a 5-year-old boy. I can't risk him."

He said the businesses he built over a lifetime, manufacturing and selling auto parts and selling real estate, will surely go bankrupt and his 35 employees will lose their jobs. He said he would try to manage his businesses from Florida and with discreet return trips every few months. But he said they require more hands-on management than that, and that the kidnappers have forced him into ruin.

He said he spent $150,000 to hire two private investigators to look into his case, and they told him his niece was abducted by a well-organized gang led by state and local police officers. They were too well-connected and too organized to fight, he concluded. "You can buy anyone with the money they are making," he said.

They have taunted him on the phone, telling him, "You will never catch us, we know too much," he recalled. And they did know a lot. "They taped our phone conversations about two or three months before the kidnapping and replayed them for us. They checked our property records, they knew about our cars and houses. They did an inventory. They said, 'Tell your mother to sell her condo to pay the ransom.'"

Gerardo said he was angry, that he would like to kill someone. But he said the forces against him were too strong to fight, so his only option was to run. He has never reported the case to the police.

"You work, you study, you get married, have kids, a life, stability," he said. "I was going to stay here always. But now we and our money are leaving Mexico."

Spending on Security

Pedro Fletes Renteria, director of a private school in Mexico City, was kidnapped as he arrived for work at 6 A.M. on March 1, 2001. Masked men with pistols forced him into a car and put him facedown on the floor with a gun to his neck. He was held for 59 days.

Fletes said he was kept for most of that time in a five-foot-square closet, with a bucket to use as a toilet. He was allowed to bathe every three days. Outside, he could hear children playing, families having parties—the sounds of Mexico City's warm springtime.

Fletes, 54, said the kidnappers knew everything about him, including his children's names and his schedule. He said the only thing they didn't seem to understand was his business: Their $5 million ransom demand was more than the school's total worth.

"I felt every emotion you can imagine, in cycles: anguish, desperation, thinking badly of my family, thinking I would die, crying," said Fletes, whose face is soft and round beneath a salt-and-pepper beard. "It was so inhumane."

After almost two months, after his family paid a ransom he won't disclose, the kidnappers drove him to a busy downtown intersection and let him out. They gave him back the suit he was wearing on the day he was taken. It had been cleaned and pressed.

Fletes said the kidnapping nearly broke him financially. He said his wife, five daughters and a son spent thousands of dollars for bodyguards and armored cars after he was kidnapped. After he was released, he hired a team of bodyguards to protect him for several months.

"But I got rid of all that," he said, tapping the desk with his hands, which flutter around him constantly like nervous birds. "It was too expensive, and I didn't want to live that way."

The costs to his school, which runs from elementary grades through high school, continue. Since his kidnapping, he has paid more than $18,000 to install a closed-circuit television security system and motion-sensing alarms. He pays more than $5,500 a month for security measures he never took before, including new guards at the doors and new identification cards and security procedures for his 1,200 students.

He said he'd rather spend that money for a new language laboratory, paint for the school's cracked yellow walls and upgrades to the school's 40 outdated computers.

"If we didn't have to spend so much for security now," he said, "we could make everything here better."

Companies in Mexico pay dearly to protect themselves because the government doesn't. Analysts said big companies typically spend between 5 percent and 15 percent of their annual budgets on security—sometimes $2 million or more.

In a country where more than 54 million people—more than half the population—live on less than $4.50 a day, business leaders said their heavy spending on security represents lost jobs and lost opportunities.

"Instead of investing in security, they could be investing in new factories or new lines of products," said Javier Prieto de la Fuente, president of Concamin, Mexico's Industrial Chamber of Commerce. "When you are dealing with global markets, even 1 percent is important. We are losing our competitive edge because of these concerns."

"We Don't Trust the Police"

While many parts of Mexico are relatively safe from the kidnapping epidemic, problems are severe in Mexico City, Guadalajara, Puebla and U.S. border areas where much of the nation's manufacturing is located. Many Japanese executives at factories near the border are forbidden by their companies to drive in private cars. Buses with armed guards carry Japanese executives between their homes in the San Diego suburbs and their factories around Tijuana.

Foreign companies pay premiums—the equivalent of hazard pay—to lure top executives to Mexico. Foreign and Mexican firms often must buy kidnapping insurance for their top corporate officers. The problem is severe enough that a company here has begun offering surgical implants of satellite location devices to help recover kidnap victims, although as of recently they had no takers.

Few, if any, companies have left the country strictly over security concerns, as Mexico is simply too big and attractive a market to abandon. Foreign direct investment continues to grow, but many here say kidnappings and other crimes are a key reason Mexico's economy has not grown faster.

Kidnapping has become so common that Fox mentioned it prominently in his annual state of the nation address [in September 2002]. Crime analysts say the federal government's new elite anti-kidnapping unit is an important step. But even Fox conceded that wiping out the "scourge" of insecurity was still "an outstanding debt to our citizens."

Fletes said he never wanted the police involved in his case.

"We don't trust the police, and we want to protect our families," he said. "I know of two other kidnapping cases right now, and neither of them has been reported."

But he said that at the moment he was kidnapped, one of the kidnappers fired shots—perhaps as a warning. That caused so much commotion that police came, and an investigation was started.

Fletes said the Federal Preventative Police was the lead agency in the investigation. But Fletes said his brother negotiated directly with the kidnappers, without any police involvement, and eventually paid the ransom himself.

Once Fletes was returned, the search for the kidnappers was turned over to the Mexico City attorney general's office, which has a special unit dedicated to kidnapping investigations.

"I can say they are very friendly, but not very effective," Fletes said. "I think their attitude is that once the victim is returned, the case is solved."

His own private investigators turned up evidence that top Mexico City police officers might have been involved in the case. Fletes's attorney, Jose Antonio Ortega, a prominent lawyer who heads the security committee of Coparmex, said telephone records show that the cell phone used by the kidnappers was also used to make calls to the home of a top official from the department's anti-kidnapping unit.

Jesus Jimenez Granados, head of the attorney general's anti-kidnapping unit, said he investigated the claims and found no evidence that the police had been involved. But he said the officers suspected of involvement had been transferred to another unit anyway. He said that on a matter as delicate as kidnapping investigations, police and investigators had to be totally beyond suspicion.

"People have to trust us," said Jimenez, a stocky bull of a man in a suit made for someone taller. "We think we're giving citizens results and earning their trust."

Jimenez said his office received 149 complaints of kidnappings last year and solved 70 percent of them. Jimenez also said police had a suspect in custody who may have been involved in Fletes's kidnapping. "It's about to be resolved completely," he said.

But Fletes remained skeptical, and scared. Sitting in his office, just a few feet from the street where he was kidnapped, Fletes said the police officers he suspects were involved in his kidnapping could "come back at any time."

Fletes said Fox's election [in 2000] was a positive sign, and that some things are beginning to change. But he said Mexico is still a land too often governed more by force and intimidation than by laws. He said his nephew had been "express kidnapped" this month by abductors who held him for a few hours and forced him to withdraw money with his ATM card—a common crime in Mexico City that is almost never solved.

"We've had a political transition," Fletes said. "But Mexico still needs a transition of justice."

Mexico's Attempts to Address Past Human Rights Abuses

By Mark Fineman

During the 1960s, 1970s, and early 1980s, leftist student activists, peasant organizers, and dissidents who were arrested by the Mexican police or army often disappeared without a trace from their homes, schools, or places of business. Their families tried to learn the fate of these "disappeared" men and women but usually found out nothing. Thirty years later, the administration of President Vicente Fox Quesada is opening files of secret government documents. This action will most likely reveal a deep vein of human rights abuses by Mexico's Institutional Revolutionary Party, which ruled the country for most of the twentieth century and used "disappearance" as a way to suppress left-leaning political activists and opponents of the status quo.

Places of detention included jails and secret prisons called safe houses, where torture was customarily used to extract information or punish individuals suspected of being subversives. The numbers of the disappeared who were executed and their bodies secretly disposed of may never be known. Nevertheless, families of the missing, aided by nongovernmental human rights organizations, continue to pressure the government of Mexico to reveal the fate of their loved ones. The following selection, taken from a newspaper article written by Mark Fineman, recounts the experience of Martha Camacho, who was seized in 1977 by government authorities and held in custody. Years after her abduction, Camacho and others like her doubt the government's recent willingness to reveal the total truth surrounding the fate of the disappeared.

Mark Fineman has served as Caribbean bureau chief for the Los Angeles Times. *He is currently a staff writer for the* Los Angeles Times *and writes about international affairs.*

The first time Martha Camacho saw her newborn son, he had a machine gun to his head. The boy was just seconds old. Camacho was one of Mexico's desaparecidos, or "disappeared ones," when she gave birth, bound and blindfolded, in a secret government safe house 24 years ago. Her husband, the father whom her son has never known, remains a desaparecido.

The "Dirty War"

The story of Martha Camacho, her son and her husband, Jose Manuel Alapizco—which is partially documented by recently released Mexican intelligence files—bears testimony to the brutality of Mexico's "dirty war," the government's clandestine crusade against leftist insurgents [in the mid-1970s]. Their story, and others like it, has fueled President Vicente Fox's stated intent to cleanse the record with truth about the hundreds of Mexicans missing since the late 1960s and '70s. It is also a part of the history of Sinaloa, the northwestern state where the war's legacy is felt with special poignancy: With at least 40 men and women who have not been seen since they were in the custody of government authorities in that era, Sinaloa ranks third in the nation in the number of "forcibly disappeared ones." Most of the missing were like Camacho and Alapizco, young teachers and students in the state capital, Culiacan, who were swept up in the heady campus activism of the 1970s. In independent-minded Sinaloa, a centuries-old culture of violence and resistance fanned that activism into the flames of armed insurrection for hundreds of the young. The state's tally of missing, along with case studies for each of them, is part of a 2,846-page report released last month [November 2001] by Mexico's National Human Rights Commission. Fox said he would appoint a special prosecutor to pursue the perpetrators and punish the guilty. Most of the Sinaloa missing were seized, like Camacho, from their homes, the commission concluded. Others were grabbed from buses or at security checkpoints. And in virtually every case, the commission's files state—without assigning blame—that the missing were then "illegally and arbitrarily" denied the most basic rights of Mexico's declared democracy: freedom and justice. It's what the com-

mission's report and its supporting documents do not say, however, that has triggered criticism, frustration and anger among the
victims' families.

Camacho, one of the rare "reappeared ones," is incensed: Her
husband's name isn't even on the commission's list of 532 disappeared. He is one of many nationwide whose cases fell through
the legal cracks. Never mind that Camacho had been a key witness before the commission in 1992 and that Alapizco's name figures prominently in its dossiers on other missing Sinaloans. As she
told her story to a *Los Angeles Times* reporter in a restaurant booth
in this hot and dusty city, Camacho, now 46, explained why she
was going public with the details for the first time: "This is a historic moment. Right now, the eyes of the whole world are fixed
on the government of Fox, which supposedly is a government of
change. It is time for the truth." Camacho had worn the blindfold
for more than a month before she gave birth that night. She had
been bound and beaten. She had been in custody since the
evening that intelligence officers and heavily armed police burst
into her small concrete house on Culiacan's Avenue 11, pointed
their rifles at her swollen belly and demanded to know where her
husband was. Alapizco was at work, Camacho insisted. He'd be
home soon. So they waited, Camacho eight months pregnant and
pleading with the gunmen not to harm her unborn child.

When her husband, a ranking member of the September 23
Communist League guerrilla movement, approached the house,
her captors opened fire—dozens of rounds, hundreds maybe.
Then they dragged her to a van and took her away. And then,
Camacho, a 21-year-old high school teacher, simply vanished
from her world. So did her 20-year-old husband of two years.
Secret federal agencies held her for 60 days, first at a military
camp and then at the clandestine safe house, where, she said, she
was repeatedly tortured. "When they took the baby out and cut
the [umbilical] cord that night—it was about 2:30 A.M.—they
lifted my blindfold for the first and only time. They were holding up my baby, with the machine gun pointed at him. And one
of them said, 'Meet your son, Thompson.' It was a Thompson
submachine gun." That was Sept. 29, 1977.

"Where Is He?"

"Meet my son," Camacho said, pointing across the table to the
bearded, 24-year-old graduate student seated opposite her,

"Miguel Alfonso Millan Camacho." In her tone was a defiant pride. That local trait and the history of a fierce and entrenched guerrilla wing of the Communist League that attacked police, burned buses, smashed stores and sought to spark a popular uprising in Culiacan in 1974 help explain the state's high number

President Fox Addresses
the U.S. Congress

Vicente Fox Quesada was elected the sixty-second president of Mexico in July 2000. His election ended seventy-one years of rule by the Institutional Revolutionary Party (PRI). Fox, a former businessman, had served as governor of the state of Guanajuato. Fox's assumption of power marked the first democratic transfer of power in Mexico's history. In 2001, President Fox addressed the U.S. Congress and spoke about issues facing the United States and Mexico. The following excerpt is taken from that speech.

As a result of last year's vote, Mexico now has a legitimate and truly democratic leadership. This has meant a change in government, but it is also a reflection of a profound change in the values and aspirations of Mexican society. I am, therefore, determined to make democracy and tolerance the principles that guide all government actions, and to ensure that public institutions in Mexico become the guarantors of the rights and highest aspirations of citizens.

I have also pledged to address the most pressing problems now confronting Mexico, some of which are perhaps unintended, but nonetheless tangible legacies from our authoritarian past. Among them, the poverty and inequality that for so many decades have condemned millions of Mexicans to a life of disadvantage and insecurity; the crippling disease of corruption, which has had such an insidious effect on the life of our country; and the fragility and weakness of our judicial system, which itself must be reformed in order to bring an end to impunity and to consolidate the rule of law of missing. That attitude and history also help explain the skepticism of the victims' families about the rights commission's recent attempt to account for them. Camacho had the same tone as she spoke of her husband. "Where is he?" she asked, disbelief ringing, as she intently scanned the list of names of long-lost uni-

---

throughout the country. . . .

It should be clear by now that no government, however powerful, will be able to defeat on its own the forces of transnational organized crime that lie behind drug trafficking. Intense cooperation is required to confront this threat, and trust is certainly a prerequisite of cooperation.

This is why since I took office last year, Mexico has enhanced its cooperation with U.S. authorities. We have arrested key drug kingpins and extradited drug traffickers wanted by the United States Justice Department. . . .

As the history of this country [the United States] shows, migration has always rendered more economic benefits to the United States than the costs it entails. Let us also not forget that migrants invariably enrich the cultural life of the land that receives them. Many among you have a parent or a grandparent who came into this country as an immigrant from another land.

Therefore, allow me to take this opportunity to pay homage to those brave men and women who in the past took on the challenge of building a new life for themselves and for their families in this country.

And let me also salute the Mexican migrants living in this country and say to them, Mexico needs you. We need your talent and your entrepreneurship. We need you to come home one day and play a part in building a strong Mexico.

When you return, when you retire, we need you to come back and help us convince other Mexicans that the future lies in a prosperous and democratic Mexico. My dear countrymen, Mexico will not forget you and will support you. We will not fail you.

Vicente Fox Quesada, address to the U.S. Congress, September 15, 2001.

versity friends and neighbors posted on the commission's Web site. "It's absurd he isn't here."

Oscar Loza Ochoa, Culiacan's veteran human rights leader and head of the independent Human Rights Defense Commission of Sinaloa, said, "It's a very partial list, because it doesn't include all the names of known missing." He estimated the total of Mexico's missing at closer to 1,100. "But I think it's a very important first step," he said. "For the first time, it opens an investigation, an interrogation, of a very dark epoch in our history." The National Human Rights Commission's vice president explained in an interview in Mexico City that, by law, its investigators could probe only cases formally filed and presented to them. Camacho said she hadn't thought she needed to do more after her 1992 testimony before the commission.

Mere mention in the thousands of pages of commission files does little to restore humanity to the missing. In the impersonal language of bureaucrats, the lists and statistics, they remain two-dimensional. And there is barely a hint of the multilayered anguish of dozens of families here, deeply scarred and forever changed by the many years of not knowing. "It is an eternal torment," said Margarita Velazquez, whose son Carlos Aleman Velazquez disappeared a month after his 18th birthday. Security forces pulled him off a bus near their lower-class Culiacan barrio, ripped off his shirt, blindfolded him with it and took him away as a suspected subversive on Aug. 26, 1977. Ever since, Dona Margarita, as his 75-year-old mother is now best known, has been searching. She also has been a pioneer in one of Mexico's first Unions of the Mothers of Disappeared Sons. For 2½ decades, these women of Culiacan have clung to an inexplicable, unshakable conviction that their sons are still alive. Dona Margarita said she has stayed in the house where she gave birth to Carlos and raised him, just so he'll know where to go when he's eventually freed. From the day Carlos failed to come home from playing basketball and a quick visit to his university, Dona Margarita has filed dozens of legal appeals. She has marched in scores of street protests, shut down highways and elbowed her way to the side of presidents. She has prayed and wept and prayed some more. Carlos' absence has burned through the lives of his six brothers and sisters as well. One of his older sisters, Maguy, swears she saw him in a car at a Culiacan street corner in 1988—11 years after he disappeared. She recalled that she tried to speak to him through the car window. The man in the car replied only that he was under the constant guard of a man nearby. To this day, Maguy says, she is tortured day and night by visions of Carlos.

The classified documents released by the rights commission last month assert that Carlos was one of six suspected rebels who fled a clandestine government safe house in Culiacan on Dec. 15, 1977. Five of those six are officially listed among the missing. Two of them, the government documents state, were killed in subsequent shoot-outs with government forces. The commission rejects that version but suggests no alternative conclusion. The classified documents call Carlos "a fugitive from justice." His sister Rosa Delia Aleman, 47, dodges the issue, calling him "a strong believer in the dignity of Mexicans." As for the rest of the once-secret information, the family rejects it entirely: "There's nothing new, nothing at all," Dona Margarita said. "And there are lies."

Witness T-47

Among the chief sources the commission cites for its doubts about the safe-house escape is Martha Camacho. The tough, blunt-spoken teacher has been a compelling witness against the "dirty war" as well as being its victim. Despite fears that her tormentors remain alive—even in positions of power—she came forward as Witness T-47 during the commission's 1992 visit to Culiacan. Excerpts from her testimony published in the commission's report [in November 2001] show that she identified several of the missing through conversations she had with them in the safe house, which served as a secret prison. Camacho and more than 20 others were held there. At least two of the detainees were suspected guerrilla members who, according to the now-declassified internal documents of the security forces, had been shot and killed in clashes two months before Camacho spoke with them. One of those was Javier Manriquez Perez, the same young recruit to the Communist League who federal agents said had fingered Camacho and her husband, even leading security forces to their front door. Manriquez was picked up by authorities early on Aug. 19, 1977, while plastering Communist League slogans in Culiacan's downtown plaza, according to one document from Mexico's now-defunct Federal Security Directorate. That paper was excerpted in the commission's case file on Manriquez published last week. Under interrogation, the document states, Manriquez said he had been recruited by Camacho's husband, Alapizco, whom he described as "recruiter and coordinator of Communist League brigades in Culiacan." The commission also found a report of Manriquez's death in his file at the directorate: It says he was shot and killed sometime in August that year while wielding a .38-caliber Trejo pistol during a security forces raid on a Communist League safe house. Sharply challenging that account, the commission's report specifically cites Martha Camacho's testimony—that she knew Manriquez to be alive in the secret prison two months later.

The Absence of a Father

The commission may have used Camacho's words to shed light on the Manriquez case, but all of her detailed testimony about her own disappearance and her husband's has so far not helped in prompting a separate investigation into Alapizco's fate. No one from the commission has approached her since 1992 to testify further, she said. But memories of her ordeal stay sharp and haunt her endlessly. Camacho was released—"I only imagine because they realized I had absolutely no link to the movement," she said—after two months in custody. For a year afterward, she never once left her parents' house. As for the son born under the barrel of a gun, she never let him out of her sight. Every night for two years, she slept holding him to her chest. She eventually remarried, "because I thought reentering a normal life would make me normal again." She bore three daughters and tried to forget the past. It wasn't until Miguel turned 16 that she told him how he had come into the world—and how his father had disappeared from it. "It changed my whole perspective on the world," said Miguel, who earned his master's degree in languages in June and now hopes to seek his doctorate in France. "It has taken a long time to assimilate all of it. There are times, dates, I don't know why, when I feel the anguish, the absence of my father. But it has contributed greatly to my desire to change things. To learn more. This is our generation's inheritance from the one before us. This should not be wasted nor forgotten." As for Camacho, she returned to her university studies four years ago—20 years after federal authorities snatched her. She completed her master's studies in June and is now writing her thesis. Her topic: The Union of Mothers of Disappeared Sons of Sinaloa and the impact of the disappearances on their lives.

Mexico City's Environmental Hazards

By Elisabeth Barrett Ristroph

According to the 2000 census, Mexico City is home to 18 million people, a fourth of the nation's population. Residents and businesses are crowded into a vast bowl-shaped valley surrounded by mountains. The stresses on services and the infrastructure of such a crowded city are great, and the ever-present smog from auto emissions, trapped inside the valley, makes breathing risky for the healthy and dangerous for the elderly and infirm. Factories in Mexico City are lax in their control of dangerous wastes, allowing the effluents to run off into the city's public drainage ditches. Although environmental controls do exist at the federal level, state and local laws are ineffectively enforced. Too often, overburdened inspectors will allow factories in violation of the laws to continue operating.

The following selection addresses the problem of Mexico City's pollution. It is based on the report of an eyewitness who accompanied pollution inspectors to a small factory. There, the reporter, Elisabeth Barrett Ristroph, witnessed how Mexico's environmental laws are actually enforced. The factory was found to have several violations. The inspectors negotiated on the size of a fine and received a bribe for keeping quiet about their inadequate enforcement of the law. The situation described is indicative of the ways environmental laws are applied in Mexico. The author avoids condemning the inspectors and the factory owners, however, and points to the many motivations behind inadequate law enforcement. A major motivation is the plight of small industries, which employ the majority of the Mexican workers.

O ur intrepid reporter accompanies Mexico City pollution inspectors to a small factory.

The infamous yellow smog that hangs over Mexico

Elisabeth Barrett Ristroph, "Law and Odour," *Alternatives Journal*, vol. 26, Summer 2000, p. 4. Copyright © 2000 by *Alternatives Journal*. Annual subscriptions $25.00 (plus GST) from Alternatives Journal, Faculty of Environmental Studies, University of Waterloo, Waterloo, Ontario N2L 3G1. www.alternativesjournal.ca. Reproduced by permission of the author.

City is a potent symbol of the limited and poorly enforced air quality regulations in the region. This mass of dangerous chemicals and particulate [particle] matter, created by the city's three million cars and 30,000 factories, is not only an eyesore: it is also a major cause of respiratory ailments and a significant environmental hazard.

For this reason, the World Bank and other international agencies have helped finance clean-up initiatives such as the "Programme to Improve Air Quality in the Valley of Mexico." Despite these programmes, air pollution remains a formidable problem.

This is due in part to rapid industrialization in a highly populated valley surrounded by mountain walls that trap pollutants. However, there are also law enforcement difficulties. Air quality initiatives aimed at the industrial sector in Mexico seem to be paper programmes that ultimately fall victim to political and economic concerns.

The Challenge of Enforcement

Inspection agencies responsible to the industrial sector suffer from jurisdictional and monetary constraints. Industrial inspections in Mexico City are co-ordinated by Profepa, the national environmental agency, but carried out by local inspectors in each ward of the city. Inspecting industries located outside the city boundaries requires the co-operation of a number of different regulatory agencies, a sometimes difficult task. Local inspectors also have limited resources at their disposal, and many inspectors lack the equipment necessary to perform their duties. According to Juan Manuel Muñoz, director of technical support under the general direction of environmental emergencies for Profepa, this results in inspections that rely on visual evidence. "The inspectors can see the emissions with their eyes but cannot measure them because they lack the proper equipment." This enables factories to contest a penalty, declaring that their emissions are not hazardous, but simply water vapour.

An Inspection Is Carried Out

After months of inquiry, I was permitted to attend a factory inspection to view how environmental laws are actually enforced. I met first with Enrique Velasques, director of Soil and Water Control for a particular ward in Mexico City.

Velasques indicated that actual industrial pollutants include carbon monoxide, carbon dioxide, nitrogen oxides, sulphur oxides, and particulate matter, and that general inspections measured the levels of all of these pollutants. He confirmed Muñoz's assertion that should a violation be noted, a citation would be given, and if not contested, a fine would have to be paid.

Two inspectors—I will call them Jesús and António—conducted the inspection. Our equipment consisted of an extension cord, a sonometer (used to monitor noise levels), and a Sensonic 2000, which measured only carbon dioxide, oxygen and carbon monoxide. Jesús and António said that the good equipment had already been taken for the morning inspections.

To be inspected was Industrias Yoser, SA de CV (the initials are the equivalent of "Inc." in Canada), a small sweater factory. Being careful not to use the word "bribe," I asked the two inspectors if it were possible that a fine would be paid this day if the equipment were not in compliance. Jesús confirmed the possibility.

After presenting our documentation, we were escorted to the four-kilo, vapour-capacity, diesel-powered boiler. Some argument ensued about where to measure the vapours, and finally the chimney just above the boiler was chosen.

The data generated from measuring the pollutant levels appeared to be less important in assessing the company's equipment than the visual part of the test. This involved removing the indicator of the now greasy Sensonic 2000 from the chimney and touching it to a sheet of paper, producing a dark smudge.

This spot was then compared to a sheet of paper containing ten such spots in varying shades of darkness, supposed indicators of the contamination level of the emissions. The inspectors squabbled with the director of the factory as to which spot most closely corresponded to the one measured. They looked to me for support. I declined opinion, agreeing that it was difficult to discern.

My fellow inspectors then ambled about the premises with the sonometer, stopping at various machines to measure the noise levels.

The factory was judged to have exceeded the maximum 50-ppm [parts per million] standard of polluting gases, generally resulting in a fine of 4000 pesos (US$500). At this point, António ushered me outside the factory.

When I asked whether the factory would now pay the fine, António congenially asked me to consider the wealth of such a micro-enterprise. Reflecting on its size and dinginess, I conceded that it would surely be impossible for such a small factory to pay the full fine and ventured that perhaps they could vie for a reduced fine.

António agreed, confiding that at times there was corruption in Mexico such that money might exchange hands in an extralegal manner. We returned inside, where Jesús and the factory officials were cordially finishing the signing of the documents. António whistled as he carried the complimentary sweaters that the pair had received.

After the inspection, Jesús confirmed that the factory had been levied a small fine, paid that very day.

The Goals and the Reality

This case represents only one factory inspection. Velasques says that this office conducts six inspections every day. Yet it is illustrative of the disjunction between the goals of the large governmental entities that are creating environmental norms and programmes, and the realities in the smaller agencies actually carrying out the inspections. Shoddy equipment, poorly paid inspectors, and an absence of watchdogs to ensure adequate enforcement all undermine national pollution control goals.

At a more fundamental level, the problem is that pollution has become integrated into the Mexican economic and political system.

There are many possible political motivations behind the tolerance of limited industrial inspection. Industrial regulation is unattractive because it threatens the viability of many small industries, the bedrock of the Mexican economy. Political and administrative weaknesses, especially in the face of economic temptations for corruption, are also evident factors.

Regardless of the political motivations behind current regulatory failures, Mexico faces a stark reality. The air quality of the city is damaging the health of its people, the environment and even the tourist industry. While strictly enforced laws may be a threat to Mexico's small and poor factories, continued emissions pose an apparently greater threat to humanity and nature.

The solution is not simple. The United States, the World Bank and the International Monetary Fund are calling for new regulations. But the truth is that regulations without enforcement (and without the funds) are meaningless.

Poor Indians and Globalization

By Sam Quinones

Globalization is an approach to doing business in the twenty-first century. Multinational corporations aim to eliminate national boundaries and cultural barriers as they try to capture a share of the market. In doing so, they often drive out local farmers or independent business owners who cannot compete with the large corporate entities and thus never get to share in the wealth generated by the multinationals. Because of these and many other factors, globalization is a controversial subject in much of the developing world, including Mexico.

In the following selection, journalist Sam Quinones examines the impact globalization has had on the Indians of Chiapas, one of the poorest states in Mexico and the scene of the Zapatista uprising. (The Zapatistas are a rebel group opposed to globalization and the government's treatment of the poor.) Quinones interviewed members of a coffee cooperative that was formed in 2000 by 650 Indian peasant growers in order to break the iron control of local coffee buyers. Quinones and those he met during his stay in Chiapas ponder small-scale development and what it might mean to the Indians' lives. This development includes teaching the basics of education such as reading and writing, and typing. Without these skills, the Indian co-op members will never be able to connect themselves via e-mail to potential buyers or advertise their existence to the outside world. Globalization in the form of connectivity is the key to their rise out of poverty, Quinones maintains.

Sam Quinones is the author of True Tales from Another Mexico: The Lynch Mob, the Popsicle Kings, Chalino, and the Bronx.

In this town [Bochil] in the highlands of Chiapas, the coffeebean buyers are easy to spot. Their two-story concrete houses, complete with garages and metal doors, occupy half a city block. The homes of the Indian peasants who grow the coffee are adobe. And therein lies an unexpected story.

The Indian peasants have no access to world coffee markets other than through the local buyers in Bochil. As a result, they are financially abused. Captive and poor, they pay for life's essentials by indebting themselves to loan sharks who abound near here.

Too Little Globalization?

I went to Bochil recently to meet the members of a coffee co-operative, known as Mut Vitz, that was formed [in 2000] by 650 Indian peasant growers to break the stranglehold of the local coffee buyers. Mut Vitz—"Bird Mountain" in the Tzotzil Indian language—has a small office, warehouse and packaging operation. But it still exports less than 10% of the 950 tons of coffee beans it produces annually.

All that would change if Mut Vitz had what it covets above all else—an Internet connection. Coffee buyers in other countries pay up to five times more than the buyers in Bochil do, but Mut Vitz can't contact them cheaply. Telefonos de Mexico, or Telmex, the former state monopoly, says that connecting the Indian cooperative to a major city that has Internet service wouldn't be profitable. So, the closest Internet connection is two hours away, in San Cristobal de las Casas, Chiapas' former capital.

On Jan. 1, 1994, the day the North American Free Trade Agreement went into effect, the Zapatista National Liberation Army (EZLN) rebelled not far from Bochil. Protesting the abject poverty in which millions of Mexican Indians live, the EZLN in part blamed globalization for the Indians' sad fate. But the case of Mut Vitz demonstrates that, if anything, Mexico's Indians suffer from too little globalization.

Globalization is connectivity to the world chiefly through technology and open markets. Its basic tools are literacy, electricity, roads, airports, telecommunications and the Internet. The Indians in Bochil, as do their counterparts in the rest of Mexico, have none of these. They are victims of centuries of disinvestment in education, communication and transportation—the essentials of connectivity.

Globalization has thrown into brutal relief just how isolated Mexico's Indians are. Some still live in areas that are accessible only by small aircraft on clear days. Many Indian villages are hours by foot from schools and health clinics.

These are obvious signs of isolation, but the less obvious ones are no less pernicious.

Acquiring Basic Education

On my way to Bochil, I met Juan Manuel Perez, a 22-year-old Tzotzil Indian. He is a student at the Center for Full Indian Development, a private vocational school in San Cristobal de las Casas. Perez's goal is to learn how to type, a skill that rivals that of reading and writing in today's high-tech economy. No one in Perez's village knows how to type. So, he spends half his day at the center in front of a sticky manual typewriter, a towel draped over his hands and the keys, copying government documents for practice.

Almost every student who arrives at the center doesn't know how to type. Many can't read or write. Some don't know how to drive a car. The school also offers courses in baking, weaving, farming and animal husbandry because the Indians' knowledge in these traditional activities is so paltry.

This lack of basic knowledge is also the bane of the Mut Vitz coffee cooperative. Only two of the co-op's members know how to use e-mail. Andres Diaz, 19, and Mariano Gonzales, 21, both sons of coffee growers, take computer training one day a month as money permits. Web site design remains a total mystery to these young men.

Improving Indians' economic lot has become a major theme of [President] Vicente Fox's administration, Congress and Indian and human-rights groups. The Mexican president has proposed an ambitious infrastructure-building program, known as Plan Puebla-Panama, to connect the most isolated and poorest communities in Mexico's southeastern states, where the country's largest Indian population lives, to seven Central American countries. It's unclear where the money to pay for all the roads, bridges, airports and telephone lines will come from, but few doubt the need for such an undertaking.

Much smaller-scaled efforts are already underway. In Chiapas, Margarito Ruiz, coordinator of the National Indigenous Assembly for Autonomy, shops for science and engineering scholarships to award his Indian students. Eleven of them are in Havana studying medicine on Cuban government scholarships.

"People who are malnourished and shoeless, that's poverty. It's not Indian culture," said Ruiz, a Tojolabal Maya Indian. "A strong society that uses cars and planes strengthens its identity because it has time to think how to develop its identity. It isn't thinking constantly how it's going to feed itself or its children who are dying."

Indian doctors or computer technicians? For many Mexicans, those are strange notions. Mexicans often imagine Indians as colorful repositories of national culture—folks trapped in time and natural habitat. But geographic and intellectual isolation is a recipe for cultural decline and poverty.

At the moment, most Indians face two fates: subsistence farming or, when that fails, selling gum on the streets of Mexico City. If globalization is allowed to reach the highlands of Chiapas, and if the Indians there and elsewhere in Mexico are given the opportunity to learn its tools, those alternatives will dramatically multiply. Indian economic self-determination, as with Mut Vitz, may only be an Internet connection away.

Patrolling the U.S.-Mexico Border

By Katherine McIntire Peters

By 1990 the population of the borderland between Mexico and the United States, a two-thousand-mile-long stretch of hostile desert that extends from Brownsville, Texas, to San Diego, California, was more than 9 million. Every day, people and goods traverse the border, sometimes legally but often illegally. The illegal traffic is often in drugs but also consists of humans—Mexican workers who trek across the border at night, often at the cost of their lives—in search of better jobs, better lives, and a better future. The border is also a "hot" zone where terrorists can enter the United States from Mexico.

In the following selection, writer Katherine McIntire Peters describes a visit to southeastern Arizona, where smugglers try to evade detection by authorities at border crossings by trekking across private ranches, state and federal parks, and Indian reservations. Peters writes in light of the federal government's attempts to control terrorist access to the United States after the events of September 11, 2001.

Katherine McIntire Peters writes for Government Executive, *a monthly business magazine for senior executives and managers in the federal government's departments and agencies.*

"You don't mind if I carry this, do you?" Larry Vance asks before he straps a .44 Magnum handgun into a holster at his waist. It's not really a question. Vance rarely leaves home unarmed. His home, a modest white frame house with blue trim, sits on a lonely patch of dirt just north of the Mexican border in the rolling, parched landscape of southeastern Arizona. Like many of the rural homes in this part of the country, it is enclosed by a high, chain-link fence, behind which a couple of agitated dogs run about, circling the narrow perimeter between the house and the fence, vigorously protesting a visitor's arrival.

On a warm Friday evening in May [2002], Vance has agreed to show me this stretch of the U.S.-Mexican border a few miles west of Douglas, Ariz., in the southeastern corner of the state, a hardscrabble world overshadowed by narcotics smuggling and illegal immigration. After a short drive down a dirt service road that hugs the border, Vance pulls his diesel pickup truck into some brush, pulls out a pair of binoculars and gets out of the truck. He doesn't have to wait too long. Soon, he picks up the movements of a small group—a dozen or maybe 15 people—picking their way north toward the border. Some nights—this is not one of them—he watches as Mexican buses drive to within a mile or so of the border, then drop off dozens of people who head north carrying the plastic water jugs and other necessities of an immigrant journey that now litter the landscape.

This isn't a place you'll find described in many guidebooks. It's a world where hundreds of would-be immigrants die every year of exhaustion and dehydration crossing inhospitable territory, where drug traffickers brazenly brandish automatic weapons, where rural residents live uneasily with intruders who appear daily, where ranchers frequently find their fences cut and reservoirs emptied of precious water, where trash left behind by the northbound tide accumulates so quickly that volunteers from a local church wage a war on litter to keep the place from becoming a garbage dump. It's a world where longtime residents, many of whose families have lived here for generations, no longer feel comfortable, or even safe, on their own land, in their own homes.

"I've been burglarized three times," says Vance, who has lived most of his 46 years here. Two summers ago, his dogs were poisoned. His fences have been cut so many times he gave up trying to keep horses some time ago. "A lot of people might wonder why I stay here," says Vance. "Well, who do you think would buy my place?"

Troubling Questions

Smugglers and illegal immigrants have been a fixture on the Southwest border for as long as anyone can remember. Dave Stoddard, a retired Border Patrol agent who grew up in southern Arizona and returned a few years ago, remembers that when he was a kid many rural residents would put food out for immigrants, most of whom were heading north to work on ranches and farms. "In those days, you could leave your doors unlocked," recalls Stoddard. Now, he, too, lives behind a chain-link fence with several dogs and a number of guns.

But for rural Arizonans like Vance and Stoddard, putting up with the smuggling and the illegal immigrants and the bandits who prey upon them became a lot more difficult beginning in the mid-1990s. Two trends converged, flooding the remote areas along the border with illicit traffic: The Mexican economy tanked just as the American economy soared, luring millions of people north in search of jobs; and federal agencies began to seriously crack down on the smuggling of both people and drugs, especially in urban centers such as San Diego and El Paso, pushing the traffic onto ranches, state and federal parklands, and Indian reservations where law enforcement was sparse.

Throughout the 1990s, the federal government spent billions of dollars to hire more Border Patrol agents and deploy more sophisticated technology—remote sensors and cameras, for example. In some ways, those investments have paid off—federal data show that illegal border-crossings are down, and drug traffickers are being driven to take ever-greater risks. But the fact remains that thousands of people enter the United States illegally every day, and the drug trade continues to overwhelm federal agents. In the wake of [the terrorist attacks of] Sept. 11 [2001] that raises troubling questions: If the feds can't keep drug smugglers and illegal immigrants from walking across the border, how can we expect them to keep out terrorists? Aren't terrorists at least as committed as narcotics traffickers?

It's no surprise that across the Southwest, rumors abound about Middle Eastern operatives working out of Mexico. Nearly everyone I spoke with during a week's visit to southern Arizona in mid-May had heard stories that Iraqis or Saudis or others of unknown origin had either been detained in Mexico or spotted trying to cross the border. Such fears were no doubt fueled by reports of a truck loaded with sodium cyanide—a deadly chemical that terrorists are known to covet—missing from Mexico City this spring. (The truck, which was apparently hijacked, and its load of cyanide were later recovered.) There is even a new lexicon springing up among ordinary citizens in which the new foreigners, real or imagined, are referred to as OTMs—other than Mexicans.

"It's not lost on us that if you can bring drugs and illegal [immigrants] through, you can certainly bring terrorists in," says Homeland Security Director Tom Ridge. In an interview in May [2002], Ridge said federal agencies would have to take a new approach on the border, particularly the Immigration and Naturalization Service [INS], which is responsible for screening people entering the country, and the Customs Service, which is charged with keeping out contraband—everything from child pornography to drugs to nuclear weapons. "You can check people and cargo if they go through traditional checkpoints or traditional infrastructure, but in both the Great Lakes on the Canadian border and [along] the Mexican border, INS' and Customs' task is much, much greater," Ridge said.

"We know we're going to have to expend resources to put additional people and deploy technology there that we probably haven't used before," Ridge said. That acknowledgement came just days before the White House announced its plan to consolidate and reorganize federal agencies into a new Homeland Security Department, and it offers some encouragement to those who believe that substantially improving border security will require a much greater investment of resources, despite the Bush administration's claims that the new department won't require any additional funding.

Watching the Detectives

What's striking about the situation in Arizona is that there, federal agencies are using some of the most sophisticated detection technologies on the market, and cooperating with each other and their state and local counterparts, as well as Mexican authorities, to an unprecedented degree, yet drugs and people still continue to flow surprisingly freely across the border.

Donna De La Torre, the Customs Service director of field operations for the Arizona Customs Management Center, has a view her peers elsewhere in the country would envy: From a command center in her Tucson office, she can watch operations as they unfold hundreds of miles away at each of the seven border crossing stations in the state, known in government-speak as ports of entry. A sophisticated, remotely controlled camera system digitally records activities 24 hours a day. It's a system whose virtues seemed especially obvious after Sept. 11. "Having visual contact with all of your operations all of the time has moved us miles ahead in terms of intelligent border management," De La Torre says.

The benefits of the camera system have accrued well beyond Customs. Digital records have been used to detect smuggling patterns, to review and improve inspection procedures, to spot sloppy or even corrupt Customs and INS agents, to refute travelers' claims of abuse, to help local law enforcement officials solve crimes and even to spot the spotters—those people paid by smugglers to spy on port operations. "The ports are under constant surveillance [by smugglers]," says Rudy Cole, director of Customs' anti-smuggling operations in Arizona. "In the past, [smugglers] knew more about our ports of entry than we knew ourselves. The cameras are helping us change that."

The camera system, which has been in use for a couple of years now, has proved far more useful than anyone initially predicted. Cameras originally were placed at border crossings several years ago to provide facility security, but then Customs began to develop a plan to link all 205 of the cameras and use them more effectively, says John O'Reilly, Customs' deputy director of field operations in Arizona. Given the remoteness of most of the ports of entry here and the absence of reliable telecommunications in some areas, getting the infrastructure in place for the network was complicated. Ultimately, one of the ports had to be connected using satellite communications.

"It's a great advantage to have the cameras," says Joe Lafata, the port director in Nogales, the busiest border-crossing station in Arizona and a 90-minute drive south of Tucson. Nogales, which sits across the border from the Mexican city of the same name, is the second largest point of entry for produce entering the country. "The cameras provide daily security for our officers and backup in the case of a passenger complaint—we can pull the video up right away and put that complaint to rest and protect the inspectors as well. It's really a topnotch system. Many of the cameras have tilt-zoom capability. We can actually shoot into some of the hills here and watch the spotters as they're watching us. They're there all the time and every once in a while you get a really nice portrait of them."

Seizing Dope

Despite long lines of traffic waiting to enter the United States at times, port operations in Nogales seem remarkably efficient. All

58,000 rail cars entering the country here every year automatically pass through X-ray machines, where Border Patrol agents work with Customs to prevent the entry of contraband and undocumented immigrants. The 250,000 commercial trucks that pass through Nogales annually from Mexico are diverted to a separate screening facility about a mile away, reducing both congestion and risk at the busy port.

Inspectors from Customs and INS together staff the primary inspection booths where all vehicles and passengers are scrutinized upon entering the port. Inspectors from both agencies work the booths interchangeably and are periodically and randomly rotated during their shifts to prevent smugglers from trying to game the system by getting in line for a particular inspector. Electronic license plate readers can alert inspectors to stolen cars moving south, and wanted drivers moving north. Customs, INS and Agriculture Department employees do more thorough inspections of selected traffic in a secondary inspection area. At the pedestrian entrance to the port, officials are testing cameras that use facial-recognition technology to scan the inbound crowd for criminals whose photos have been entered into a database. Every two seconds the camera records four faces, each of which is compared with the photos in the database at more than 60 points on the face. If there is a potential match, the camera sends an alert to a cellular phone worn by an inspector.

The facial-recognition technology is particularly attractive to Lafata because it adds significantly to an inspector's capabilities without placing a lot of additional demands on the inspector's time or attention. "All of our nonintrusive technologies [X-ray systems, for example] are great, but very labor-intensive. You put in one unit that costs $4 or $5 million dollars to examine trucks and then you also have to expend another six to eight people a day to run that operation," Lafata says.

For a couple of days after Sept. 11, the drugs stopped flowing at Nogales, Lafata says. "It seemed that the smugglers just dropped off the map. But it couldn't have been three days to where they started moving again." Despite the increased scrutiny of people and vehicles at all the ports of entry, smuggling hasn't slackened.

"We are overwhelmed with narcotics trafficking," says Customs' Richard Cramer, the Office of Investigation's resident agent in charge at the port. "They're hitting us underground, over ground, with every imaginable method." In December [2001],

Customs agents discovered an 85-foot tunnel from a home in Nogales, Ariz., to a flood-control channel that parallels the border in Mexico. In April [2002] they found another tunnel under the port itself. The flood-control channel presents a particularly vexing problem, Cramer says. The channel must be kept open; otherwise, the city will flood during heavy rain. But the possibilities for transporting drugs or other contraband through the channel are practically endless.

Cramer's staff of 40, including administrative personnel, is too small for the job. "My agency is very good about providing the other resources we need, such as equipment and facilities, but I could certainly use more agents. But justifying them is not as simple as saying 'Look at all the drugs.' It's difficult to quantify success. We also do long-term investigations. We can seize dope all day, and we can arrest the mules [drug carriers] but if we don't arrest those that are actually involved in the high-level trafficking, then we're spinning our wheels."

The Wild West

West of Nogales, about 40 miles as the crow flies, but closer to 80 miles if you're taking the only paved road, sits the tiny border town of Sasabe, population 32. Cowboys on horseback still round up the cattle out here, and automobiles share the road with animals. The town, which features a few small houses, a gas station and a store where the 81-year-old proprietress sells everything from car stereos to wood-burning stoves, was for sale until recently. The owner, a Mexican national, took it off the market for lack of interest, according to one local resident.

The paved road ends in Sasabe, at the small white Customs house, built in 1932 and restored in 1991. Across the border, the road turns to gravel in El Sasabe and continues south into Mexico for 65 miles before it hits pavement again. Seventy-five to 100 cars pass through here a day, along with the occasional truck hauling adobe blocks or mesquite wood north. Because the Agriculture Department doesn't send inspectors to this remote outpost, Customs officers are trained and certified to inspect the wood for pests and levy fines for violations. In addition, they also monitor the National Weather Service equipment housed in the basement of the port building.

Michael Kring, the port director, is an influential figure here. As the only law enforcement agency other than the Border Patrol for miles around—the local sheriff's office is more than 70 miles away—Customs sometimes is tapped for unlikely duties. When medical emergencies occur, people on both sides of the border turn to Customs for medical evacuations. When someone becomes stranded during the summer monsoons, Customs will stage a rescue. In negotiations with Mexican officials in Sasabe over a burning dump that was affecting air quality at the port, Kring exerted economic leverage: "There's only two gas stations in this whole area—and they're on my side. So they'll cooperate with me. You want to cross the border, you put the dump out," Kring laughs.

"We do a little bit of everything out here," he says. Mostly though, port officials seize drugs. There were so many high-speed chases through Sasabe that a few months ago, Kring had concrete barriers installed on the border. "I got tired of people trying to run me over going through the gate. Once, the gate ended up about 20 feet into Mexico." About a year and a half ago, Kring was struck and seriously injured by a southbound car he attempted to stop. "He had some kind of load," Kring says. Southbound contraband tends to be firearms—Mexico doesn't manufacture them, so they're a pretty popular import among the smuggling set—and cash from drug sales.

Inspectors here have seized 13 drug shipments since Oct. 1, [2001], the start of the fiscal year, already more than the port saw last year or the year before. There are no X-ray machines in Sasabe, just a handful of inspectors who know what a proper engine or automobile frame looks like and are trained to recognize alterations. "You look around and you see something that's been tampered with or messed with and you know something's going on," Kring says. "Tanks inside of tanks are always good—propane tanks with water tanks inside them, gas tanks that have other tanks inside them. We see wheels that have compartments inside them. There's different ways of beating us. If you can think of it, they've already thought of it."

The inspectors can be creative too. Kring usually has a canine unit for at least part of the day now, which has helped the inspectors enormously. Sometimes an inspector would bring in a pet dog just to throw people off, and, confronting the pooch, some smugglers would give themselves away with fear. Once, an inspector taped some wires to a radio and walked around vehicles as if he had some newfangled drug detector. But these days, even Sasabe is getting sophisticated technology. An X-ray machine for vehicles is slated to arrive soon, as will a tower for another camera.

The five Customs inspectors, including Kring, and four INS inspectors who work at the Sasabe border station know most of the locals so well they've memorized their license plates. They know their routines and they're pretty quick to recognize when something's amiss. But it's not the locals who present the biggest challenge at the port, Kring says; if they wanted to transport contraband, they'd know how to bypass the official border crossing.

Across the border, El Sasabe has become something of a staging area for illegal immigrants and drugs. "They're staging 1,000 people a day there," Kring says. Much of Kring's information comes from his Mexican counterpart, with whom he has an unusually good relationship. "He grew up over here and I've known his father for many years. You'd be surprised how supportive the Mexicans are here," Kring says, especially if they think they have information about non-Mexicans crossing the border. "We've had rumors of certain folks being on the other side. The ones we did catch were from Brazil. You're in a high smuggling area of both illegals and drugs. We've caught Chinese coming across. We've caught Brazilians. In Douglas, they caught some Germans."

Says Rudy Cole, Custom's anti-smuggling director in Tucson, "We get reports. Border Patrol found some documents out in the desert that looked like they came from the Middle East but that was never confirmed. Then the Mexicans apprehended some people they first reported as Middle Easterners, Saudis they thought, and then they said they were Brazilian. Of course we didn't have our mitts on the people so all we could get was secondhand information. But we relayed it to the FBI."

Armed and Dangerous

If the ports of entry—the official crossing stations—are dangerous, the land between them is particularly perilous. On the Tohono O'odham Nation reservation, many residents live in fear, says Henry Ramon, the soft-spoken vice chairman of the tribe. "The border here is just a regular barbed wire fence. We're seeing 1,200 to 1,500 people crossing a day. It is very hard on the environment. There have been shootouts and people are scared."

In a particularly troubling incident here in May [2002], a Border Patrol agent reported being fired upon by Mexican soldiers, just hours after federal agents seized a ton of marijuana nearby. (Mexican officials denied any troops were in the area and have suggested that criminals dressed as soldiers may have been responsible.) It's not the first time Mexican soldiers, or people who appear to be Mexican soldiers, have been found in southwest Arizona. Corruption among Mexican military and law enforcement officials and their collusion with drug traffickers have long vexed the relationship between the two countries, a number of U.S. federal agents here say.

On the reservation, issues of sovereignty are even more complex. The Tohono O'odham Nation covers nearly 3 million acres of the Sonoran Desert in south-central Arizona and shares 75 miles of border with Mexico. Tribal lands extend into Mexico, making immigration a sensitive issue for the tribe. The tribe's 24,000 members, many of whom have no proof of citizenship because they never were issued birth certificates, live on both sides of the border. Tribal members historically have been sympathetic toward the few immigrants who made it through this remote corner of the desert, and traditionally have helped them with food and shelter as they made their way north. But in recent years, the sheer number of immigrants and the growing influx of drug smugglers have overwhelmed the tribe.

"We never complained before, but we just got to a point where we can't do it any more," Ramon says. The burden on already-limited tribal resources has been enormous. Increasingly, young people are using drugs and tribal members are succumbing to the big money offered by traffickers in exchange for cooperation, says Ramon. And the illegal immigrants are overwhelming the tribe's already precarious health care system. In April [2002] alone, the tribe rescued more than 350 people, most of whom were so dehydrated they had to be treated in the tribe's only hospital (in Sells, Ariz.), forcing some tribal members to seek medical care hours away in Tucson.

The Tohono O'odham Nation is one of 25 tribes whose reservations cover hundreds of miles of border with Mexico and Canada. Because remote tribal lands are particularly inviting to anyone wishing to enter the United States unnoticed, and because federal law enforcement agencies may not enter tribal lands without permission from the tribe, the situation is causing some alarm in Washington. In January [2002], Attorney General John Ashcroft met with tribal leaders, including Ramon, and asked them to allow federal agents onto their land. "The meeting was very productive," says Ramon. "We're willing to help, but we need help in return." The Tohono O'odham have long had a unique relationship with federal law enforcement officials—the tribe has the only Native American anti-smuggling unit in the Customs Service, and the Border Patrol works cooperatively with the tribal police department on the reservation. But the tribe needs to boost the capabilities of its own police force, says Ramon, not just invite more federal agents onto tribal land.

Retired Border Patrol agent Stoddard believes the entire Southwest is dealing with issues of sovereignty. "I would venture to say that from Brownsville, Texas, to San Diego, there is a corridor, and this corridor is right on the border, in some areas it is a few hundred yards thick, in other areas it's as much as maybe 20 miles, but this entire area is literally a no-man's land. United States citizens living in this area are not being protected by the United States government. People from Mexico are being given special privileges to vandalize, steal vehicles, burglarize, and do whatever they want. That's why so many homeowners here are living in a fortress. That's why many of them run around armed all the time," he says.

Vance, the son of a Mexican immigrant, agrees. "My father didn't speak a word of English when he came here. He became a naturalized citizen, and he was a loyal American." Vance, who resents outsiders who suggest that angry landowners are anti-Mexican, believes that Mexico is trying to recapture lands lost in the Mexican–American War, a theory not uncommon here.

Gaining Control

In the opinion of retired Army Gen. Barry McCaffrey, who worked closely with law enforcement agencies on the border as director of the White House Office of National Drug Control Policy during the Clinton administration, substantially improving border security is not only achievable, it is essential. "I don't think intellectually it's much of a challenge to imagine us going from zero control over our borders, which certainly would have been my characterization five years ago, to significant control over our borders," he says.

But two factors will be key, he says: an immigration policy that acknowledges the U.S. reliance on foreign, especially Mexican, labor, and a more sophisticated border law enforcement organization with a mission akin to that of the French national police. The agencies responsible for border management, primarily Customs and the INS, which includes the Border Patrol, are not large enough and don't coordinate their operations effectively, he says. He supports the Bush administration's proposal for consolidating those agencies into a new Department of Homeland Security, but with an important caveat: Agencies need many more people and significantly better funding to be effective in the war against terrorism.

"You want a Border Patrol, in my view, that's 40,000 people and has its own aviation, maintenance, logistics, and training system," he says. "You want to tell them you're not just chasing migrants, you're saving lives, you're enforcing any relevant federal law, and you're working in cooperation with the international community."

Just as important, he says, will be immigration reform. "We've got [an immigration policy] right now that I think is unbelievably unfair," says McCaffrey. "My underlying conviction is that too many people in the country don't want to pay minimum wage and minimum housing standards and health care to these workers who grow our food and run our tourism industry."

"Our agriculture system won't work without Mexican workers. Our meat-packing industry won't work. The construction industry won't work. You have to get those workers on a bus, pay them minimum wage, make sure they've got running water and lights, allow them legally to send their money back to families," McCaffrey says. Reducing the flood of illegal immigrants may not stop terrorists from crossing the border. But it would make it a lot easier for federal agencies to focus on homeland security.

And it would reduce the flow of people through Larry Vance's backyard.

Chronology

ca. 7000 B.C.
Agriculture begins to appear in Mexico with the cultivation of seeds and root crops; the growing of maize opens the way to the development of advanced civilizations.

ca. 1200–400 B.C.
The Olmec culture—Mexico's first established culture—flourishes in the lowlands of eastern Mexico.

ca. A.D. 200–900
Zapotec culture flourishes around the ceremonial city of Monte Albán.

ca. 300–600
The Mayan culture of the Yucatán Peninsula, notable for its hieroglyphics, use of the calendar, and numbering system, spreads throughout southeastern Mexico.

ca. 600–900
Mayan advancements in science and art reach their apex at cities such as Copán, Palenque, and Uxmal.

ca. 800
The Toltecs—a culture that fused Mayan, Zapotec, and Mixtec cultures—build a large urban center in the Valley of Mexico. About three hundred years later, their empire collapses.

ca. 1100
The Aztecs, a Nahuatl-speaking Indian group from northern Mexico, arrive in the Valley of Mexico.

1345
The Aztecs found the city of Tenochtitlán on an island in the middle of one of the lakes in the Valley of Mexico.

1502

Montezuma II becomes emperor of the Aztecs.

1519

Hernán Cortés launches an expedition to Mexico that consists of eleven ships and five hundred conquistadores.

1521

Cortés and his fellow Spaniards, aided by their Indian allies, seize the Aztec capital of Tenochtitlán after a three-month siege.

1535

The viceroyalty of New Spain is established with Mexico City (built on the ruins of the Aztec city of Tenochtitlán) as its capital.

1546

The Maya of eastern Yucatán rise up in rebellion against the Spanish colonists.

1680

Pueblo Indians of northern Mexico's Rio Grande Valley attempt to overthrow Spanish rule but are reconquered.

1810

Father Miguel Hidalgo calls for a revolt against Spanish rule.

1821

Mexico's first independent government is established.

1822

Agustín de Iturbide is proclaimed emperor of Mexico.

1824

Mexico adopts a constitution and becomes a federal republic.

1836

Texas declares its independence from Mexico; this action leads to a war between the United States and Mexico.

1846–1848

Mexico and the United States are at war; a defeated Mexico cedes half of its territory (consisting of present-day California, Arizona, New Mexico, and Texas).

1859

President Benito Juárez issues the Reform Laws establishing separation of church and state and freedom of religion.

1862

French troops occupy Mexico in an attempt to collect a debt; military intervention by Napoléon III is his attempt to spread French power and influence in the Americas.

1864

Mexico becomes an empire ruled by Maximilian, an Austrian archduke and puppet of Napoléon III.

1867

French troops withdraw from Mexico, leaving Maximilian undefended against guerrilla fighters; the emperor is captured and executed.

1867–1872

The republic is restored and led by liberal reformer Benito Juárez until his death.

1876–1911

Under the presidency of Porfirio Díaz, Mexico's economy grows and modernizes but political opposition is suppressed.

1911

Political dissident and presidential candidate Francisco Madero calls for the establishment of democracy, workers' rights, and land reform; peasants rise up in support of Madero.

The Díaz government loses control as rebel leaders Pascual Orozco, Pancho Villa, and Emiliano Zapata seize cities, towns, and large estates; Francisco Madero is elected president.

1913

General Victoriano Huerta seizes power and imprisons Madero, who is killed while supposedly attempting escape; the revolution continues in earnest as rebel leaders in the states attack the forces of Huerta.

1917

A new constitution is approved providing for the inviolability of the nation's shorelines and natural resources, separation of church and state, and the right of workers to form unions and to strike; the Mexican people also gain the right to land and free public school education.

1920

Álvaro Obregón becomes president and begins the reconstruction of Mexico according to the ideas contained in the Constitution of 1917.

1925

A national bank, the Bank of Mexico, is established as part of the expansion of the role of the state; in addition, land redistribution is carried out, schools are built, and the railroad system is expanded.

1926

Anticlerical laws are passed by the government, leading to an uprising by enraged Catholics; tens of thousands are killed in the ensuing Cristero rebellion.

1934

Lázaro Cárdenas is elected president and sets out to reform Mexican society; as part of his program, education is extended for all Mexicans through the building of rural primary schools.

1938

The federal government seizes the Mexican petroleum industry and turns over the foreign-held properties to worker control.

1940

Cárdenas's government is responsible for redistributing nearly half of Mexico's farmland to peasant farmers through the *ejido* system of communally held farms.

1942

Mexico enters World War II in June against Germany, Italy, and Japan.

1945

Mexico becomes one of the founding members of the United Nations.

1951

The Christopher Columbus Pan-American Highway opens; it

extends the length of Mexico from Ciudad Juárez to the border with Guatemala.

1952

The National University of Mexico is dedicated; its buildings are covered with mosaics by some of Mexico's most famous artists, including David Alfaro Siqueiros, Diego Rivera, Juan O'Gorman, and Chavez Morado.

1958

Women, having won the vote in 1953, vote for the first time in a presidential election.

1965

The Mexican government establishes the Border Industrialization Program in which U.S. or other non-Mexican companies send parts or components to Mexican assembly plants along the border to be assembled into products by Mexican workers.

1976

Mexico's currency, the peso, is devalued twice as the government attempts to stabilize an economy suffering from recession and inflation and drastic price increases.

1980

As a result of the discovery of extensive oil fields in Tabasco and Campeche in the 1970s, Mexico becomes the world's fifth largest producer of oil; the government uses its income from oil to create jobs.

1981

A decreased demand for oil and lower prices for petroleum-based products lead to an economic crisis characterized by governmental debt, high unemployment, and rising consumer prices.

1990

The population of the borderland between Mexico and the United States—an expanse of land stretching from Brownsville, Texas, to San Diego, California—reaches more than 9 million.

1994

Mexico, along with the United States and Canada, signs the North American Free Trade Agreement; the day after the treaty goes into effect, rebels of the Zapatista National Liberation Army (EZLN) seize four towns in Chiapas in protest against poverty and the loss of land among indigenous farmers.

2000

Vicente Fox Quesada takes office, ending seventy-one years of uninterrupted rule by the Institutional Revolutionary Party (PRI); the new president promises to deal with economic problems and to end decades-old police and political corruption.

FOR FURTHER RESEARCH

General

Gilbert M. Joseph and Timothy J. Henderson, eds., *The Mexico Reader: History, Culture, Politics.* Durham, NC: Duke University Press, 2002.

Michael C. Meyer and William H. Beezley, eds., *The Oxford History of Mexico.* New York: Oxford University Press, 2000.

Patrick Oster, *The Mexicans.* New York: William Morrow, 1989.

Henry Bamford Parkes, *A History of Mexico.* Boston: Houghton Mifflin, 1969.

Terry Pindell, *Yesterday's Train: A Rail Odyssey Through Mexican History.* New York: Henry Holt, 1997.

Great Indian Civilizations

Richard E. W. Adams, *The Origins of Maya Civilization.* Albuquerque: University of New Mexico Press, 1977.

Michael D. Coe, *The Maya.* London: Thames & Hudson, 1966.

———, *Mexico: From the Olmecs to the Aztecs.* New York: Thames & Hudson, 2002.

David Drew, *The Lost Chronicles of the Maya Kings.* Berkeley and Los Angeles: University of California Press, 1999.

Miguel Leon-Portilla, *Aztec Thought and Culture.* Norman: University of Oklahoma Press, 1990.

Matthew Restall, *The Maya World: Yucatec Culture and Society, 1550–1850.* Stanford, CA: Stanford University Press, 1997.

Dennis Tedlock, *Popul Vuh.* New York: Simon & Schuster, 1986.

Spanish Conquest and Rule

Georges Baudot, *Utopia and History in Mexico: The First Chronicles of Mexican Civilization, 1520–1569*. Niwot: University Press of Colorado, 1995.

Robert S. Chamberlain, *The Conquest and Colonization of Yucatan, 1517–1550*. Washington, DC: Carnegie Institute, 1948.

Hernando Cortés, *Letters from Mexico*. New Haven, CT: Yale University Press, 1986.

Bernal Díaz del Castillo, *The Discovery and Conquest of Mexico, 1517–1521*. New York: Farrar, Straus & Giroux, 1970.

Peter Gerhard, *A Guide to the Historical Geography of New Spain*. Norman: University of Oklahoma Press, 1993.

Charles Gibson, *Spain in America*. New York: Harper & Row, 1966.

Hugh Thomas, *Conquest: Cortés, Montezuma, and the Fall of Old Mexico*. New York: Simon & Schuster, 1993.

Michael Wood, *Conquistadors*. Berkeley and Los Angeles: University of California Press, 2000.

Alonso de Zorita, *Life and Labor in Ancient Mexico*. New Brunswick, NJ: Rutgers University Press, 1963.

Independence to Empire to Republic

Timothy E. Anna, *Forging of Mexico, 1821–1835*. Lincoln: University of Nebraska Press, 1998.

John S.D. Eisenhower, *So Far from God: The United States War with Mexico, 1846–1848*. New York: Random House, 1989.

Enrique Krauze, *Mexico: Biography of Power, a History of Modern Mexico, 1810–1996*. New York: HarperCollins, 1997.

Ramón Eduardo Ruíz, *Triumphs and Tragedy: A History of the Mexican People*. New York: W.W. Norton, 1992.

Reform and Revolution

Anita Brenner, *The Wind That Swept Mexico*. New York: Harper & Brothers, 1943.

Charles Cumberland, *Mexican Revolution: The Constitutionalist Years.* Austin: University of Texas Press, 1972.

Martin Luis Guzman, *The Eagle and the Serpent.* Gloucester, MA: Peter Smith, 1969.

John Mason Hart, *Revolutionary Mexico: The Coming and Process of the Mexican Revolution.* Berkeley and Los Angeles: University of California Press, 1987.

Alan Knight, *The Mexican Revolution.* 2 vols. Cambridge, UK: Cambridge University Press, 1986.

Ralph Roeder, *Juárez and His Mexico: A Biographical History.* New York: Viking Press, 1947.

Ramón Eduardo Ruíz, *The Great Rebellion: Mexico, 1905–1924.* New York: W. W. Norton, 1980.

John Womack, *Zapata and the Mexican Revolution.* New York: Knopf, 1969.

Postrevolution to Modernization

Francisco E. Balderrama, *Decade of Betrayal: Mexican Repatriation in the 1930s.* Albuquerque: University of New Mexico Press, 1995.

Jean Charlot, *The Mexican Mural Renaissance, 1920–1925.* New Haven, CT: Yale University Press, 1963.

Hayden Herrera, *Frida: A Biography of Frida Kahlo.* New York: Harper & Row, 1983.

Stephen R. Niblo, *Mexico in the 1940s.* Wilmington, DE: Scholarly Resources, 1998.

John Womack, *Rebellion in Chiapas: An Historical Reader.* New York: New Press, 1999.

Twenty-First Century

Peter Andreas, *Border Games: Policing the U.S.-Mexico Divide.* Ithaca, NY: Cornell University Press, 2000.

Marilyn P. Davis, *Mexican Voices/American Dreams: An Oral History of Mexican Immigration to the United States.* New York: Henry Holt, 1990.

Oscar J. Martinez, *Border People: Life and Society in the U.S.-Mexico Borderlands.* Tucson: University of Arizona Press, 1994.

Websites

Democracy and Human Rights in the Americas, www. worldpolicy.org/globalrights/mexico/mexico.html. This site contains information about Mexico's human rights issues. It is maintained by the World Policy Institute, a think tank devoted to tracking and reporting on topics with global scope and importance.

Internet Modern History Sourcebook, www.fordham.edu/ halsall/mod/modsbook.html. This site provides primary-source readings from various epochs and regions of the world, including information on Mexico's history.

Latin American Network Information Center (LANIC), www. lanic.utexas.edu. A site devoted to those interested in the economies of Latin American nations. It contains information on industry, agriculture, exports, and imports, and tracks the latest data on business being conducted in Latin America.

Mexican History and Culture, www.mexican-embassy.dk/ history.html. This site, maintained by the Mexican embassy, provides a wealth of information for anyone interested in Mexico's history, government, economy, and society.

Mexico: A Country Study, http://memory.loc.gov/frd/cs/ mxtoc.html. This site, in the electronic archive of the Library of Congress, contains information on Mexico, including its geography, climate, natural resources, history, governmental structure, economic output, and international relations.

INDEX